Trial and Error

Trial and Error

The American Controversy
Over
Creation and Evolution

Updated Edition

EDWARD J. LARSON

OXFORD UNIVERSITY PRESS
New York   Oxford

Oxford University Press

Oxford   New York   Toronto
Delhi   Bombay   Calcutta   Madras   Karachi
Kuala Lumpur   Singapore   Hong Kong   Tokyo
Nairobi   Dar es Salaam   Cape Town
Melbourne   Auckland

and associated companies in
Beirut   Berlin   Ibadan   Mexico City   Nicosia

First published in 1985 by Oxford University Press, Inc.,
200 Madison Avenue, New York, New York 10016

First issued as an Oxford University Press paperback, 1989

Library of Congress Cataloging in Publication Data
Larson, Edward J.
Trial and error.
Bibliography: p.   Includes index.
1. Evolution—Study and teaching—Law and
legislation—United States—History. 2. Creationism—
Study and teaching—Law and legislation—United
States—History. I. Title.
KF4208.5.S34L37   1986   344.73'095   85-7144
ISBN 0-19-503666-2   347.30495
ISBN 0-19-506143-8 (ppbk.)

Printing (last digit) 9 8 7 6 5 4 3 2 1
Printed in the United States of America

Preface to Paperback Edition

The paperback edition of this book continues the saga of the American legal controversy over creation and evolution through the 1987 Supreme Court ruling against the Louisiana statute mandating balanced treatment for "creation science" and "evolution science" in public-school science instruction. Due to the time of its publication in 1985, the previous edition ended with the trial-court ruling against that law. Although the controversy will continue in some form, the Supreme Court ruling offers a convenient breaking point for this narrative because it necessarily concludes one phase of the creationist legal effort. I want to thank Oxford University Press for publishing this revised and expanded edition. I also want to thank my colleagues at the University of Georgia who have assisted me in preparing this edition.

Athens, Georgia   E.L.
June 1, 1989

Preface to First Edition

What legal rights and restrictions have applied to the teaching of evolution and creation in American public schools since the advent of Darwinism? What do the granting of those rights and the imposing of those restrictions indicate about the place of science and religion in modern American society? How has the legal system coped with conflicting demands for such rights and restrictions? To address these questions, I have chronicled the American legal controversy over creation and evolution.

This book has been made possible by the help of many friends. First and foremost, historian of science Ronald L. Numbers, an expert on the history of modern creationism, gave me continual guidance, encouragement, and critical advice during my research and writing. Without him, this book simply would not exist. Historians David C. Lindberg and John B. Sharpless also provided ongoing encouragement and advice while constitutional scholar and educator Robert M. O'Neil took time to review my manuscript. Although none of these individuals are in any way responsible to any weaknesses of this book, they deserve much of the credit for its strengths.

Various institutions and individuals have contributed to this book by making research materials readily available. The bulk of the documents used in my research came from the collections of the Library of Congress, and I thank the staff of that library for their assistance. The cooperation of a wide variety of other institutions and individuals enabled me to round out my research. These sources included Yale University Library as caretaker of the papers of Justice Abe Fortas, Princeton University Library as home of Justice John M. Harlan's papers, the Marion County, Indiana, Superior Court for providing the *Hendren* court file, the United States Supreme Court library as a repository for appellate documents in the *Epperson* case, John Ball for assisting with access to *McLean* court documents, Wendell Bird for sharing public documents relating to the recent Louisiana litigation, and the Texas Board of Education for giving me up-to-the-minute reports on its regulatory actions. Access to information about creationist activities was generously provided by researchers at the Institute for Creation Research, Nell and Kelly Segraves, and Mel Gabler. Special thanks go to Carolyn Agger for granting me permission to view the Fortas papers. Other institutions and individuals helped as well. I deeply appreciate all of their assistance and hope that I have proven worthy of their trust.

Finally, I wish to acknowledge my debt to those that encouraged and supported my work on this book. John Brabner-Smith, Thomas E. Petri, William H. Ellis, and my parents, Jean and Rex Larson, stand out in this respect. To these five, I dedicate this work.

Seattle, Washington   E.L.
March 12, 1985

Contents

Trial and Error

Introduction

A popular crusade against instruction on the theory of evolution in public high schools erupted in America during the early 1920s. Led by the influential Democratic politician William Jennings Bryan, the crusade focused on enacting state statutes to bar teaching human evolution and, at least in part, represented a response to the spread of secondary education, which was then carrying evolutionary concepts to the general public to an unprecedented extent. After a series of near misses and the imposition of lesser restrictions in several places, in 1925 Tennessee became the first state to outlaw evolutionary teaching. Bryan, an attorney as well as a politician, took his crusade to the courtroom when the American Civil Liberties Union (ACLU) instigated a judicial challenge to the Tennessee statute. In the ensuing trial of science teacher John Scopes, Bryan and Clarence Darrow, who represented the defendant, sparred over science, religion, and academic freedom.

Feeding on the public reaction to that trial, which upheld the anti-evolution law, the controversy over evolution intensified during the second half of the twenties. Anti-evolution legal activities reached new heights at that time, but encountered stiffening opposition and increasing ridicule, especially in the North. The legal controversy finally cooled into a quiet standoff by 1930, but only after textbook publishers bowed to the demands of anti-evolutionists by de-emphasizing the offending theory in most high-school texts. Aroused popular opposition to evolutionary teaching had successfully restricted public science instruction.

The legal controversy heated up three decades later, when widespread demands for better science instruction led to the creation of the federally funded Biological Science Curriculum Study, which gave a prominent place to evolution in its popular tenth-grade textbooks. Other texts soon followed suit. When these widely used evolutionary textbooks came into contact with the surviving laws against evolutionary teaching in the mid-sixties, the United States Supreme Court in *Epperson v. Arkansas* used newly expanded constitutional restrictions against the establishment of religion to void the old statutes. This ruling made much of the modern acceptance of evolution. Public support for evolutionary teaching proved a half-hearted patron, however, for while significant efforts to outlaw evolutionary teaching never reoccurred, publication of the new evolutionary texts touched off widespread demands for both giving equal time to creationist instruction and presenting evolution as an unproven theory. These new demands pre-dated *Epperson*, and reflected the popular uncertainty about evolution.

Because these demands of equal time for the *biblical* account of creation ran up against the same constitutional barriers invoked by *Epperson* against anti-evolution laws, creationists increasingly concentrated on securing equal time for *scientific* evidence that purportedly supported their beliefs. The Arkansas and Louisiana legislatures complied in 1981 by mandating balanced treatment for "creation science" and "evolution science" in public schools, bringing the ACLU back on the scene to challenge both laws in court. The first statute fell a year later in *McLean v. Arkansas*, and the second in 1985. Nonetheless, the creation-evolution legal controversy has remained at or near the boiling point, as both sides continue to battle over the content of high-school biology instruction.

This study analyzes the legal controversy both as a central manifestation of the popular response to evolutionary thought in America and as an episode in the use of law to redress the relationship of science and society. Based on an examination of all statutory and judicial actions arising out of the controversy, it emerges that the creation-evolution legal actions primarily represented efforts to reconcile public science—that is, publicly supported science teaching and related activities—with popular opinion. This process was reflected in legal actions during the twenties banning evolutionary teaching in response to strong public opposition to Darwinism, in the Supreme Court's over-turning of such bans after the public seemed to display a marked deference to scientific opinion, and finally in increasing activity toward granting equal time for creationism where public opin-ion favored such fairness for competing "scientific" ideas. Re-gional and demographic currents appeared in this popular opinion over time, with concern about evolutionary instruction settling toward the rural South during the mid-twenties and later spreading to suburban areas in the South and West. Mean-while, partisan leadership of the anti-evolution issue gradually passed from Democrats in the twenties to Republicans in the sixties.

Typically, legislators showed greater responsiveness to pop-ular opinion than judges, but even the courts operated within parameters established by popular sentiment. Public science could never deviate too far from popular opinion. In crafting this reconciliation, both legislators and judges avoided ruling on the scientific merits of evolution or creation, which they typically viewed as being beyond the scope of their compe-tence, by basing their decisions on non-scientific factors, such as the religious nature of creationism or the social ramifications of evolutionary teaching. Scientific opinion inevitably influ-enced these decision-makers, but often only to the extent it was distilled through popular opinion either directly in the accep-tance of a theory of origins or indirectly in the cultural respect afforded science generally.

This study is organized into five chapters. The first chapter provides historical background by examining evolutionary teaching in America during the years leading up to the anti-evolution crusade. This is done primarily by reviewing the treatment of evolution in textbooks of the period, beginning with the gradual incorporation of evolution into high-school texts during the late nineteenth century and continuing through the increasingly dogmatic presentation of that doctrine during the early twentieth century. By tracing this incorporation process back before the anti-evolution crusade and analyzing the treat-ment of evolution in pre-crusade texts, the first chapter identifies exactly what crusaders were fighting against and explores the timing of their drive.

The next two chapters examine the initial anti-evolution crusade and its impact. In particular, Chapter Two traces the reform heritage of Evangelicalism within the Progressive Era, the rise of the anti-evolution issue among fundamentalist evangelicals, and the enactment of the first anti-evolution laws leading up to the *Scopes* trial. From this analysis, the crusade against evolution emerges as a mass movement fitting the interventionist pattern common to Progressive reforms. The third chapter tells the *Scopes* story, highlighting the judicial attitudes toward scientific and popular opinion reflected in that litigation. The account then follows the impact of that case on the ongoing anti-evolution movement through 1960.

The final two chapters carry the story up to 1985. Chapter Four traces the readmission of evolution to the classroom during the sixties, leading to *Epperson*, which struck down the Arkansas anti-evolution law, and parallel legal actions in Tennessee and Mississippi. The budding creationist legal response to this development is noted. The last chapter reviews the crossfire since 1970, as creationists initiated lawsuits and legislation designed to qualify evolutionary teaching while evolutionists struggled to consolidate their earlier gains.

The study closes with brief concluding remarks. As those remarks observe, the creation-evolution legal controversy persisted because popular opinion remained deeply divided over evolutionary teaching in public schools. That split prevented any amicable compromise and drove both sides to seek legal relief. Yet that same division precluded either side from accepting an unfavorable legal resolution as final. So the legal controversy continued, with the law mostly serving to provide forums where both sides could present their arguments in the hope of obtaining at least temporary legal protection for their cause.

1

Scene of the Crime

Evolution in American Education
Before 1920

The legal battles of the creation-evolution controversy, to a great extent, have centered on the contents of high-school science textbooks. This stands out when one looks back over the battlefields. In 1983 the parties seeking judicial enforcement of the Louisiana statute requiring parity for "creation science" and "evolution science" in public schools complained that the science textbooks used in that state presented only evolution. The 1982 federal court ruling against a similar Arkansas law rested in part on a finding that no acceptable creation-science textbooks existed. During the 1970s and 1960s, California and Texas creationists sought more favorable treatment for creation science in school textbooks through lawsuits and state school-board actions. The 1968 Supreme Court case striking down statutes prohibiting the teaching of evolution arose when the illegal theory appeared in a required textbook. The 1925 indictment of John Scopes leading to his famous trial rested on his teaching evolutionary passages in an assigned textbook. Indeed, America's first anti-evolution legal action was a 1923 Oklahoma statute prohibiting the inclusion of Darwinism in textbooks distributed by the state.

Textbooks became the battleground for the creation-evolution controversy largely because they represented the most tangible evidence of and influence on course content, which was the real prize at stake. Yet before *Scopes* and the half-decade of anti-evolution legislative activity that preceded it, the offending doctrine gradually entered science textbooks without organized opposition. This process simply reflected tendencies within the American scientific community, where evolution had replaced special creation as the dominant view shortly after Darwin published his theory in 1859.

Before Darwin, American scientists typically accepted the biblically orthodox view that God directly created every type of species, with each thereafter reproducing true to form. In contrast, Darwin proposed that the interaction of several biological mechanisms naturally caused some descendants of older species gradually to evolve over countless generations into the ancestors of new species. A popular 1912 high-school biology textbook summarized those key Darwinian mechanisms. "We have seen in our study thus far (1) that no two individual plants are exactly alike, (2) that enormous numbers of seeds are produced by plants, and (3) that there is inevitable competition or struggle for existence," the text explained. "The question, then, that confronts us is this: Which of the many competitors will survive in the struggle, reach maturity, and finally reproduce themselves? Obviously those plants that vary from the rest in such a way that they can best adapt themselves to the surrounding."[1] Those survivors of "natural selection" then continue this process of change, eventually breeding new species. Alternative evolutionary mechanisms proposed during the late-nineteenth century included the neo-Lamarckian concept that members of a species physically adapt to changed environmental conditions. The inheritance of these adaptions then account for the evolution of new species without the need for a competitive struggle for survival.

Evolutionary ideas quickly leaped from the writings of Darwin to the beliefs of most American scientists and from there into the content of public education. By 1880 the American scientific community so embraced these new concepts that the hostile Presbyterian *Observer* could identify only two working American naturalists who did not accept some form of evolution.[2] Following the lead of scientific opinion, science educators began adding evolutionary concepts to high-school textbooks almost immediately, and had fully incorporated the doctrine into biology teaching materials by the turn of the century.* The increasingly evolutionary character of the secondary-school textbooks published during the period from 1859, when Darwin announced his theory in the *Origin of Species*, until the anti-evolution crusade began in earnest about 1920 provided the backdrop for the ensuing legal actions.

Paper Menagerie

The earliest texts published after the *Origin of Species* generally were simply revised editions of pre-Darwinian books. Only one of these textbooks added evolutionary concepts. This was Asa Gray's *First Lessons in Botany*, later renamed *The Elements of Botany*, the leading high-school botany text of the late nineteenth century.[3] First published in 1857, Gray's text remained in print for decades, undergoing extensive revisions in 1887. The author was a Harvard professor of botany and America's foremost Darwinist. Darwin first shared his theory with Gray in 1857, making Gray the only American taken into Darwin's confidence prior to the publication of *Origin of Species*. Gray later arranged the publication of Darwin's book in America and became a visible defender of Darwinism.

Gray, however, wrote the original version of his text before learning about natural selection. Consequently, it took a pre-Darwinian, special-creation viewpoint. This is clearly expressed in Gray's statement that "the Creator established a definite number of species at the beginning, which have continued by

*This conclusion arises from a review of all multiple-edition high-school life-science textbooks published in the United States during the period from 1859 to 1920 that are now contained in the generally comprehensive collections of the Library of Congress. (See the Appendix for a complete listing.) Botany, zoology, and geology texts are included in this review in addition to standard biology texts, with these first three types of texts being more common before the turn of the century, when the combined study of biology emerged as the core of the modern high-school life-science curriculum. Single-edition texts are excluded on the assumption that they were little used and therefore are not indicative of the content of secondary-school instruction. Applying similar logic, the more often republished texts are given special attention.

propagation, each after its kind."[4] The 1887 version of Gray's text omitted this creationist affirmation.[5] Similarly, the later edition dropped Gray's claim that even the very similar species of White, Red, and Scarlet Oak "we take for granted, have not originated from one and the same stock, but from three separate stocks."[6] In its place, Gray suggested that "nearly related species probably came from a common stock in earlier times."[7]

To explain this new view of the origin of species, Gray modified the discussion of varieties. In the original version, varieties are presented as individual differences from the special norm that "are not likely to be reproduced by seed," and even where they are reproduced, naturally "dwindle and perish, or else revert to the original form of the species."[8] In contrast, the later version inserted a new rule—fundamental for natural selection—that "[n]o two individuals are exactly alike; a tendency to variation pervades all living things." The text then retained the statement that individual differences are usually not inherited, but where they are inherited, now they are only "*likely* to dwindle and perish, or else revert to the original form of the species." After leaving this opening, Gray observed, "In an enlarged view, varieties may be incipient species."[9] Evolution thus replaced fixity of species, though without describing the mechanism of natural selection or mentioning either Darwin by name or the term "evolution."

With these textual modifications came a subtle change in the role of the Creator. Studying the gradations of species connecting the "beautiful diversity of forms" was originally enough "to convince the thoughtful botanist that all are parts of one system, works of one hand, realizations in nature of the conception of One Mind."[10] After evolution, the resemblances between species merely "show that they are all part of one system, realizations in nature, as we may affirm, of the conception of One Mind."[11] God still lies behind nature, but the secondary cause of evolution replaced His creative hand as the immediate instrument of speciation.

As an orthodox Christian who developed a teleological interpretation of Darwinism, Gray admitted evolution into his text by merely adjusting the role given to God. Yet removing God as the direct cause for special characteristics led Gray to add evolutionary explanations for these. For example, the original text simply noted the different types of flowers and described them.[12] The later text added that these types "represent different adaptations to conditions or modes of life, some of which have obvious or probable utilities, although others are beyond particular explanation."[13] After describing some such adaptations facilitating cross fertilization, Gray commented that "there must be some essential advantage in cross-fertilization or cross-breeding. Otherwise all those various, elaborate, and exquisitely adjusted adaptations would be aimless."[14] Such a concern was foreign to the original edition, where "the Creator's plan" provided all the explanation needed.[15] With evolution, Gray gave the high-school student a naturalistic purpose for various plant characteristics.

The entry of evolution into high-school zoology textbooks differed from the story for botany because America's leading mid-nineteenth-century zoologist, Louis Agassiz, never joined his Harvard colleague Asa Gray in converting to the new theory. Therefore, post-Darwinian editions of *Principles of Zoology*, Agassiz's high-school and college textbook written in collaboration with like-minded zoologist A. A. Gould, retained a creationist flavor. "The records of the Bible, as well as human tradition, teaches us that man and the animals associated with him were created by the word of God," Agassiz affirmed in every edition of his text, "and this truth is confirmed by the revelations of science, which unequivocally indicate the direct interventions of creative power."[16] But this was as far as Agassiz went in supporting the Genesis account.

From the original 1848 edition to the final revised 1873 edition, *Principles* contained an identical presentation of Agassiz's non-biblical view that whole animal populations were created essentially where they subsequently lived in a series of Divine acts occurring at intervals over a very long earth history. Massive biological extinctions punctuated this history into four distinct ages without any intervening development. Agassiz opposed both the Bible and evolution by denying "a direct linkage between the faunas of different ages. There is nothing like parental descent connecting them."[17] Apparent animal relationships were instead attributed to their common origin in the mind of their Creator. "To study, in this view, the succession of animals in time, and their distribution in space, is, therefore, to become acquainted with the ideas of God himself," Agassiz assured his student readers in a catechismal phrase answering more to German Idealism than either orthodox Christianity or prevailing scientific opinion.[18]

Creationist concepts also survived in the chief holdover geology textbook, *Elementary Geology* by Amherst College president and famed geologist Edward Hitchcock. As a believing Christian who had come to terms with geological evidence suggesting that the earth was not recently created in six literal days, Hitchcock's text included lengthy sections reconciling the geological record with the Genesis account of creation by equating geological ages with biblical days or, alternatively, positing a gap in the Genesis account.[19]

Hitchcock died in 1864 without accepting organic evolution. His final revised edition of *Elementary Geology*, issued in 1860, advocated this viewpoint by asserting that the absence of intermediate life forms in the fossil record refuted the "absurd" supposition that "from a mere mass of jelly vitalized, higher and more complicated organic forms have been eliminated, until man at last was the result." Here, Hitchcock also mentioned the nebular hypothesis of cosmic evolution and the supposition of spontaneous generation as further parts of an overall "hypothesis of creation by laws," warning his student readers that "[w]hen this hypothesis is fully carried out, it is intended and adopted to vindicate atheism."[20] Although these general concepts of naturalistic creation predate Darwin, Hitchcock only added this warning after the publication of *Origin of Species* increased their scientific credibility.[21]

At least Hitchcock recognized the challenge of Darwinism. Other pre-Darwinian geology textbooks revised after 1859 omitted evolution altogether.[22] Outside Gray's work, the same could be said for all holdover botany and zoology textbooks.[23] These textbooks, typically written by science educators rather than research scientists, lagged far behind those of the masters in incorporating scientific advances.

This creationist flavor continued in the first entirely new post-

Darwin high-school geology, James Dwight Dana's popular 1863 *Text-Book of Geology*.[24] A devout Christian as well as a prominent Yale geologist and editor of the *American Journal of Science*, Dana held out against accepting organic evolution until 1874. His text reflected his belief in special creation. Following the lead of his close friend Edward Hitchcock, Dana traced the "evolution" of the earth's features over indefinitely long geological ages through the operation of ongoing natural agencies and unfolded the fossil record of prehistoric species.[25] Reflecting his personal beliefs, Dana gave a creationist interpretation to the fossil record. Dana saw the sequence of species recorded in fossils showing "that the life of the world underwent constant changes through exterminations and creations." Dana also saw an "upward progress in the grand series of species" over the ages and "a striking degree of harmony between the species" in each age.[26] But while Darwin interpreted this as evidence for evolution, to Dana "[i]t demonstrates the oneness in plan and purpose of all nature, and thereby the oneness of its author."[27]

Dana did not stop here, but went on to tell his high-school audience, "Geology affords no support to the hypothesis that species have been made from pre-existing species, and suggests no theory of development by natural cause. In other words, it has no facts sustaining the notion that *Man* was made through the gradual progress or improvement of some one of the *Apes*."[28] In fact, this "development-hypothesis" was not even "true Science" because it was refuted by the central evidence that species do not shade into one another, higher species sometimes appear earlier than lower species, and the earth has suffered total exterminations of whole families that subsequently reappeared.[29] In accordance with this limitation on hypothetical science, Dana stated, "Geology has no theory of creation to present." Instead, he fitted historical geology into the Genesis account, with the geological ages equated to the days of the Mosaic record and the creation of life forms tied to divine commands.[30] "Geology may seem to be audacious in its attempts to unveil the mysteries of creation," Dana concluded at the end of his text, "[y]et it is at least sufficient to strengthen faith in the Book of books," the Bible.[31]

In 1874, after years of personal struggle, Dana accepted a

limited version of theistic evolution and promptly incorporated it into a revised edition of his *Text-Book*. Given the harshness of his earlier anti-evolution statements, this required a significant textual revision and the result, both in word and spirit, constituted only a partial recantation. Dana's revised text confessed that the fossil record revealed a basic pattern of biological evolution punctuated by "remarkable" breaks suggesting the Divine creation of certain basic life forms, including man.[32] Omitting his earlier discussion of the day-age theory, Dana instead reconciled geology with Genesis by observing that the first chapter of the Bible merely identifies four Divine creative fiats and "plainly implies that, after the fiats, that is, through these expressions of the Divine Will, the new developments went forward successively to the completion of the grand system."[33] With this, the only attempt to reconcile the biblical account with organic evolution in any of the reviewed high-school texts, Dana retained his concluding affirmation that geology "strengthens faith" in the Bible.[34]

Shortly after Dana's death in 1895, his textbook was radically revised by Wesleyan University geologist William North Rice to affirm the evolutionary development of all species, including man.[35] Any attempt to reconcile geology with Genesis or to support Scripture was eliminated in favor of a new concluding comment that "science, as such, knows nothing of efficient cause or of purpose; but it leaves full scope for faith . . . that the whole process of the evolution of Man and his dwelling place has been guided by infinite Wisdom."[36]

The large number of editions and printings of their texts relative to those of other authors suggests that Dana, Agassiz, and Gray dominated the limited high-school life-science textbook market during the first post-Darwinian generation. A few science educators, however, challenged this dominance with new textbooks during the 1860s and 1870s. These textbooks totally omitted evolutionary concepts. The most popular of these works came from J. Dorman Steele, a New York high-school teacher with an uncommon knack for popularizing science.[37] Steele eventually published simple high-school textbooks in every scientific discipline.

All Steele's textbooks avoided evolution. Both his zoology and botany texts assumed a low profile on the origins issue by using a catalog format that simply described individual existing species without discussing relationships.[38] Such a format became popular with zoology texts of the era.[39] Nevertheless, a growing bias toward evolution appeared in the order of presentation. In his initial 1877 zoology text, Steele followed a nonevolutionary order of presentation by opening his paper menagerie with man, followed by other animals in order of their decreasing complexity. Mimicking similar textbooks of the time, a revised 1887 edition of Steele's work co-authored by Brown University zoologist J. W. P. Jenks shifted to an evolutionary arrangement, introduced by the comment that zoology "would naturally begin with the more simple forms, and finally conclude with those of highest development."[40] Evolution itself, however, went without mention. In 1905, Steele's publisher added that the new arrangement followed "the later view of Naturalists," without any further elaboration of that later evolutionary view.[41]

Steele's geology text ducked the origins issue by simply affirming that God created the universe and all its inhabitants, without detailing the manner of creation. Faced with the most sensitive question of human origins, Steele characteristically concluded that science is impotent to determine if "the one all-wise Creator" made man by "fiat, or by some intermediate process of secondary causes."[42]

Enthroning Evolution

The first generation of American scientists trained after the publication of *Origin of Species* began writing high-school textbooks in the 1880s. These texts were invariably evolutionary. Charles E. Bessey's texts offer a prime example. Bessey studied under Asa Gray at Harvard in 1873 and at the University of Nebraska he went on to radically alter American botany by emphasizing laboratory methods and prairie-related ecological concepts. Bessey first entered the textbook field with *Botany for High Schools and Colleges* in 1880, and four years later supplemented this basically college text with a "Briefer Course" high-school *Botany*. Both versions were published by Henry Holt and Company as part of its popular American Science Series.

Bessey's textbooks were thoroughly evolutionary, with his briefer *Botany* describing the introduction, extinction, and distribution of species over geological time.[43] The enlarged 1896 edition of Bessey's briefer *Botany* added a chapter recounting the evolutionary history of angiosperms.[44] Both editions preached Bessey's evolutionary doctrines that "similar conditions have brought about similar vegetations" as opposed to the creationist view that the fit between an environment and its biological life reflects Divine design.[45] Like all good preaching, Bessey's goal was conversion. "The mission of the true teacher is to burn the thoughts in, brand his students for life," Bessey once said.[46] His textbooks carried out this philosophy. "It was intended to train the scientific mind," historian Ronald C. Torbey said of Bessey's first textbook. "A student working through the book would be mentally disciplined with a critical method and a internalized philosophy of pragmatism."[47]

While Bessey moved into the botany textbook market, Joseph LeConte successfully challenged Dana's hold on geology textbook sales.[48] Unlike the cautious approach taken in Dana's book, LeConte's 1884 text boldly affirmed evolution. This befit the author, a prominent University of California geologist and leading advocate of neo-Lamarckian evolution. "Geology is essentially a history," LeConte began. "It is a history of the *evolution* of the earth and of its inhabitants."[49] The fossil record of each geological era then was unfolded and given an evolutionary interpretation. For example, the Paleozoic era was presented as producing the first vertebrate animals—Devonian fishes, which "were not typical fishes, but connecting links between fish and reptile, and from this intermediate form, as from a trunk, true fish and reptiles were afterward separated and developed as branches."[50] Similarly, the evolution of present mammals from common ancestors during the Cenozoic era was traced in general terms, illustrated by the "genesis of the horse" through forty different species.[51]

Man's participation in this evolutionary development was

discussed, but not resolved in LeConte's text. Humanity was traced back to the drift-river man of the Quaternary period, but this man was described as being as "thoroughly human as any of us."[52] In the first edition of his text, LeConte then observed, "We have not yet been able to find any transition forms or connecting links between man and the highest animals."[53] LeConte's 1898 revision added a footnote here stating, "Such a link is supposed, by many, to have been recently found in Java, and named Pitheranthropus. We wait for more evidence."[54] Clearly, LeConte felt free to suggest the possibility of human evolution to his high-school audience, the earliest text in our sample to do so.

Even though LeConte was a liberal Christian who strove to reconcile evolution with religion, he never mentioned Creation or God in his textbook.[55] To the contrary, his discussion of the antiquity of man expressly warned against this. "The amount of time which has elapsed since man first appeared is still doubtful," LeConte wrote. "Some estimate it at more than a hundred thousand years—some only ten thousand. The question should not be regarded as of any importance, except as a question of science."[56] LeConte thus told his nineteenth-century high-school audience that religious considerations about the age of man were unimportant. Although LeConte's text never mentioned special creation, it also did not mention natural selection. New species evolve and old species become extinct, but a competitive struggle for survival was never mentioned. Yet, rather than suggesting a desire to protect his young readers from such doctrines, this merely reflected LeConte's own neo-Lamarckian brand of evolution that stressed progressive specific adaptation rather than competition.[57] At every turn in his text, LeConte described changed environmental conditions causing rapid evolutionary progress.[58]

A spate of high-school botany, zoology, and geology textbooks appeared around the turn of the century as the number of high schools multiplied but before the curriculum reform movement succeeded in merging the life sciences into a single course in biology. This expanding market brought a wide variety of authors into the field, from top research scientists to industrious high-school teachers. Nine of these texts were popular enough to go through multiple revised editions, often under differing names: all espoused evolution.

Each of these turn-of-the-century life-science texts at least implied that evolutionary concepts are true. For example, Boston high-school instructor Joseph Y. Bergen's 1901 *Foundations of Botany* described the "savage competition going on among living things" and analyzed how natural selection, "acting on an enormous scale through many ages, may well be supposed to have brought about the perpetuation of millions of such variations as are known to be of constant occurrence among plants."[59] Darwin's *Origin of Species* was expressly cited as the source of these concepts. Cornell horticulture professor Liberty Hyde Bailey was even more dogmatically evolutionary, entitling one section of his 1900 botany text as "The Fact of Struggle for Existence." Referring to this "fact," Bailey asserted, "We shall observe that this is true; but we are compelled to believe it by considering the efforts which all plants make to propagate themselves."[60] After reviewing other key Darwinian concepts, Bailey concluded, "Variation, hereditary, natural selection, and other agencies bring about a *gradual change in the plant kingdom:* this change is evolution. This hypothesis that one form may give rise to another is now universally accepted amongst investigators."[61]

Turn-of-the-century zoology textbooks gave new prominence to evolutionary concepts by replacing the old animal catalog format with a presentation focusing on biological concepts, including evolution. Three leading zoologists from Stanford—David Starr Jordan, Vernon Kellogg, and Harold Heath—developed this approach as they jointly and independently published a variety of high-school texts during the first few years of the new century. Their leading text, the 1903 *Animal Studies*, was structured around a central chapter, entitled "The Struggle for Existence," that summarized the doctrine of natural selection.

The authors then used this concept in succeeding chapters to explain various animal structures, habits, and distributions. For example, in explaining animal coloring, the text stated, "We have already seen that by the action of natural selection and heredity those variations or conditions that gave animals advantages in the struggle for life are preserved and emphasized. And so it has come about that advantageous protective resemblances are very widespread among animals."[62] The authors placed no limits on the power of evolution to account for current life forms. Indeed, they wrote that "all backboned or vertebrate animals are related to each other through being descended from a common ancestor."[63] So that there could be no mistake, man's evolutionary origins were repeatedly suggested to the high-school readers of the text.[64] Many other turn-of-the-century texts also presented human evolution as fact, the first texts to do so.[65] By 1915, one of Kellogg's texts simply asserted, "Although there is much discussion of the causes of evolution there is practically none any longer of evolution itself. Organic evolution is a fact, demonstrated and accepted."[66]

Not satisfied with enthroning evolution, several of these texts criticized creationist concepts. Colgate University professor Albert P. Brigham's 1900 geology text commented that even though the "missing link" connecting humans to any lower form remains undiscovered, religious considerations about human evolution are inappropriate. "In this, as in all questions, the truth should be sought without prejudice or fear. The antiquity of man and his possible evolution from lower forms of life are questions of science. No answer which science may render is inconsistent with the highest view of our origin and destiny."[67] Eugenicist Charles Davenport, director of the Carnegie Institution's Department of Experimental Evolution, went a step further in his 1911 basic zoology text. "We have seen how the Greeks regarded the evolution of the organic world as a part of cosmic philosophy. Through a narrow interpretation of the Mosaic account of creation, the Christian church was led away from those broad views," Davenport wrote in summarizing the history of zoology. "It was the great service of Charles Darwin to offer such a theory, accompanied by proofs so numerous and presented in a fashion so judicial as to win acceptance by all."[68] Finally, Cornell botany professor George Atkinson's 1912 *Botany for High School* asserted that evolution "has been accepted

because it appeals to the mind of man as being more reasonable that species should be created according to natural laws
rather than by an arbitrary and special creation."[69]

Special significance attached to the American Book Company's *Botany All the Year Round* as the only multiple-edition life-
science text of the period written by a Southern high-school
teacher. Despite the muscle anti-evolution sentiment soon exerted in the South, the author, Eliza F. Andrews of rural Georgia, felt free in 1903 to instruct students that "the geological
record shows that the simplest forms of life were the first to
appear and from these all the higher forms were gradually
evolved."[70] A 1911 revision of Andrews's text added a section
entitled "The Course of Plant Evolution," which concluded with
an admonition for open-mindedness asserting that "in questions of this sort it is wise to keep in mind the blunt remark of
a famous old American statesman that 'only fools and dead
people never change their opinions.' "[71] Andrews joined all her
fellow turn-of-the-century life-science textbook writers in completely omitting any mention of God, which represented a total
reversal from both the pre-Darwinian creationist texts and the
transitional theistic evolutionary works of Gray and Dana.

Around the turn of the century, high-school botany, zoology, and historical zoology began to be combined into a single
course of biology.[72] The first high-school biology textbook appeared in 1907, with at least eight more following before 1920.[73]
Gerald Skoog reviewed eight texts published during this period
in his quantitative analysis of the topic of evolution in twentieth-century biology textbooks. In these texts, he counted 18,498
words dealing with topics related to evolution, of which 3,949
words dealt with the Darwinian thesis; 2,092 words dealt with
natural selection; only 98 words dealt with special creation; and
no words dealt with the evolution of man or mammals, the fossil record of man, or the issue of religion and science. Even
though Skoog did not calculate comparison figures for the total
number of words in these texts, he concluded that "evolution
was not stressed in the textbook of this period."[74] These figures indicate, however, that creation received much less attention than evolution. Further, a qualitative analysis of such biology texts popular enough to go through multiple editions reveals

a strong evolutionary flavor. This should not be surprising given the fact that the period ended with a popular crusade against teaching evolution in public schools.

Although Skoog cited in support of his conclusion that the 1912 two-volume edition of *Elementary Biology*, written by New York high-school teachers James E. Peabody and Arthur E. Hunt, never used the term "evolution," neither did *Origin of Species*. The "Plants" volume of *Elementary Biology* did contain a sub-chapter, entitled "The Struggle for Existence and Its Effects," presenting evolutionary concepts. The reader was also pointed to the source for these concepts by a picture of Darwin and a reference to "his great book on the 'Origin of Species,' published in 1859—a book which has doubtlessly influenced human thought more than any other book of modern times."[75]

The high-school biology text most widely used at the inception of the anti-evolution crusade was George W. Hunter's 1914 *A Civic Biology*.[76] Hunter, himself a former high-school biology teacher, included sections on both evolution and heredity in his textbook. In the former, the doctrine of evolution was defined as "the belief that simple forms of life on the earth slowly and gradually gave rise to those more complex and that thus ultimately the most complex form came into existence."[77] The fossil record spanning "millions of years" was given as evidence of this evolution. Man is presented as a product of this evolution, with the Caucasian race being "finally, the highest type of all."[78] Leaving no doubt about his bias, Hunter concluded his textbook with a biographical sketch of Charles Darwin. "His wonderful discovery of the doctrine of evolution was due not only to his information and experimental evidence, but also to an iron determination and undaunted energy," Hunter wrote of Darwin. "He gave the world the proofs of the theory on which we today base the progress of the world."[79] A decade after its introduction, this popular text became the flash point of legal controversy when a Tennessee high-school teacher named John T. Scopes was indicted for lecturing from it on evolution.

The final high-school biology textbook published before the anti-evolution crusade was the 1918 *Civic Biology* by Clifton F. Hodge and Jean Dawson. The problem format and practical bent of this text de-emphasized academic theories, but the authors still managed to join the choir singing the praises of evolution. It is "criminal" not to try to learn and obey the evolutionary "laws of life," readers were admonished. These laws were the law of geometrical increase that "[a]ll things tend to increase in geometrical ratio," the law of variation that "[n]o two things are exactly alike," the law of heredity that "[o]rganisms tend to produce offspring like themselves," and the law of natural selection that "[n]ature selects the fittest to survive." These laws, coupled with artificial selection, have "resulted in the species and varieties, strains and breeds, that we now see in the world."[80] "Charles Darwin," the authors wrote, "by lifelong application and sacrifice, marked the greatest advance in discovery of the laws of life that the world has known."[81] Thus, these three biology textbooks dating from the 1910s, far from not stressing evolution and almost in defiance of Christianity, exalted Darwinism as having supreme influence on modern thought, providing the base for future progress, and representing the greatest ever advance in understanding the laws of life. As if to dare the coming anti-evolution crusaders, *Civic Botany* affirmed, "it is as impossible now to take the ideas of descent and of natural selection out of the world as to take a star out of the sky."[82] But this would not dissuade crusaders empowered to move mountains and to make the sun stand still.

Overall, this analysis of botany, zoology, geology, and biology textbooks indicates that evolutionary concepts appeared in many high-school science textbooks throughout the late nineteenth and early twentieth centuries. Indeed, it is hard to imagine a more fully evolutionary (albeit neo-Lamarckian) presentation than that found in LeConte's popular 1884 geology textbook. By the turn of the century, evolution had clearly supplanted creationism in high-school textbooks. Throughout, the treatment of organic origins by textbooks of the period mainly reflected each author's own position on that issue, without any apparent effort to shield students from evolutionary concepts. To the extent that textual content was an indication of teaching, public high schools were teaching evolution decades before the anti-evolution crusade, with the presentation seeming to grow more dogmatically Darwinian over time. A review of teaching journals, policies, and manuals reinforces this conclusion.

From the first publication of *School Review* in 1893, that leading national teachers' journal encouraged evolutionary teaching. The first volume of that journal contained an article entitled "Biology in Secondary Schools" suggesting that plant species be studied in the order of their increasing complexity "because this order of study will give some notion of the evolution of the plant kingdom."[83] In the same year, the National Education Association's influential Committee on Secondary School Studies recommended just such a format for both botany and zoology courses.[84] A 1900 article in *School Review* by a Chicago high-school teacher stated, "The fundamental theory of the evolution of organic life and an explanation of the powers of 'natural selection' should surely be unfolded when data enough have been mastered to make it intelligible. I have found that even first-year high-school pupils are keen to appreciate the greater conceptions of biology if they are given the chance."[85] *School Review* never expressed any interest that creationist theories also be unfolded.

Secondary-school teachers were not only encouraged to teach evolution by turn-of-the-century journal articles, they were instructed to do so by a 1904 normal-school textbook for future high-school biology teachers. The author of the botany section of that manual advised teachers that "the modern doctrine of evolution, which was arrived at first by the study of animals and plants, is a far too important generalization from the point of view of education as well as science to be neglected in the high school."[86] The author of the zoology section expressly agreed with this advice, but reprinted evolutionist T. H. Huxley's caution that a detailed study of evolution was "too difficult for the young mind."[87] This approach of introducing the broad concept of evolution to high-school students without dwelling on its details was recommended by the influential American Society of Zoologists in 1906.[88]

Perhaps the best testimony to the substitution of evolution for creation in the turn-of-the-century classroom appeared in a 1902 history of high-school zoology instruction carried in the second volume of *School Science*, the first professional journal for secondary-school science teachers. That article traced evolutionary instruction in high-school zoology back to 1870.[89] "The last seventy-five years have seen great advance in the teaching of zoology," the article concluded. "In aim it has progressed from the narrow ideal of religious and memory training to the broader conceptions of mental, moral and physical development according to the most recent physiological and psychological researches. Subject matter has broadened through the discoveries of eminent naturalists, as, for example, Darwin, Huxley and many others of less prominence."[90]

A decade later, *School Science* even more explicitly advocated instruction in evolution over religion. Expressing concern that rural areas were "holding out" against evolution, a journal article written by a small-town Indiana schoolteacher suggested a strategy for teachers to incorporate evolution into high-school science. The article observed that all teachers and students know that high-school science must include evolution, but that "most" parents object out of their ignorance about evolution. These parents were never taught evolution, and "[t]o them Darwin, evolution, and natural selection are synonyms for Satan, sin, and eternal damnation."[91] Teachers were advised to use Parent-Teacher Associations to teach parents about evolution, "and then we can go ahead with the pupils."[92] Teachers were further advised to teach students cautiously but clearly about "the anthropoidal descent of man" and that "it is our duty, if called upon, to correct for them some of the ideas which previous training in the Sunday school or home has led them."[93] Two years later, in 1916, *School Science* again published a call for incorporating evolution into high-school biology—with this call bearing the endorsement of the National Education Association.[94]

Russian Dolls

Teaching journals, policies, and manuals dating from the 1890s through the 1910s thus second the evidence from science textbooks that evolutionary instruction penetrated public high-school life-science courses by the turn of the century. At most, such sources occasionally recommended caution in teaching evolution; they never supported creationist concepts. This finding, however, simply discloses the outermost in the nest of Russian dolls involved in explaining the timing of the anti-evolution crusade: for if evolution reached the high-school science classroom well before 1920, why was the crusade to impose legal restrictions on evolutionary teaching so slow in coming?

Since evolution commanded a prominent position in high-school life-science courses from before 1900, the crusade could have followed an increase in such course work relative to other subjects. But no such relative emphasis of the life sciences occurred immediately preceding the crusade. Indeed, the life sciences were taught in most secondary schools throughout the period. One survey limited to the North Central states revealed a gradual increase in the percentage of high schools offering life-science courses during the period 1860 to 1900, with botany rising from 70 percent to 83 percent, zoology rising from 20 percent to 45 percent, and the newly combined study of biology capturing 10 percent.[95] This trend leveled off during the first quarter of the twentieth century, with a dramatic decline in number of high schools offering separate courses in botany or zoology roughly offset by an increase in the number offering biology. One national survey of secondary schools comparing the years 1908 and 1923 showed a decline in the number of schools offering botany from 81.5 percent to 29.9 percent and zoology from 52.2 percent to 1.8 percent, with biology jumping from 26.5 percent to 83.8 percent.[96]

Although only a portion of the students in schools offering life-science courses actually took those courses, there is no indication that this portion was increasing. To the contrary, the United States Bureau of Education statistics for the years 1910, 1915, and 1922 indicated a steady decline in the percentage of high-school students taking botany or zoology that was not offset by the increase in the percentage taking biology.[97] During the 1910s, science-education leaders repeatedly expressed concern about dropping enrollment in high-school science courses, especially for the life sciences, but never attribute this to any unpopularity of evolution.[98] Clearly, the timing of the anti-evolution crusade cannot be attributed to a new emphasis on evolutionary life-science teaching within secondary education.

Thus, opening the second Russian doll simply leads to a third; for if most high schools were teaching evolutionary life sciences all along, then a general expansion of secondary education to include more youth could produce a reaction from those opposed to such teaching. Historians Ronald L. Numbers and Kenneth K. Bailey have suggested just this as one irritant for the anti-evolution crusade, and the available evidence backs them up.[99] "It was in the period between 1880 and 1920 that the American high school assumed its familiar shape and characteristics," historian of education Edward Krug has concluded.[100] This was certainly a period of tremendous expansion for American secondary education. The federal Commission of Education did not even record national high-school enrollment figures in 1880, and by 1890 this figure stood at only 202,963 pupils, representing 3.8 percent of the 14 to 17 age group.[101] This statistic doubled every decade during the rest of the period, jumping to 519,251 pupils in 1900, to 915,085 pupils in 1910, and to 1,851,968 pupils in 1920. The number of public high schools also increased dramatically, rising from 2,526 schools in 1890, to 6,005 schools in 1900, to 10,213 schools in 1910, and to 14,326 schools in 1920.[102]

The public perception of such a change is the stuff of which popular crusades can be made. Reviewing his thirty-six years as an educator in a speech before the New York Chemistry Teachers' Club in 1917, John Woodhull observed, "We have several high schools in New York City now that have more pupils than all the United States had when I began to teach. The pupils now number about 1,500,000 against, say, four or five thousand in the whole country then."[103] Regardless of the accuracy of Woodhull's figures, he clearly perceived a tremendous increase in secondary education.

Although public elementary education expanded to include most children at least fifty years earlier, it had not carried evolution. Historian Ruth Elson's analysis of over a thousand nineteenth-century elementary-school textbooks uncovered almost no hint of evolution and none at all of natural selection.[104]

This presumably continued throughout the period since even proponents of evolutionary teaching believed that the theory was too difficult for younger children.[105] It was the expansion of public secondary education that carried evolution to an increasing number of America's youth, and this expansion coincided with the anti-evolution crusade. Crusaders recognized this connection from the beginning. In a 1921 speech that helped launch the anti-evolution crusade, William Jennings Bryan cited the small percentage of children going to high school and college in the past as the only reason Darwinism "has not done more harm."[106] The rapid expansion of secondary education thus gave new immediacy to the danger.

The expansion of public secondary education, which carried along evolutionary science teaching, does not exhaust the possible explanations for the timing of the anti-evolution crusade. Historian James R. Moore saw the passing of the early "evangelical evolutionists" as one explanation, since the most prominent Christians seeking to reconcile orthodoxy with evolution died before the crusade.[107] These evangelical evolutionists include Asa Gray, who collaborated with geologist George Frederick Wright in efforts to popularize an orthodox-Christian interpretation of Darwinism. Joseph LeConte expended similar effort promoting a liberal-Christian interpretation of evolution. The Christianity of Gray and LeConte could certainly have helped to defuse religious opposition to the evolutionary content of their texts. Their passing, followed by Wright's death in 1919, could have upset the balance working toward the reconciliation of the evolutionary and Christian world views.

Beyond this, the sudden emergence of the anti-evolution crusade reflected a growing disquiet about evolutionary thought based on political and religious concerns that, coupled with an increased public interest in the content of high-school education stimulated by the growing number of secondary-school students, created an eager response when the cry sounded to "drive Darwinism from our schools."[108] Coming from William Jennings Bryan, the era's greatest orator and lay Christian leader, this cry hardened the vague anti-evolution feelings of countless thousands into a fighting conviction.

2

Outlawing Evolution

1920–1925

"I have supported the four [Constitutional] amendments that have been adopted since I entered politics—Popular election of Senators, Income Tax, Prohibition, and Woman Suffrage," Bryan reported at the height of his anti-evolution efforts. "I also had a part in the passage of the Currency Bill and in every other reform that has been adopted in the last thirty three years."[1] Probably no other American, save the authors of the Bill of Rights, could rightly claim credit for as many Constitutional amendments as the Great Commoner. But this is attributable as much to the progressive reform era in which Bryan flourished as to the legendary oratory, driving energy, and reforming spirit contributed by the Commoner to the progressive cause. Although only sixteen amendments have been added to the Constitution during the nearly two centuries since that document was ratified and the Bill of Rights adopted, fully a quarter of those, the four identified by Bryan, were added in just one decade. That decade, the second of the current century, represented the culmination of a generation of populist and progressive agitation that made unprecedented use of law as a means of reform, with constitutional enactment simply standing as the highest form of law. Bryan was a chief agitator throughout this period.

The turn-of-the-century Progressive Era, broadly defined to include the period from 1875 to 1925, generated a tremendous variety of different reform movements and drew in a wide spectrum of participants. "Never before had the people of the

United States engaged in so many diverse movements for the improvement of their political system," historians of the era Arthur S. Link and Richard L. McCormick observed in 1983. "Yet in the goals they sought and the remedies they tried, the reformers were a varied and contradictory lot."[2] Some progressive reforms aimed at protecting certain individuals from economic exploitation (especially children, farmers, women, and workers) by such means as child labor laws and railroad rate regulation. Other reforms focused on increasing popular control over government and combating political corruption through provisions for legislation by initiative, direct election of senators, women's suffrage, and the like. A third group of reforms sought to rationalize business competition by antitrust and labor law restrictions. Finally, certain reforms attempted to improve the quality of urban life, by, for example, sanitation and consumer protection laws.[3] What these progressive reforms shared, according to the Link-McCormick thesis and an earlier analysis by historian David Kennedy, was a common pattern of development rather than a common ideology.[4]

Link and McCormick found this common development pattern arising from a shared "belief in interventionism" that underpinned the efforts of progressive reformers. This belief typically led progressives first to encourage others to bring their behavior voluntarily into line with some desired standard and then to coerce laggards into comformity by force of law. Elaborating on this pattern, Link and McCormick noted that a "familiar scenario during the period was one in which progressives called upon public authorities to assume responsibility for interventions which voluntary organizations had begun."[5] In his history of populism, which can be viewed as the first progressive reform movement, Lawrence Goodwyn found this familiar scenario, which he broke into the four stages of organizational formation, participant recruitment, public education, and movement politicization, with the first three falling within Link's voluntary phase and the last representing Link's coercive phase.[6] In both analyses, law became the final means of implementing reform.

Freed from the need to find a unifying ideology joining Progressive Era reforms, Link saw progressivism lapping over its traditional boundaries into the 1920s. This broke with the established historical interpretation that saw progressive idealism replaced by a conservative reaction after the First World War.[7] Nevertheless, as Link noted, it accounts for the continued strength of progressives in Congress following the war, the enactment of certain progressive reforms during the twenties, and the strong showing by Progressive Party presidential candidate Robert La Follette in 1924.[8] Even though the two Presidents most closely connected with the progressive cause, Theodore Roosevelt and Woodrow Wilson, died or became inactive at the onset of the twenties, Bryan, La Follette, and other priminent progressives survived to carry on the fight. Indeed, Bryan, saw the 1922 Congressional elections as a "progressive" victory and he pushed hard for progressive candidates at the 1924 Democratic National Convention, which led to his brother's nomination for vice president.[9] The anti-evolution crusade fits snugly into both this historical setting and the interventionist pattern outlined by Link, McCormick, and Goodwyn for all progressive reform movements.

"A Double-Barrelled Shotgun"

William Jennings Bryan, William Bell Riley, and John Roach Straton were easily the three most prominent leaders of the national anti-evolution crusade. Of these, Bryan certainly stood out most in the public mind during the early 1920s as he used both his prominence as a respected politician and his magnificent speaking voice to battle evolutionary teaching. In testimony to this, Riley called Bryan "his greatest co-laborer, the mightiest lay-leader associated with the fight against evolution."[10] By this testimony, Riley left for himself the title of the mightiest religious leader in the fight. Riley could rightly lay claim to this title as the founder and guiding force of the strongest religious organization supporting the anti-evolution crusade, the World's Christian Fundamentals Association (WCFA). Bryan was officially representing the WCFA when he participated in the *Scopes* trial.[11] For this trial, Bryan summoned the last member of this triumvirate, Straton, as a expert witness on religion.[12] Straton opposed evolution as vehemently as anyone, and was most often suggested as Bryan's successor in leading the anti-evolution crusade after the Commoner's death in 1925.[13] Long before the anti-evolution movement arose, all three of these men were deeply involved in other progressive reform movements.

Bryan was perhaps America's premier progressive. When Bryan was but a young Nebraska politician and former congressman, his famed "Cross of Gold" speech to the 1896 Democratic National Convention led his party into the progressive camp on the key issue of currency reform. The Democratic party nominated Bryan for president three times on a progressive platform while he simultaneously carried the endorsement of the populist People's party in 1896. Throughout his adult life, Bryan campaigned tirelessly for countless liberal progressive reforms. In summarizing Bryan's career, the influential progressive editor William Allen White wrote that Bryan "stood for as much of the idea of socialism as the American mind will confess to."[14]

Typically, Bryan joined reform movements in their final politicized stage, as they pressed for a legislative remedy. Bryan recognized this role. "[M]y work is not the work of a pioneer. While the work of a pioneer is a very honorable one," Bryan wrote during the anti-evolution crusade about his efforts generally, "my intention has been to deal with the questions which seem solvable in the immediate future or at least in my life time."[15] Thus Bryan skipped the pioneering stages, when reform ideas were generated, supporters recruited, and the public educated about the issue, only to take the lead of political efforts to enact reform legislation when those efforts became ripe for success. This was his pattern in the anti-evolution crusade as well.

Bryan's progressive activism never let up during his life, and it continued while he fought evolution during the twenties. "Bryan's increasing preoccupation with Darwinism and evolution did not in any way curtail his promotion of political questions and reforms," biographer Lewis W. Koeing observed. "In the most absolute sense, his endeavors in religion and politics were interlocking. He could not do one to the exclusion of the other."[16] A year before his death, he offered himself as a candidate for delegate to the 1924 Democratic National Convention "running as a progressive."[17] He subsequently served as a leading progressive voice at that convention. Earlier that same year, he was feted by the liberal New York Progressive Club for his lifetime achievements.

The traditional picture painted by H. L. Mencken and Richard Hofstadter of Bryan as a broken, seedy, and even reactionary figure during his anti-evolution years wilts under recent scholarship. Rather, Bryan remained a progressive leader advocating new and defending old reforms, promoting international peace reminiscent of his days as Wilson's Secretary of State, and trying to revive progressivism within his party.[18] The most that can be fairly charged against Bryan on this score is that his progressivism remained rural, agrarian, and dry while the main currents of Democratic reform shifted to urban, industrial, and wet. When a political cartoonist drew Bryan as a big-game hunter shifting his aim from a Republican elephant to a Darwinian monkey, Bryan responded, "You should represent me as using a double-barrelled shotgun firing one barrel at the elephant as he tries to enter the treasury and another at Darwinism—the monkey—as he tries to enter the school room."[19] At the time of his death, Bryan was planning to run for the Senate, where he hoped to rally the progressive forces within the Democratic party.[20]

Although William Bell Riley lacked Bryan's progressive pedigree, he was active enough during his early career for historian Ferenc Szasz to maintain that Riley "was a social radical when he arrived in Minneapolis in 1897, on the left, and a social radical when he died in 1947, but on the right. Riley went from radical to radical by standing still."[21] Even though historian C. Allyn Russell challenged this as "an overstatement," he agreed that Riley was active in social concerns.[22] Riley pastored the prestigious First Baptist Church in Minneapolis during the first half of the present century. There he built a small religious empire, including four schools, that served as the base for his national promotion of Evangelicalism. Riley was active in the prohibition movement before the First World War, when prohibition was a central progressive reform. He also championed turn-of-the-century legal and political efforts to enforce anti-gaming, anti-prostitution, and Sunday closing laws, all of which placed him in the company of progressives.[23]

From his experiences with progressive causes, Riley clearly appreciated the role of law in coercing reform, even though his main answer to social problems remained individual Christian conversion and regeneration. "For six years 'evangelism' has been the watchword of Evangelical Christians," Riley said in 1906 of the movement alternatively called either Evangelicalism or, after 1919, Fundamentalism by its followers. "For the same length of time 'reform' has been the shibboleth of every successful politician. It is most natural that these movements should come together."[24]

John Roach Straton personified this merger of Evangelicalism and progressivism better than Riley. Straton was a prominent Baptist minister in Chicago, Baltimore, and Norfolk during the 1910s, before assuming the pulpit of New York City's huge Calvary Baptist Church from 1918 until his death in 1929. Throughout his ministry, Straton was a leading proponent of progressive social service among theologically conservative Christians. "Christianity is a means of *social* salvation as well as a means of individual salvation," Straton affirmed as he advocated this double-barrelled gospel of progressivism and Evangelicalism in a lifetime of sermons, articles, tracts, and debates.[25]

Speaking to the more than six thousand original fundamentalists at the 1918 inaugural convention of the WCFA, Straton asserted that "[t]here is a logical and vitally important place" for Christian social service.[26] "The ministers and the church of Christ are traitors to their trust," Straton exclaimed three years later as the anti-evolution crusade got under way, "unless they battle heroically against such evils as unjust wages, especially to women workers, child labor, and the hell-black social evil, lawlessness, and the awful shame and disgrace of the liquor traffic."[27] These key progressive issues of the minimum wage, child labor, and prohibition were just the beginning for Straton. He had a curiosity about socialism and regularly called for the redistribution of wealth in America through welfare and income taxation.[28]

Straton did not limit his role to that of the evangelist advocating voluntary right conduct, but appealed to lawmakers to coerce reform. In his role as executive secretary of the Social Services Commission of the Interchurch Federation of Baltimore, Straton wrote a newspaper editorial outlining his hopes for the 1914 Maryland legislature. "New laws are necessary under the changed economic, political, social and moral conditions of today," Straton wrote. The editorial went on to identify these needed reforms, including legislation to improve working, housing, and prison conditions; to redistribute wealth; and to expand the rights of women.[29] Before entering the ministry, Straton had planned a career in law and politics.[30] His continuing interest in legislation showed that he never completely forgot his earlier ambitions.

Despite his progressive social convictions, Straton never adopted a purely social gospel that sought a material rather than a spiritual salvation. "The true aim of social service, indeed, is to open the way for spiritual service. Mere reform, apart from Christ, can not permanently heal the sores of our society," Straton exclaimed. "To improve environment gives a better chance for the transforming truths of God to reach the hearts and change the lives of men—and that is the Christian philosophy of social service."[31] Just as child labor, grinding poverty, and liquor could destroy spiritual sensitivity according to Straton, so could a belief in evolution.[32] So Straton crusaded against evolutionary teaching along with other perceived social ills. Commenting on Straton and Riley, each of whom came from rural southern origins to serve in urban northern ministries, Ferenc Szasz observed, "They were both active in the strong ferment of reform which swept through the cities during this period, and they might well be seen as representatives of the rural wing of the progressive movement. Their concerns with reform continued into the 1920's, but their emphasis changed considerably from their progressive days."[33] In Bryan, these two strong-willed ministers found a soulmate who had led this rural wing of the progressive movement for a generation and, by the twenties, also was ready to battle evolution.

The channel connecting the anti-evolution movement with a progressive heritage of using law as an instrument of coercing reform runs deeper than just the personal experiences of the three leading anti-evolutionists. As the anti-evolution crusade was getting under way around 1920, American evangelicals were just concluding their most exhilarating foray into the political realm of legislating reform since freeing the slaves—prohibition. The Eighteenth Amendment to the U.S. Constitution outlawing the public sale of alcoholic beverages was overwhelmingly ratified in 1919. This amendment culminated a forty-year struggle to reform American drinking habits, first by voluntary regeneration and finally by federal coercion. Historically, this struggle emerged with the first stirrings of populist reform, accelerated during the Progressive Era, and culminated in the waning days of Wilsonian reform.

In many ways, prohibition was the product of a typical progressive reform movement, and has been recognized as such by recent scholarship.[34] Historian Jack S. Blocker's quantitative analysis of prohibition leaders found them "educated, mobile geographically and probably occupationally, winners in politics as in battle, living in close contact with the dominant social forces of the country—urbanization and industrialization," and, most critically, religious, with "four-fifths belonging to evangelical denominations."[35] Finding links between the leaders of the mid-nineteenth-century abolitionist and late nineteenth-century prohibitionist movements, Blocker noted that the prohibitionists "adopted from conservative abolitionism a belief in the need for political action. It was a paradoxical program because political action involved coercion, which implied that some men would remain unreformed. Their only resolution was majoritarianism, which retained a radical faith in regeneration along with the conservative expectation that a minority could not be reformed."[36]

Passage of the Eighteenth Amendment in 1919 left these evangelical prohibitionists free to agitate for other reforms. It also left them with the experience of successfully invoking law to reform social and moral behavior—successful, that is, until the Twenty-first Amendment repealed prohibition in 1933. Even though the anti-evolution crusade never reached anywhere near the following enjoyed by the prohibition movement, most leaders (and probably most supporters) of the new crusade were drawn from the ranks of the prohibitionists.[37] Bryan, Riley, and Straton were seasoned prohibitionists. Key regional anti-evolution leaders also supported prohibition, including the Rev. Frank Norris of Dallas, Mississippi's Rev. T. T. Martin, and the Rev. John Porter of Kentucky. So did the three major southern Protestant denominations—the Southern Presbyterian General Assembly, the Southern Baptist Convention, and the Southern Methodist General Conference.[38] Although none of these denominations officially endorsed anti-evolution laws, their members provided the grass-roots political support that led to the enactment of the laws.

Just as abolitionism once served as an inspiration for the prohibition movement, so too the prohibition movement served as an inspiration for the anti-evolution crusade—but with each reflection, the image grew dimmer. Other pale reflections of the prohibition struggle appeared in Progressive Era efforts by evangelicals to enact blue laws and legally restrict such morally offensive conduct as gambling, dancing, smoking, and the showing of lewd movies.[39] Just four years before he proposed the first anti-evolution bill, Porter harkened back to the good old days when the Continental Congress had the wisdom and courage to outlaw gaming.[40] He soon called for similar legislative wisdom and courage to outlaw evolutionary teaching.

A further progressive element hallmarking the anti-evolution crusade appeared in the crusaders' concern for adolescent development. More than anything else, the crusaders opposed evolutionary teaching because it harmed the spiritual and moral development of students. "[T]he teaching of evolution is being drilled into our boys and girls in our high schools during the most susceptible, dangerous age of their lives," crusader T. T. Martin warned. "Ramming poison down the throats of our children is nothing compared with damning their souls with the teaching of evolution, that robs them of a revelation from God and a real Redeemer."[41] Such an earnest concern for adolescents was typical of the Progressive Era, and reflected an emerging conception of the teenage years as a special period of impressionability and spiritual vulnerability that replaced an older view of youth as either miniature adults or undergoing a longer, less defined transition from childhood to adult maturity.[42] This changing conception of youth generated a host of progressive reform movements aimed at protecting and nurturing adolescent development. These included movements for compulsory school attendance, secondary education, child-labor laws, separate juvenile-justice systems, playgrounds, industrial education, foster homes for orphans, and widows' pensions.

These movements concerned with adolescent development drew in many future anti-evolution crusaders. Bryan, of course, joined all of the movements named above. He was especially active in those promoting public education.[43] During the same year that he launched his anti-evolution crusade, he proposed creating a federal Department of Education.[44] Three years later, in 1924, the chairman of the Illiteracy Commission of the National Education Association, a prospective Democratic National Convention delegate, advised Bryan that "most of us would rather see you President than any man on this earth, and we know that education would be one of your chief interests."[45] The author of these sentiments must have been familiar with Bryan's views on evolutionary teaching because she lived in Frankfort, Kentucky, where Bryan personally led a strong anti-evolution effort just two years earlier.

The three major southern Protestant denominations also displayed a keen interest in secondary education during the Progressive era by supporting church-related high schools during the late nineteenth century before the public secondary-school movement reached the South and by endorsing the extension of public education thereafter.[46] Throughout the period, these denominations called for a Christian influence in education, laying a foundation for opposing allegedly heretical evolutionary teaching. For example, in 1904, long before attention was focused on evolutionary teaching, the Southern Presbyterian General Assembly officially advocated "protecting public schools from the evils of influences unfavorable to Christianity;" while in 1917 the Southern Baptist Education Commission endorsed the appointment of only Christians as public-school teachers.[47]

No reform movement captured the progressive spirit of protecting adolescent development better than the drive against industrial labor by children. Here the element of legal coercion entered in much the same way as it entered the anti-evolution effort. Reflecting the earlier view of adolescence, government leaders praised industrial child labor as benefiting youth and society in the colonial and early national periods. This attitude began to change during the nineteenth century, as industrialization and the modern view of adolescent vulnerability spread. Despite efforts by early progressive reformers to educate the public about the dangers of child labor, a record number of American children were working in gainful occupations at the turn of the century. About this time, a massive grass-roots reform movement sprang up across the country in opposition to child labor. Local, state, and eventually national child-labor reform organizations emerged, participants were recruited to the cause, muckraking public education efforts appeared, and, ultimately, state and federal legislation was enacted to restrict the industrial employment of minors.[48]

In the North and nationally, these efforts precipitated around the secular settlement houses and grew to include the business and social elite offering little direct participant overlap with the anti-evolution movement, though Straton fought for child-labor reform in Baltimore and New York while Bryan supported the movement nationally. But in the South, where white children manned the expanding textile mills, the movement was closely linked to the churches, many of whose members later opposed evolutionary teaching. All three major southern Protestant denominations actively supported child-labor laws during the early twentieth century.[49] Ordained ministers pioneered the effort in the key southern textile states of Alabama, North Carolina, and Georgia.[50] Although southern religious opposition to child labor was not centered in the church's evangelical wing, a heritage of successful religious agitation for legal regulation protecting children was established. Bryan called on this in one of his major stock anti-evolution speeches. Appealing for popular support against evolutionary educators, Bryan cried, "We have to enact child labor laws to keep college graduates from dwarfing the bodies and souls of little children."[51] This offered precedent for enacting protective legislation against evolutionary teaching.

Despite a tendency among some evangelicals to shun political involvement based on the otherworldliness of the Christian hope and the biblical doctrine of a fallen world, progressivism drew many theologically conservative Christians into movements clamoring for the coercive regulation of individual behavior and the protection of children.[52] Bryan and Straton as individual evangelical leaders, and prohibition and child-labor reform as movements, stand out nationally in this respect, but beyond them lay countless other people and causes linking Evangelicalism and progressivism.

For example, *The Fundamentals*, a series of early twentieth-century booklets distributed by the millions with the goal of defining evangelical doctrines, only touched on politics in its last article, but there sided with key progressive concerns. "Some are quite comfortable under what they regard as orthodox preaching, even though they know their wealth has come from the watering of stocks and from wreaking railroads, and from grinding the faces of the poor," the article affirmed. "The supposed orthodoxy of such preaching is probably defective in its statements of the social teachings of the Gospels."[53] The Rev. Mark A. Matthews of Seattle personified this union at the local level during the early twentieth century when he led local progressive reform efforts from the pulpit of the largest Presbyterian congregation in the world. Matthews's concern for children led him to draft the law creating Seattle's first juvenile court, to open the Northwest's first kindergarten, and to advocate that all youth have a right to go to college. It also led him to condemn evolutionary beliefs as "detrimental to spiritual growth" and to lament about teachers that "the schools are full of heretics."[54]

In 1906 Riley prophesied the coming together of the religious movement for fundamentals and the political movement for reform. This merger occurred over many issues during the Progressive Era. Thereafter, once evangelicals perceived a danger to youth from evolutionary teaching, they quite naturally sought a legal remedy. "The thirty-seven anti-evolution bills that were introduced into twenty state legislatures between 1921 and 1929," historian Lawrence Levine concluded, "were products of the American faith that legislative action can bring into being pure morals, right thinking, and patriotic action."[55] The same can be said of much progressive lawmaking.

Sowing the Wind

Evangelicals did not at first perceive evolutionary teaching as a grave threat requiring a legislative remedy. The evangelical movement had been coalescing for a half-century before generating the anti-evolution crusade in the twenties. Evangelicalism arose within mainline Protestant denominations and among independent revivalist churches, erupting as a major social force under the appellation "Fundamentalism" shortly after the First World War. Although fundamentalists lacked a unifying organization and differed among themselves on many fine points of doctrine, they typically shared the epistemological touchstone of biblical literalism. From this touchstone emerged a common belief that the human race was created by God, that all people deserve damnation for their sins, and that God lovingly sent Jesus Christ as a sacrifice for human sin, leading to salvation for anyone personally accepting that sacrifice.

Fundamentalism, however, defies easy analysis. Social historians traditionally attributed the postwar rise in Fundamentalism to widespread disillusionment over the outcome of the Great War and other attempts at liberal social engineering coupled with a concern over a perceived collapse of public and private morals. These tensions were seen as aggravating existing disquiet stemming from industrialization, urbanization, and other forces of social change, leading many to seek comfort in the oldtime religion. As such, Fundamentalism became part of the postwar return to normalcy.[56] In contrast, historians of religion recently began uncovering theological and intellectual roots for Fundamentalism reaching far back into the last century. In particular, Ernest R. Sandeen traced the origins of postwar Fundamentalism to the nineteenth-century revival of millenarianism throughout America and the emergence of the doctrine of biblical literalism at Princeton Theological Seminary.[57] George Marsden and Ferenc Szasz later merged Sandeen's findings into the broader cultural setting by interpreting Fundamentalism as an accelerating reaction by millenarians and other theologically conservative Protestants against the spread of biblical liberalism within the church and secularizing forces within society.[58] In this context, biblical liberalism, often called "modernism," meant giving a figurative interpretation to at least some scriptural passages based on the application of textual higher criticism.

By the end of the Great War in 1918, Evangelicalism had assumed the dimensions of a potentially powerful social movement, but lacked a specific common objective other than the general defense of biblical orthodoxy within the church. Source materials generated by the movement clearly indicate that stopping evolutionary teaching had not yet become a common goal. During the four decades bracketing the turn of the century, the evangelical message of scriptural authority and individual regeneration went out in countless local church meetings and regional summer Bible conferences.[59] Beyond this, evangelical spokesmen commonly vied with politicians, educators, and paid entertainers on the secular summer Chautauqua circuit. Such meetings, conferences, and lectures were especially popular in the days before movie theaters and radio. They played a decisive role in recruiting and educating participants for the evangelical movement, thereby accomplishing the second and third stages of Goodwyn's pattern for popular reform movements. A similar program of local interest-group meetings, regional conferences, and Chautauqua lectures rallied Americans to populism and other mass reform movements of the Gilded Age.[60]

Although most of the discussion about evolution at such public assemblies presumably went unrecorded, clearly no anti-evolution-crusade mentality existed there prior to the First World War. One indication of this appeared in the lectures given by William Jennings Bryan. As America's foremost orator and a favorite political and religious speaker, Bryan cut a popular figure on the Chautauqua and Bible conference circuits.[61] "The Prince of Peace," one of Byran's most popular and often repeated prewar speeches, handled the evolution issue with kid gloves. After opening with the observation that evolution does not resolve the ultimate issue of origins because the theory does not explain how the evolutionary process itself started, Bryan added that, "I do not mean to find fault with you if you want to accept the theory." Then, after noting certain logical and moral objections to evolution, Bryan assured his audience, "While I do not accept the Darwinian theory, I shall not quarrel with you about it; I only refer to it to remind you that it does not solve the mystery of life or explain human progress."[62] No call to war sounded here.

Further indicators suggest that only a mild creationism creased the warm summer air of the Chautauqua and Bible conferences. J. Dorman Steele published his popular high-school science textbooks in "Chautauqua Editions" for use in summer adult-education programs offered at those assemblies. Although clearly affirming creation by "the Almighty Worker" and tracing human ancestry to a single pair "created 'in the image of God'," these texts applied a figurative interpretation to the Genesis account.[63] Similar evidence comes from the influential fourteen-point creed of the great Niagara Bible Conference, which as the leading assembly of its type brought together prominent evangelicals for a week each midsummer during the last quarter of the nineteenth century.[64] This creed, "the bond of union with those who wish to be connected with the Niagara Bible Conference," focused on the role of the biblical Christ. Other than a general affirmation of the divine inspiration of all Scripture, the origins issue was covered by a simple assertion that man was "originally created in the image and after the likeness of God." The creed neither condemned evolution nor affirmed any particular means of biological creation.[65]

Printed tracts provided a second major medium carrying the evangelical gospel before the First World War. Here too, because the evangelical movement lacked a recognized authoritative voice, no tract presented the definitive evangelical position on evolution. Yet the most widely distributed evangelical tracts of the era, the twelve booklets called *The Fundamentals*, echoed the same conciliatory creationism that sounded at public assemblies. Three million copies of *The Fundamentals* were distributed free of charge between 1905 and 1915. These booklets contained more than one hundred articles written by a representative spectrum of leading evangelical spokesmen.[66] In an early article entitled "Science and the Christian Faith," the ordained minister and Scottish professor James Orr endorsed theistic evolution for subhuman life forms. " 'Evolution,' in short, is coming to be recognized as but a new name for 'creation,' only that the creative power now works from *within* instead of, as in the old conception, in an *external*, plastic fashion," Orr assured his evangelical readers. "Here, again, the Bible and science are felt to be in harmony."[67]

A somewhat harder line appeared in a *Fundamentals* article by George Frederick Wright, the Calvinist minister and geologist who collaborated in Asa Gray's earlier efforts to reconcile Darwinism and orthodox Christianity.[68] Wright's article maintained Gray's position that God must be the source of the special variation driving Darwinian natural selection. But he limited such theistic evolution to closely related species, with God directly creating the most distinctive special types, including man. After punching a series of scientific holes in broader versions of Darwinism, Wright assured evangelicals that "evidence for evolution, even in its milder form, does not begin to be as strong as that for the revelation of God in the Bible."[69] In the only other discussion of evolution in *The Fundamentals*, two jointly published articles by active ministers presented scientific-sounding arguments against Darwinism. One of these articles, by an anonymous author, took special aim at evolutionary preaching from the pulpit while the other, by Henry H. Beach, tackled evolutionary teaching in schools. Foreshadowing the coming crusade, this second article, dating from 1912, argued that the "teaching of Darwinism, as an approved science, to the children and youth of the schools of the world is the most deplorable feature of the whole wretched propaganda."[70] Despite this singular blow, *The Fundamentals* displayed much greater concern over biblical higher criticism than Darwinism and nowhere suggested outlawing evolutionary teaching.

The war experience did not immediately dispel the conciliatory air enveloping creationism, but it did supercharge the atmosphere of the evangelical movement generally. "Between 1917 and the early 1920's American conservative evangelicals underwent a dramatic transformation," historian George Marsden observed. "After 1920 conservative evangelical counsels were dominated by 'fundamentalists' engaged in holy warfare to drive the scourge of modernism out of church and culture." Marsden saw this change as a reaction to both the increasing radicalism of theological liberals and the cultural disruptions following the war.[71] The 1919 World's Conference on Christian Fundamentals cemented this change. This influential Bible conference attracted 6000 evangelicals to Philadelphia to hear the leaders of their movement denounce modernism and explain the fundamentals of their biblically orthodox faith. More critically, the conference generated two significant new elements: a coordinated battle plan of promotional and educational Bible conferences to build popular support; and a permanent interdenominational organization to direct the fight, the WCFA.[72] These steps finally addressed the organizational stages of Goodwyn's pattern for reform movements, leaving only the ultimate political stage to come.

Yet evolutionary teaching still was not singled out for attack. Delegates were welcomed by conference organizer William Bell Riley, who warned that their Protestant denominations were "rapidly coming under the leadership of a new infidelity, known as 'modernism'," followed by his invocation that the "conference is called to oppose the false teachings of the hour."[73] One by one, seventeen prominent fundamentalists trooped to the podium to expound their basic biblical beliefs while emphasizing, as one speaker put it, that " 'Modernism' is the product of Satan's lie."[74] "It is ours to stand by our guns," Riley said in closing the conference. "God forbid that we should fail Him in the hour when the battle is heavy."[75] Fundamentalism clearly had assumed a militant posture, but the future target of evolutionary teaching escaped serious assault.

Officially the conference went on record against both believing and teaching the theory of human evolution, but speakers did not dwell on either matter.[76] Even a glancing blow delivered by one speaker rejecting all forms of evolution on scriptural grounds was followed merely by a dismissal of evolutionary teaching as "just hot air"—hardly the vicious one-two punch against Darwinism and evolutionary teaching that soon characterized fundamentalist meetings.[77] Indeed, none of these early materials heralded an anti-evolution crusade, though in retrospect they all can be seen as preparing the way for such a crusade by reinforcing creationist convictions. "When the Fundamentals movement was originally formed, it was supposed that our particular foe was the so-called 'higher criticism'," Riley later recalled, "but in the onward going affairs, we discovered that basal to the many forms of modern infidelity is the philosophy of evolution."[78] After this discovery, however, the key fundamentalist media of Bible conferences, printed tracts, and the Chautauqua, carried the call to arms. The comparison of evolutionary teaching to "hot air" brings to mind the biblical warning against sowing the wind. The warning is apt, for evolutionary teaching soon reaped the prophesied whirlwind.

Bryan turned against the teaching of human evolution with a vengeance in early 1921. Characteristically, this change was marked by a new speech, "The Menace of Darwinism," which Bryan repeatedly delivered to Bible conferences and Chautauqua audiences during the remainder of his life. A second antievolution speech, "The Bible and Its Enemies," joined Bryan's repertoire later that year. Both speeches were printed as tracts and distributed by the thousands to ministers, fundamentalist laymen, politicians, and college students.[79] Bryan broke out of the starting blocks so fast that the friendly promotional material appended to the initial 1921 printing of the "Enemies" speech already used the phrase "Mr. Bryan and his crusade against Evolution."[80] These speeches rallied opposition to evolution. Just as critically, these speeches set the tone of that opposition, with other crusade leaders adopting Bryan's basic arguments and agenda.

Both speeches made the same pitch. The first part of each speech attacked Darwinism as both unscientific and unconvincing. Bryan appealed to the traditional Baconian definition of science to attack the scientific standing of Darwinism. The Commoner correctly summarized this definition, which was widely accepted by English and American scientists from the mid-1600s to the mid-1800s, by asserting that "science to be truly science is classified knowledge; it is the explanation of facts. Tested by this definition, Darwinism is not science at all."[81] "Darwin does not use facts; he uses conclusions drawn from similarities. He builds upon presumptions, probabilities and inferences," Bryan noted, accurately summarizing Darwin's hypothetico-deductive method only then gaining widespread acceptance among scientists.[82]

Despite this analysis and unlike the approach taken either earlier in *The Fundamentals* or later by scientific creationists,

Bryan's speeches acknowledged that scientists generally accepted the evolutionary hypothesis, but this did not settle the matter for the old populist campaigner. Instead, the Commoner appealed to his people, arguing that "the scientist can not compel acceptance of any argument he advances, except as, judged upon its merits, it is convincing."[83] For Bryan, this meant convincing to the common person. While maintaining that scientists and public-school teachers were entitled to their own opinions on evolution, Bryan feared that teaching Darwinism as true in public schools improperly compelled (rather than convinced) students to accept the doctrine.[84]

Bryan believed that the Darwinian theory of human evolution was not convincing to the popular mind. His speeches addressed this point with a series of ridiculing arguments zeroing in on several weakness in the theory, including Darwin's scientifically discredited law of sexual selection, shaky evolutionary explanations for the development of individual organs, and the absence of transitional forms. Satisfied that "the people, as a rule, do not believe in the ape theory," Bryan felt free to move against Darwinism regardless of scientific opinion.[85] "When reform starts in this country, it starts with the masses," Bryan claimed in one of his anti-evolution speeches. "Reforms do not come from the brains of scholars."[86] The application of this observation to evolutionary teaching could not be clearer—popular opinion should control public science. In Bryan's words, "Man is infinitely more than science; science, as well as the Sabbath, was made for man."[87]

Challenging the scientific basis and popular standing of evolution merely left Bryan where he had been nearly twenty years earlier with his "Prince of Peace" speech. But his anti-evolution speeches now moved on, explaining his new-found militant opposition to the Darwinian doctrine of human development with the observation that "a groundless hypothesis—even an absurd one—would be unworthy of notice if it did no harm. This hypothesis, however, does incalculable harm."[88] First and foremost, Bryan cited anecdotal and statistical evidence suggesting that belief in human evolution "leads people away from God" by giving them a materialistic rather than divine origin.[89] Here again, Bryan expressed his view on the relative place of science by observing that, "it is better to trust in the Rock of Ages, than to know the age of the rocks; it is better for one to know that he is close to the Heavenly Father, than to know how far the stars in the heavens are apart."[90]

Second and probably most crucial for Bryan's conversion, Darwin served to "lay the foundations for the bloodiest war in history."[91] World peace emerged as one of Bryan's chief concerns during his tenure as Secretary of State, culminating in his resignation from the cabinet in protest over Wilson's drift toward American involvement in World War I. Subsequent war relief work drew Bryan together with Stanford evolutionists David Starr Jordan and Vernon Kellogg. Kellogg's published accounts of those efforts linked German militarism to a Darwinian survival-of-the-fittest mentality.[92]

Beyond these pre-eminent concerns, Bryan feared that Darwinism encouraged the exploitation of labor by justifying selfish competition and discouraging reform by basing human improvement on slow physical evolution rather than rapid moral regeneration.[93] Bryan clearly carried his past progressive concerns with him into his anti-evolution crusade. Indeed, stopping the spread of evolutionary belief seemed vital to Bryan for maintaining the spirit of progressivism. As these supposed dangers followed primarily from a belief in human evolution, Bryan limited his efforts to defending the special creation of man without attempting a broader defense of pre-human creationism that marked the later creationist movement.[94] Consequently, anti-evolution legislation during the twenties typically barred only the teaching of human evolution while post-1960 creationist legislation sought the teaching of universal cosmic creationism.

To counter this menace of Darwinism, Bryan initially proposed three reforms that carried him to the brink of advocating anti-evolution laws. Only creationists should be allowed to preach in Christian churches. Only fundamentalist Christians should teach in church-supported schools. Finally, "in schools supported by taxation we should have a real neutrality wherever neutrality in religion is desired."[95] Bryan, always sensitive to the rights of religious minorities, appreciated that the disestablishment of religion precluded teaching the Genesis account in public schools.[96] But, Bryan added, "If the Bible cannot be defended in these schools it should not be attacked, either directly or under the guise of philosophy or science."[97] Though not yet calling for laws to enforce this third reform, Bryan assumed his final position that public education should be silent on the issue of human origins. Silence thus became the aim of anti-evolution lawmaking in the twenties, again in contrast to the recent creationist bills seeking equal time for creationism and evolution.

Bryan's slick, well-publicized arguments quickly steeled vague fundamentalist concerns over evolution into a crusading militancy against teaching as fact a Darwinian view of human origins.[98] "I think you have dealt a body blow to the materialism of the Darwinian theory," the Methodist chaplain of the University of Nebraska wrote to alumnus Bryan in early 1921.[99] By year's end, Kentucky's Baptist State Board of Missions, led by the Rev. John W. Porter, called for outlawing evolutionary teaching. Bryan immediately endorsed this call, and appeared on the spot to appeal for anti-evolution legislation before a joint session of the state legislature on January 19, 1922. In response to this appeal, state representative George W. Ellis promptly introduced the nation's first anti-evolution bill, and the dam burst. During the following decade, forty-five such bills surfaced in twenty different states.[100] Though the Kentucky bill died, Ellis continued crying for "open war against Infidel Evolution in Kentucky."[101] John Roach Straton began advocating similar legislation for his home state of New York in February 1922.[102] By fall, William Bell Riley had opened a third front in Minnesota. "The whole country is seething on the evolution question," Riley reported the following year, as he swung the full weight of the WCFA behind enacting anti-evolution legislation.[103] The season for lawmaking opened.

"A Two-Horsed Layman"

Spring 1923 offered the first real test of Bryan's legislative strategy. State legislatures of the day typically only assembled in general session during the first few months of odd-numbered years. The crusade got under way too late to influence the 1921 legislative sessions, and the scattered 1922 assemblies only generated near misses in Kentucky and South Carolina. But by early 1923 Bryan had focused the attention of the fundamentalist community on the anti-evolution issue and formulated his justification for a coercive legislative remedy. In a characteristic populist appeal to majoritarian control over governmental functions, Bryan reasoned, "Those who pay the taxes have a right to determine what is taught; the hand that writes the pay check rules the school."[104] Bryan addressed this appeal directly to several joint legislative assemblies during the year, as six southern and border-state legislatures grappled with anti-evolution measures.

America's first anti-evolution law passed with little fanfare in Oklahoma during early 1923. Even Bryan did not known about the measure until after its enactment, though the deed was done in his name. That deed, in a fitting combination of progressive support for public education with fundamentalist opposition to evolutionary teaching, provided for the free distribution of elementary school textbooks but precluded any mention of Darwinism in those texts. The restriction popped up without warning as a House floor amendment to the free-textbook bill. The immediate emotional passage of the surprise amendment testified to the effectiveness of the two-year-old crusade against evolutionary teaching.

Oklahoma crusaders flexed their muscles even before the 1923 legislature convened. In November 1922 the state Baptist General Session called for legislation banning "the teaching of evolution in our public school system."[105] Responding to the popular mood, several Oklahoma lawmakers made campaign promises or post-election pledges to support anti-evolution measures. "I promised my people at home that if I had the chance to down this hellish Darwin here, that I would do it," one freshman legislator told his colleagues in his maiden floor speech.[106] Shortly after his election but before taking office, another freshman representative wrote to Bryan asking for help drafting an anti-evolution bill. In explaining his request, the legislator described the heated controversy over evolutionary teaching that "rent asunder" his local high school and forced the school superintendent's resignation. He then added, "a number of our prominent citizens are requesting me to introduce a measure into the House of Representatives which will prevent, not only in our Public High Schools but all State Educational institutions in any way supported by State taxes, to have any teachers, or any text books, which present Darwinian Evolution."[107] Bryan complied with this request by sending reprints of his anti-evolution speeches, but never became directly involved with the Oklahoma effort. The Commoner's physical presence proved unnecessary—his spirit sufficed.

On February 22nd, in the midst of the routine consideration of a popular measure for the state to provide free textbooks to school children, the Democrat-dominated Oklahoma House "was thrown into an uproar" by the surprise introduction of an anti-evolution amendment.[108] The proposal, offered by a Bryan Democrat representing a rural district, provided "that no copyright shall be purchased, nor textbook adopted that teaches the 'Materialistic Conception of History' (i.e.) the Darwin Theory of Creation versus the Bible Account of Creation."[109] As a dozen legislators clamored for recognition to speak, a supportive moderator immediately put the issue to a vote, which the amendment passed by a narrow margin. Fearing that the amendment endangered final passage of the free-textbook measure, surprised sponsors of the bill moved for reconsideration of the amendment, touching off a furious debate that revealed the depth and populist tenor of anti-evolution sentiment.

Amid hoots of disapproval, the House Majority Leader appealed to scientific progress. "This is a step toward the dark ages. In progressive Oklahoma we can not afford to establish such a precedent as this," he pleaded.

The sponsor of the amendment rejected this elitist argument with a call for popular control over public science. "I'm neither a lawyer or a preacher," he shouted, "but a two-horsed layman and I'm against this theory called science!"

A freshman legislator passionately seconded this populist cry. "I have been a party to none of the groups or cliques in this house and have listened to the eloquent gentlemen here until my heart has cried out in rebellion," the new lawmaker proclaimed. "If you want to be a monkey, go out and be a monkey, but I am for this amendment and will strike this infernal thing while I can." A fellow Democrat agreed, declaring that it was time to place the party behind Bryan again.

Order nearly collapsed when a proponent of the textbook bill vilified amendment sponsors and accused them of offering the amendment solely to scuttle the bill. One anti-evolutionist tried to rush the accuser, physically, shouting "let me take care of him." Another expressed his sincere concern for school children, affirming "If you announce that I am opposed to giving free books to the children of this state, if you announce that I have offered a single amendment to kill this bill, you lie!"

Finally convinced of the sincerity of amendment supporters, the Majority Leader withdrew his opposition. "I am not against religion," he assured his colleagues. "I believe in the holy Bible. My father was a Quaker preacher and I believe just as you other men believe." Without further ado, the amended free-textbook bill passed the House by a vote of 87 aye to 2 nay.

The free-textbook bill breezed through the Democrat-controlled Oklahoma Senate with the anti-evolution rider firmly attached.[110] A Republican senator's motion to strip the amendment gained little support against the populist arguments for the restriction. "I object to Darwin or Spencer or any so-called evolutionists giving our children their spiritual life," one senator intoned during floor debate. "Let's leave their hellish teachings out. Practically all of our church members of this state are opposed to the teaching of Darwin." The vast majority of senators agreed and the motion to strike the House amendment died on an unrecorded vote: public opinion was allowed to control public science. Senators were unwilling to take the next step, however, and they tabled on a voice vote a Democrat senator's amendment to bar state schools from teaching Darwinism altogether.

Oklahoma Governor John C. Walton, a progressive Democrat, signed America's first anti-evolution measure into law on March 24, 1923, just a month after its introduction. Walton privately opposed the restrictive amendment as a reactionary, Klan-inspired blot on an otherwise enlightened free-textbook bill; but he supported the bill more than he opposed the amendment, so he accepted the lot.[111] For reasons wholly unrelated to the

anti-evolution rider, the entire free-textbook program was re-
pealed shortly after Walton's impeachment in 1925, but for now
Bryan was delighted. Hoping for a bandwagon effect, the
Commoner began touting the measure before he even saw it.
"The State of Oklahoma has recently passed a law eliminating
Darwinism from the text books of the public schools of the state,"
Bryan wrote to the mayor of New York. "The question is up to
other states and I beg to bring it to your attention for such ac-
tion as you may deem proper to take."[112]

Despite strenuous personal efforts by Bryan and other anti-
evolution legislators in several states during 1923, only Florida
followed Oklahoma in legislating against Darwinism. Action by
Florida was fitting. Bryan had "retired" to the Sunshine State a
few years earlier and immediately became a powerful force in
state politics. He repeatedly considered running for the U.S.
Senate from his new state and racked up an unprecedented
statewide vote in his race for Democratic National Convention
delegate in 1924. But in 1923 his state political objective was an
anti-evolution measure—and the Democratic state legislature
readily complied.

In an April 11th letter to one state senator, Byran requested
"legislation prohibiting the teaching in public schools or colleges, atheism, agnosticism, or the teaching as true of Darwinism or any other evolutionary hypothesis that links man in blood
relation with any form of animal life below man." To stop such
teaching, Bryan continued, "it is very important that there should
be a simple declaration, declaring it unlawful." He added two
important notes of caution, however, that were followed in the
Florida measure but disregarded in later, more radical legislation. First, Bryan stressed, "I do not think there should be any
penalty attached to the bill. We are not dealing with a criminal
class and a mere declaration of the state's policy is sufficient."
Second, Bryan suggested that the measure should only apply
to teaching human evolution as true. "A book which merely
mentions it as a hypothesis can be considered as giving information as to views held, which is very different from teaching
it as a fact."[113] By incorporating these qualifications, the Florida legislation passed quietly while later anti-evolution laws
touched off continuing controversy.

A week after this letter, the Florida State Assembly unanimously approved Bryan's proposition in the form of a concurrent resolution.[114] Tracing Bryan's language, this measure resolved it as improper for any public-school teacher "to teach or permit to be taught Atheism, or Agnosticism, or to teach as true Darwinism or any other hypothesis that links man in blood relation to any form of lower life." The measure retreated from Bryan's recommendation that such teaching be outlawed in favor of a weaker statement declaring it to be "improper and subversive to the best interests of the people."[115] But even this can be traced to the Commoner's opinion that a declaration of state policy would suffice to resolve the problem. After Bryan appeared on the scene in early May to lobby for the resolution, the state Senate added its unanimous assent and the Governor gave his approval. America's second anti-evolution measure became effective on May 25, 1923, though without the force of law or any appreciable impact on teaching policies.[116] The event passed unnoticed in the press, leaving the resolution to stand as a silent tribute to popular opposition to evolutionary teaching. Most of the publicity given the measure came directly from Bryan, who hailed the resolution as expressing his views on the controversial issue.[117]

The Florida resolution stands out as the only approved measure expressly stating the key concept that anti-religious evolution should not be taught in public schools because pro-religious creationism could not be taught.[118] This notion of neutrality through silence reflected the stated positions of Bryan, Riley, and other anti-evolution crusaders.[119] Presumably, this concept was an unstated assumption of all the anti-evolution legislation dating from the twenties. Decades in advance of current scientific creationists, Bryan recognized that neutrality could alternatively come from presenting students with opposing views on the origins issue. He even tried unsuccessfully to get schoolbook companies to "publish books that present the other side, so that students can read both sides and thus reach their own conclusions."[120] But Bryan's main objective remained silencing evolutionary teaching through law. Tennessee soon took center stage in a series of events leading to the showdown at the county courthouse in Dayton.

Pressure for anti-evolution legislation built steadily in Tennessee. During the spring offensive of 1923, committees of both houses of the Tennessee legislature killed bills outlawing evolutionary teaching. Crusaders redoubled their efforts in the face of these defeats, with Riley campaigning against evolution throughout Tennessee and the South later in the year. Bryan followed in early 1924, giving a speech in the Tennessee capital against evolutionary teaching that local supporters reprinted and distributed by the thousands to state residents and lawmakers.[121] Tennessee's progressive Democrat governor, Austin Peay, joined Bryan on the platform for this speech. The legislative off-year of 1924 yielded the introduction of only one anti-evolution bill anywhere in the country and no official action in Tennessee, but preparations continued for the following year when lawmakers would again convene in Nashville and most other state capitals. Six southern and border-state legislatures then faced anti-evolution measures, but only Tennessee acted favorably.

Bills outlawing evolutionary teaching appeared in both houses of the solidly Democratic Tennessee legislature soon after that body convened in January 1925. While the Senate Judiciary Committee promptly defeated the bill in its chamber, the lower house quickly and quietly passed its bill. "[I]t shall be unlawful for any teacher," the House measure declared, "to teach any theory that denies the Story of Divine Creation of man as taught in the Bible, and to teach instead that man has descended from a lower order of animal." The prohibition applied to teachers at all state-supported schools, with violations carrying a small monetary fine.[122]

Despite the radical nature of this bill, no substantive debate guided the House action. Less than a week after its introduction, the measure sailed through by a margin of 71 to 5 during an afternoon session in which the House hurriedly dealt with a wide variety of non-controversial issues. The anti-evolution measure duly came up for floor action after the House already had considered over two dozen bills in barely twice that many minutes and faced a couple dozen more on the daily agenda. As the House ground through its calendar, all bills sparking debate were held over for another day. When the anti-evolution bill reached the floor, one legislator requested just such a hold be placed on the measure. The sponsor of the bill objected, seeing no need for any debate because everyone understood the issue. Another representative backed up the sponsor by a parliamentary call for the previous question, and the bill passed without further discussion.[123]

Plenty of discussion ensued before the state Senate joined in passing the bill on Friday, March 13th.[124] The bill became the focus of considerable public attention during the intervening period, with public meetings, petitions, church sermons, newspaper editorials, and letters to the editor of state papers devoted to the topic. Local ministers eagerly joined in on both sides of the debate, with modernists vehemently opposing the legislation while fundamentalists embraced it.[125] The state House of Representatives even re-entered the fray by adopting a resolution defending its passage of the bill. Responding to a local pastor's elitist denunciation of the House's allegedly "asinine performance" in approving the measure, the House resolution affirmed that the legislature acted on behalf of all the people, not just a fanatical group. The resolution went on to admonish ministers to stay out of politics.[126]

After the Senate Judiciary Committee initially rejected the House bill, the fundamentalist Senate Speaker delayed further consideration until after an upcoming four-week recess, hoping to bring constituent pressure to bear on opponents. Meanwhile, the leading Senate proponent hastily wrote Byran for help. "I am writing you to know just what form of legislation you would suggest," the senator noted. "Other members have asked me to write you for suggestions before the matters comes up for final passage. If necessary we can defer final action for a few days longer in order to have the benefit if your advice." The senator concluded by inviting Bryan to address a joint session of the legislature after the upcoming recess.[127] Bryan wrote back by return mail recommending only one change—drop the penalty. Confident that teachers would respect a simple declaration, the Commoner argued that a penalty simply offered a ready target for critics without increasing the impact of the law. As a model, Bryan offered the Florida resolution.[128] Bryan's recommendation and presence proved unnecessary for passage; the recess alone sufficed. The day after returning, the Judiciary Committee reversed itself and sent the measure to the Senate floor with a favorable recommendation.

Senate debate focused on religion, education, and popular opinion.[129] Opponents argued that evolutionary teaching does not undermine religion and that the legislature should not promote one religious view of origins in public education. Supporters vigorously countered both points. "If you take these young tender children from their parents by the compulsory school law and teach them this stuff about man originating from some protoplasm," the powerful Senate Speaker replied, "they will never believe the Bible story of divine creation." Another proponent added, "We do not ask that Christianity be taught in the schools, but we do ask that nothing contrary to that belief be taught." Ultimately it was popular opposition to evolution that carried the day. One wavering senator, after expressing his regret at having to vote on the issue, announced his support "on the grounds that an overwhelming majority of the people of the state disbelieve in evolutionary theory." Another senator opined that 95 percent of Tennesseans supported the bill. With no senator contesting this estimate, the House bill cleared the Senate by a margin of 25 to 6.

Showing their support for education, the entire state legislature then boarded a special train for a weekend inspection tour of the state university in advance of hiking state funding for that institution. As this trip suggested, the Tennessee legislature's opposition to evolutionary teaching never spread to public education generally, or to an attempt to control the beliefs of public-school teachers. During the same session in which they passed the anti-evolution bill, both houses of the Tennessee legislature increased funding for education and rejected measures prohibiting the employment of teachers believing in atheism or evolution.[130] The state legislature set its sights solely on evolutionary teaching, and hit the target. The scant legislative opposition was scattered between the political parties and among both rural and urban lawmakers, without any apparent pattern beyond personal conviction.[131]

The Tennessee House of Representatives erupted in applause on March 23, 1925. The governor had signed the anti-evolution bill into law! During the preceding week, liberal clergy and scientists from Tennessee and across America entreated Governor Peay to veto the measure—but the governor's faith stood firm.[132]

"The people have the right and must have the right to regulate what is taught in their schools," Governor Peay explained in a written statement announcing his decision to sign the bill. "Right or wrong, there is a deep and widespread belief that something is shaking the fundamentals of the country, both in religion and morals. It is the opinion of many that an abandonment of the old-fashioned faith and belief in the Bible is our trouble in a large degree. It is my own belief." Accordingly, Peay willingly joined in outlawing evolutionary teaching. In doing so, he described the act as a popular "protest against an irreligious tendency to exalt so-called science, and deny the Bible in some schools." Although he hoped this protest would discourage such abuses, Governor Peay doubted that the law would ever be enforced. According to Peay, the bill allowed such wide latitude in teaching "the time and manner of God's processes in His creation of man" that no current science textbook violated the law. Further, Peay believed that the law "may not be sufficiently definite to permit of any specific application or enforcement."[133] In making this prediction, the governor never foresaw the staging of a test case where the prosecution and defense cooperated in putting the new law on trial. Even as the applause died down in the Tennessee House chamber, that test case began taking shape. Ultimately the jury was popular opinion.

3
Enforcing the Law
1925–1960

"We are looking for a Tennessee teacher who is willing to accept our services in testing this law in the courts," the New York based American Civil Liberties Union announced soon after the anti-evolution statute passed. "Our lawyers think a friendly test can be arranged without costing a teacher his or her job. Distinguished counsel have volunteered their services. All we need now is a willing client." This announcement appeared in a Chattanooga paper on May 4th, preceded by the assurance of the city school superintendent that the test case would not occur there.[1] But the paper served a wider area. Out in the rising hill country forty miles north of Chattanooga, eager civic boosters in Dayton read into the announcement an opportunity to put their town on the map.

The procedure of a public-interest legal organization bringing a test case challenging the constitutionality of the anti-evolution statute surprised backers of the law. Traditionally, constitutional challenges occurred in defense of an unwilling defendant charged with violating a statute. Governor Peay reasonably assumed that such charges would never be filed. During the 1920s, however, the ACLU sought to shatter many traditional assumptions in defense of its concept of individual freedom—and the Tennessee anti-evolution statute became its most famous target. A respected group of eastern social activists and liberal lawyers formed the Civil Liberties Bureau during the First World War to defend the rights of Americans opposed to the war. After the war in 1920, the Bureau took the name American Civil Liberties Union and expanded its mission to the defense of civil rights generally, focusing on free speech for political radicals and labor organizers. The initial position statement of the ACLU put the new Union on a collision course with the anti-evolution movement as well. "The attempts to maintain a uniform orthodox opinion among teachers should be opposed," the ninth article of the position statement affirmed. "The attempts of education authorities to inject into public schools and colleges instruction propaganda in the interest of any particular theory of society to the exclusion of others should be opposed." [2]

A secularized missionary zeal fired the new ACLU. The initial annual report pledged, "By demonstrations, publicity, pamphlets, legal aid, bail, test cases in the courts, financial appeals,—by all these methods of daily service the friends of progress to a new social order make common cause." [3] The report never adequately defined this new social order, but it clearly included absolute freedom of speech, legal protection for labor-union activities and political agitation, and expanded minority rights. [4] ACLU leaders realized that this new social order required enlightening popular opinion, and sought this through court trials dramatizing restrictions on civil liberties. "The chief activity necessarily is publicity in one form or other, for ours is a work of propaganda,—getting facts across from our point-of-view," the first report declared. [5]

At its inception only a year earlier, the World's Christian Fundamentals Association also vowed to battle for popular opinion, but with the very different goal of restoring traditional religious values. [6] The promotional efforts of these two organizations to advance their very different concepts of the ideal social order set the stage for the sensational Tennessee "monkey trial," where both sides accused the other of using the trial to publicize its own views. [7] At first, however, the ACLU did not see Fundamentalism as a clear and present danger to its cause. None of the Union's first four annual reports on the conditions of civil rights in America, covering the five years from 1920 though 1924, identify religious groups among the "agents of repression" or cite anti-evolution sentiment as a threat to educational freedom. This changed with the passage of the Tennessee anti-evolution law. Thereafter, throughout the twenties,

"Fundamentalists" and anti-evolution laws featured prominently in the ACLU reports, joining Klan-supported limits on
Catholic schools, the American Legion's push for patriotism in
the classroom, and mandatory religious instruction as the
gravest threats to academic freedom.[8]

The Union's goal of publicizing the perceived threat to freedom posed by the Tennessee anti-evolution statute through a
test case coincided with the goals of Dayton civic leaders to
publicize their town. The manager of a local coal company,
George W. Rappelyea, conceived the idea of staging an anti-
evolution test case in Dayton after reading the ACLU announcement in a Chattanooga paper on May 4th.[9] The next day,
he shared his idea with other local businessmen, lawyers, and
school officials, who agreed to the scheme to boost business.
Together, they secured the consent of a young science teacher
named John T. Scopes to stand trial. Not being a biology teacher,
Scopes doubted whether he had ever violated the law, but he
had conducted a review for the biology final exam and the course
textbook he had used, Hunter's *A Civic Biology*, prominently
featured evolution. On these grounds, Rappelyea swore out a
warrant against Scopes and wired the ACLU for help while the
school-board chairman called the Chattanooga newspaper.[10]

Under Tennessee's then new declaratory judgment act, Scopes
did not need to be charged with violating the anti-evolution law.
Instead, as a Tennessee teacher with a direct professional interest in the law, Scopes could have requested a judgment declaring the statute unconstitutional without risking criminal conviction.[11] The ACLU probably anticipated this course when it
advertised that the case would not endanger the teacher's job.
But the Dayton civic leaders apparently never considered this
course, and the ACLU welcomed the drama of a criminal trial.

The Dayton civic leaders were not the only interested party
meeting in Tennessee on Tuesday, May 5th. In an ironic coincidence, the annual convention of the WCFA, then assembled
in Memphis, that same day formally debated the question of
"why taxpayers should permit evolution and modernism to be
taught at will by school teachers while the reading of the Bible
is barred."[12] Led by William Bell Riley, the convention formally
commended the governor and legislature of Tennessee for

"prohibiting the teaching of the unscientific, anti-Christian atheistic, anarchistic, pagan rationalistic evolutionary theory."[13] The following weekend, Bryan arrived to address the convention, adding his voice to the chorus against evolutionary teaching. The Great Commoner joined in praising the state legislature for passing the anti-evolution statute, while tempering his remarks by repeating his opposition to any such law carrying a criminal penalty and cautioning that religion should not be taught in public schools. He then added in passing, "I notice that a case is on the docket for trial involving the evolution statute in your state. I certainly hope it will be upheld. It ought to be."[14]

Recognizing the interest of its organization in the pending *Scopes* case, the WCFA leadership soon asked Bryan to represent the Association at the trial.[15] Even though he had not argued a case in decades, Bryan agreed to do so "without compensation," and thereafter became a special prosecutor for the state, vowing "a battle royal between the Christian people of Tennessee and the so-called scientists."[16] As a master politician, Bryan recognized the propaganda potential of the *Scopes* trial. "The American people do not know what a menace evolution is," Bryan observed while preparing for trial. "I am expecting a tremendous reaction as a result of the information which will go out from Dayton."[17] Writing for Riley as well as himself, WCFA activist J. Frank Norris exclaimed, "It is the greatest opportunity ever presented to educate the public and will accomplish more than ten years' campaigning."[18]

The ACLU had not yet chosen Scopes's defense team when Bryan joined the prosecution. Originally, ACLU Executive Director Roger N. Baldwin and other Union strategists had planned to attack the law solely for unconstitutionally restricting academic freedom without specifically addressing the underlying conflict over evolutionary teaching. With Bryan now threatening to raise that broader matter anyway, the ACLU responded in kind. "Many would have presented the simple issue that the law on its face violated constitutional guaranties," noted the chief ACLU representative at the trial, Arthur Garfield Hays. "The defense went further and sought to show that such laws result in hate and intolerance, that they are conceived in bigotry and born in ignorance—ignorance of the Bible, of religion, of history, and of science." After describing the positive public response to these broader arguments, Hays concluded, "It is possible that laws of this kind will hereafter meet the opposition of an aroused public opinion. That was not without our purpose. . . . That people should derive light and education from court proceedings may be novel, but can hardly be objectionable."[19] Foreseeing this unique opportunity to promote evolutionary thought as well as academic freedom, the ACLU set about assembling a crack, publicity-conscious defense team.

Almost immediately after Bryan stepped to the fore, Clarence Darrow and Dudley Field Malone jointly volunteered their services for the defense. After thirty years of defending political and labor radicals against criminal charges in sensational trials, Darrow stood out as the most famous defense attorney of the day. Like Bryan, Darrow gave popular lectures throughout the country supporting pacifism, workers' rights, and the Democratic party. Darrow even supported Bryan's presidential campaigns. But Darrow broke sharply with Bryan on religion, proudly proclaiming his personal rejection of Christianity, doubts about the existence of any god, and acceptance of materialistic evolution. In the *Scopes* trial, Darrow saw an ideal chance to promote his agnostic, evolutionary beliefs while defending academic freedom.[20] A lifelong progressive, Malone had also supported Bryan's presidential campaigns and had served as the Commoner's Third Assistant Secretary of State in the mid-1910s. After the war, Malone assumed the role of a dapper New York lawyer, developing a lucrative international divorce practice, traveling in the most glamorous circles, speaking widely for radical causes, and defending the civil rights of women, blacks, and political reformers. No longer a practicing Catholic and concerned about preserving freedom to teach evolution, Malone was drawn like a moth to the limelight of the *Scopes* trial.

Neither of these men had worked closely with the ACLU before, and Union leaders wanted someone in Dayton who had. To fill this role, the ACLU originally secured the participation of Bryan's successor as Secretary of State, Bainbridge Colby, but Colby withdrew shortly before the trial. Hays, an urbane Wall Street lawyer and founding ACLU national committee member, then replaced Colby at Dayton. Former Republican presidential nominee and future Chief Justice Charles Evans Hughes agreed to argue Scopes's case before the United States Supreme Court, should the need arise. With this star-studded defense team, the ACLU prepared to use the trial to promote public acceptance of academic freedom for evolutionary teaching. After Darrow explained this to Luther Burbank in the hope of securing the famed horticulturist's expert testimony, Burbank commented that the trial "appears to me as a great joke, but one which will educate the public."[21]

Both sides went to Dayton seeking to use a judicial forum to influence popular opinion. Their arguments addressed the world, not the jury. The world listened. Hundreds of reporters descended on Dayton from across America and Europe. Pioneering live radio broadcasts and newsreel footage carried the event with unprecedented intimacy to a fascinated public. Millions followed the progress of the eight-day trial, which was billed as a battle between religion and science. "We are told that more words have been sent across the ocean by cable to Europe and Australia about this trial than have ever been sent by cable in regard to anything else happening in the United States," Bryan observed in his farewell speech to the court. "The people will determine this issue." Darrow, in his final speech, agreed.[22] When the *Scopes* court convened on July 10, 1925, the Dayton town fathers could only marvel at the success of their little publicity stunt.

Popular Prejudice

Creationists held the high ground of popular opinion in Tennessee; enactment of the anti-evolution statute showed that. After toying with the idea of attacking evolutionary teaching head on at trial to justify the statute, the prosecution opted to stand on the basic proposition that the legislature has the right to control the content of public-school instruction.[23] Thus, at trial, lead prosecutor Thomas Stewart simply argued that the law "was formed and passed by the legislature, because they thought they saw a need for it. And who, forsooth, may interfere?"[24] This position made sense for at least three reasons. First, it was legally sound. "It has been held by the supreme court that the Tennessee legislature has the right to arbitrate and to judge as to how they shall proceed in the operation of the schools," Stewart correctly maintained. "[T]he Tennessee legislature is the proprietor of the schools and directs the handling of the school funds."[25]

Second, establishing this point promised substantial gains for the anti-evolution movement. Any doubts about the validity of the legislative restrictions against evolutionary teaching would fall by beating Darrow and the other prominent ACLU lawyers in a highly publicized case. The prosecutors believed that a vigorous defense would simply magnify the impact of a decision upholding the statute, regardless of the grounds for that decision.[26] Anti-evolution laws could then be enacted in other states where public opinion supported such restrictions. "As a result of the Scopes trial under your splendid leadership, I believe that Legislative bills will be introduced in the Legislatures of many states," an influential evangelical financier wrote Bryan during the trial. "[T]o my mind this is the psychological period of time, in which to push for similar legislative action in certain other states."[27]

The most compelling reason for the prosecution's narrow legal argument emerged only as both sides prepared for trial. Arguing the merits of evolutionary teaching required expert witnesses testifying about the scientific basis for evolution and the social or religious consequences of belief in evolution. Bryan's early enthusiasm for a battle royal between religion and evolution cooled as the balance of experts willing to duel this broader issue became increasingly tilted in the favor of evolution. While the defense quickly assembled over a dozen leading scientists and liberal theologians to testify in favor of human evolution, the prosecution struggled to find reputable expert witnesses for its side. The evangelical Baptist triumvirate of Riley, Straton, and Norris agreed to testify that the theory of human evolution contradicts the Bible.[28] A wider spectrum of conservative religious leaders agreed to lend their names to an Advisory Committee designed to offset the prestigious committee of scientists supporting Scopes.[29]

Anti-evolution scientists proved harder to find. "By all means you have present at the trial Pro. George McCready Price whose work on Geology utterly demolishes evolution," Norris wrote Bryan, adding that Price "is a scholar of unquestioned standing."[30] Norris correctly singled out Price as one of the few persons then pursuing science who rejected evolution, but exaggerated Price's standing. A devout Seventh-Day Adventist, Price was a self-taught geologist without professional standing who served as a science instructor at various church schools and wrote numerous creationist books during the first half of the twentieth century. At trial, when Bryan named Price as a scientist whom he respected, Darrow shot back, "You mentioned Price because he is the only human being in the world so far as you know that signs his name as a geologist that believes like you do." The thrust hit home. Bryan failed to name any others.[31] But, because he was overseas at the time, even Price declined Bryan's summons to Dayton. "I am in full sympathy with your efforts," Price wrote from England, "but it seems to me that in this case, it is not a time to argue about the scientific or unscientific character of the evolution theory, but to show its utterly devious and 'sectarian' character, and its essentially anti-Christian implications and tendencies. This you are very capable of doing."[32]

The other potential scientific expert witnesses contacted by Bryan were even less supportive.[33] Only the respected Johns Hopkins University physician Howard A. Kelly reluctantly agreed to come, convinced that the "Christian must stand very literally with the Word regarding the creation of man," but he warned Bryan that he accepted the evolution of other biological species.[34]

Given this response by their potential experts, the prosecution could not present a credible attack against evolution on either scientific or religious grounds. Samuel Untermyer discouraged any remaining thoughts of tackling evolution head on at trial. A distinguished New York trial attorney, Vice President of the American Jewish Congress, and a devoted public servant who had recently defended the ACLU in one of its major free-speech cases, Untermyer stood with Bryan on evolutionary teaching and volunteered his services for the anticipated appeal, where he believed that the real battle would occur.

Untermyer firmly believed that the legislature possessed the authority to determine school curricula and observed that the trial looked "rather like clear sailing for the prosecution."

Untermyer correctly guessed, however, that "what the Defense will try to do will be to obscure the issue and to endeavor to establish by a swarm of experts that the theory of evolution is a scientific theory." To avoid this, he advised Bryan, "I would seek to exclude all discussion by experts or otherwise on the subject of evolution (which, to my view, has nothing whatsoever to do with the case, whether true or false) and rest squarely on the proposition that the plain letter and spirit of the law have been violated."[35] The prosecution followed this advice. In one his last letters to local counsel before boarding the train for Dayton, Bryan wrote, "If we can shut out the expert testimony, which is intended to prevent the enforcement of the law by proving that it ought not to have been passed—a perfectly absurd proposition—we will be through in a short time. I have no doubt of our final victory, but don't know how much we will have to go through before we reach the end."[36]

The prosecution successfully maintained its position at trial, keeping all expert testimony from the jury while presenting unchallenged evidence that Scopes taught human evolution. The able defense made two major efforts to break out of this fatal straitjacket.

The defense first raised a series of constitutional objections to the anti-evolution statute, primarily claiming that the law unreasonably infringed on individual freedom.[37] "My contention is that no law can be constitutional unless it is within the right of the state under the police power, and it would only be within the right of the state to pass it if it were reasonable, and it would only be reasonable if it tended in some way to promote public morals. And, Your Honor, and you, gentlemen of the jury, would have to know what evolution is in order to pass upon it." This trial argument by defense counselor Hays correctly summarized the limits on state action under the Fourteenth Amendment to the federal Constitution. Hays compared the anti-evolution statute to a hypothetical law against teaching that the earth revolves around the sun. Surely the hypothetical law would be constitutionally unreasonable, Hays reasoned, and the anti-evolution statute should be too. "The only distinction," Hays argued, "is that evolution is as much a scientific fact as is the Copernican theory, but the Copernican theory has been more fully accepted." Pleading that public opinion against evolution should not be allowed to save the statute, Hays hoped to prove the unreasonableness of the statute by showing the scientific acceptance of evolution.[38]

In reply, the prosecution stuck to its narrow legal theory, maintaining that the law did not infringe upon individual freedom because it only applied to persons who chose to teach at public schools. Of course the legislature could not constitutionally proscribe private evolutionary teaching, the prosecution acknowledged, but it had the authority "to direct the expenditure of the school funds of the state, and through this act to require that the money shall not be spent in the teaching of theories that conflict or contravene the Bible story of man's creation." In short, the prosecution maintained that popular opinion acting through the elected legislature should control public scientific education. "That is the very crux of this lawsuit. That is absolutely the question involved here," Stewart argued.[39]

Both sides presented these constitutional arguments to the court with the jury excused, because, under American legal practice, the judge decides issues of law—including the constitutionality and interpretation of statutes. The jury then applies the given law to the facts of a particular case. For the *Scopes* trial, this meant that trial judge John T. Raulston would decide the legal issues. Raulston, the elected circuit judge for east-central Tennessee, very much represented the outlook of his electorate. After a day of deliberation, he sided with the state and upheld the statute on the basis of several recent federal and state supreme court decisions generally affirming legislative control over public education.[40] To him, the statute seemed reasonable.

With the jury again excused, the defense later tried to reach the broader issues underlying the anti-evolution debate by disputing the interpretation of the statute. Since the law expressly prohibited the teaching of "Evolutionary Theory," Darrow asked "to show first what evolution is." Because the law went on specifically to ban such teaching as denying the biblical "Story of the Divine Creation of man," Darrow sought leave to show "secondly, that any interpretation of the Bible that intelligent men could possible make . . . isn't in conflict with the theory of evolution."[41] The prosecution again frustrated the defense by successfully arguing that the law needed no expert interpretation. The intent of the law is clear, the prosecution claimed, adding that "they cannot come in here and try to prove that what is the law is not the law." Reinforcing this point, the prosecution added that evolution was not on trial, only the power of the state to restrict public evolutionary teaching.[42]

In addressing both the reasonableness and the meaning of the statute, the defense offered its assembled scientific and theological expert witnesses to explain evolutionary theory, to show the scientific acceptance of the concept, and to discuss the compatability of evolution with Christianity.[43] However, only one, Johns Hopkins University zoologist Maynard M. Metcalf, took the stand before the prosecution invoked prevailing evidentiary rules to check this attempt to educate the court, and the public about evolution.[44]

At the time, strict nationally accepted court rules discouraged expert testimony. As the prosecution correctly argued, expert witnesses could only testify about their own opinions on issues beyond ordinary understanding.[45] This effectively shut off the expert testimony at Dayton. No scientist could testify about the general scientific acceptance of evolution because that would involve testifying about the opinions of other scientists.[46] The judge foreclosed the remaining issues from expert testimony by ruling that the "ordinary, non-expert mind can comprehend the simple language" of the statute.[47] Bryan captured the populist spirit of this approach to statutory interpretation when he claimed, "Your Honor, it isn't proper to bring experts in here to try to defeat the purpose of the people of this state by trying to show that this thing that they denounce and outlaw is a beautiful thing that everybody ought to believe in."[48]

The wily Darrow turned this apparent defeat for the defense into the most famous *tour de force* in legal history: he called Bryan to the stand as an expert on the Bible. Of course, Darrow did not have a right to examine the opposing counsel and expert testimony already had been foreclosed, but the prosecution never raised these points. When the startled judge asked, "Mr. Bryan, you are not objecting to going on the stand?'' the confident orator replied, "Not at all."[49] Darrow had set Bryan up for a fall earlier in the trial by vilifying the Commoner's intelligence.[50] Beyond this, Bryan had put himself forth as somewhat of an expert on the Bible for years by speaking widely on religious topics and by writing a syndicated weekly column on Christianity printed in newpapers throughout the country. Bryan would not now refuse the great agnostic's challenge. So he took the stand before all America, only to expose his cause to public ridicule.

Through Bryan's testimony, Darrow sought to show that certain passages of the Bible, like the account of creation, cannot logically be accepted as literally true. Bryan fell for this scheme by admitting under close questioning that, despite his expertise, he had no notion about how Joshua lengthened the day by making the sun (rather than the Earth) stand still, whether the Noachian flood that allegedly destroyed all life outside the ark also killed fish, where Cain got his wife, or how the snake that tempted Eve moved before God made it crawl on its belly as punishment. Striking closer to home, Bryan acknowledged his acceptance of a long earth history and a day-age interpretation of the Genesis account. Further undermining his stance against evolution, Bryan confessed that he knew little about comparative religion or science. Bryan refused all the prosecution's efforts to defend him, proclaiming at the height of his ordeal, "I am simply trying to protect the word of God against the greatest atheist or agnostic in the United States. I want the papers to know I am not afraid to get on the stand in front of him and let him do his worst. I want the world to know."[51]

The world soon knew of Bryan's ordeal. The assembled media, which sympathized with Scopes from the start, ridiculed the anti-evolution movement in their coverage.[52] The jury, however, heard none of the testimony, being excused at the time because Bryan's testimony technically addressed a purely legal question of statutory interpretation.[53] Even Darrow told the jurors in his closing argument that, based on the scant evidence presented to them, they must convict Scopes. "We think we will save our point and take it to a higher court and settle whether the law is good," Darrow concluded.[54] Darrow and Bryan both acknowledged at the end, however, that ultimately popular opinion would determine whether evolution could be taught.[55] At the time of Scopes's conviction, Bryan remembered his ordeal on the stand the day before and feared its impact on his cause. "I shall have to trust to the justness of the press, which reported what was said yesterday, to report what I will say, not to the court, but in the press in answer to the charge scattered broadcast over the world."[56] He never got that chance; a week later the Great Commoner died in his sleep in Dayton. The anti-evolution movement lost its prime mover, but momentum carried it on.

With Bryan dead and the trial phase over, the *Scopes* litigation quickly lost most of its glamour.[57] Nevertheless, the ACLU vigorously pressed Scopes's appeal to the Tennessee Supreme Court in an unsuccessful effort to have the anti-evolution statute declared unconstitutional.[58] Although the appeal raised several constitutional challenges to the law, the debate centered on the issues of individual freedom versus state authority over public employees.[59] Comparing Scopes's conviction to the execution of Socrates, Darrow closed his emotional appellate argument by proclaiming that "we are once more fighting the old question, which after all is nothing but the question of the intellectual freedom of man."[60] Not so, replied the state, "It is not part of any one's 'liberty' to perform labor for the state."[61]

The thrust and parry continued. Recognizing the strength of the government's position, a brief supporting Scopes submitted on behalf of the Tennessee Academy of Science reasserted the unreasonableness of the restriction. "The cases relied upon by the State involved reasonable regulations made by the legislative body in relation to public work—not unreasonable, arbitrary, and capricious regulations."[62] The state countered that "the common belief of the people, expressed through their chosen representatives, is a sufficient justifying standard for valid police power legislation, even though such belief may be wrong, and even though 'science may yet show it to be wrong.' "[63] Turning Scopes's freedom argument on its head, the state described the law as the "deliberate, thoughtful enactment of a sovereign people, which was designed to protect their children in their own public schools in their beliefs in the divine origin of man, which in turn measures their responsibilities to God and to their fellow-man."[64] Looking into the other end of the telescope, the state thus saw the key freedom issue as being the right of parents to protect their children from evolutionary teaching rather than the "liberty of mind and of thought and of education" identified by the defense.[65]

Here the legal debate ended and the court ruled. Finding "little merit" in the contention that the statute violated constitutional liberties, the Tennessee Supreme Court decided that Scopes "had no right or privilege to serve the State except on such terms as the State prescribed. His liberty, his privilege, his immunity to teach and proclaim the theory of evolution, elsewhere than in the service of the State, was in no wise touched by this law."[66] After taking this position on the key issue, the *Scopes* court proceeded to uphold the statute, ruling that the state may "say what kind of work shall be performed in its service—what shall be taught in its schools."[67] The court brushed aside Scopes's secondary claim that passage of the statute violated the duty of the state legislature under the Tennessee Constitution to promote education and cherish science. "If the Legislature thinks that by reason of popular prejudice, the cause of education and the study of Science generally will be promoted by forbidding the teaching of evolution in the schools of the State, we can conceive of no grounds to justify the court's interference."[68] Regardless of the truth of evolution, the Tennessee Supreme Court concluded, popular opinion justifies restricting evolutionary teaching.

Scopes's defense team expected this decision upholding the locally popular anti-evolution statute—even welcomed it as a necessary step toward a review by the United States Supreme Court—but they cried foul when the Tennessee high court then reversed Scopes's conviction for a technical error in sentencing. Without a conviction, Scopes had nothing to appeal. Malone's immediate charge of "a subterfuge on the part of the State of Tennessee to prevent the legality of the law under which Scopes was convicted being tested" appears well founded.[69]

The fatal error in sentencing was simply that the judge, rather than the jury, imposed the $100 fine. Yet at trial, Judge Raulston had instructed the jury to set the amount of the fine unless "you are content with a $100 fine, then you may simply find the defendant guilty and leave the punishment to the court." After the state duly questioned this procedure, the trial judge described it as the usual practice, and both sides expressly waived any objection.[70] The defense never raised the point on appeal.[71] That should have foreclosed the issue. Yet the court used it to overturn the conviction, and then averted a retrial by requesting that the prosecution dismiss the case to conserve "the peace and dignity of the State."[72] All subsequent ACLU efforts to continue the lawsuit failed.[73] Even without further litigation, however, *Scopes* left a lasting imprint on the ongoing anti-evolution movement.

Seeds Scattered

The *Scopes* trial shook American popular culture the way a hail storm shakes a tin-roofed Tennessee mountain shack. Neither side clearly won the case, as is apparent from comparing the outcome against the stated objectives of the ACLU defense team. "Our objective in going to Tennessee was," Malone stated, "first, to expose the ignorance and intolerance which had produced such a law, and, secondly, to test its constitutionality by ultimately carrying the question to the United States Supreme Court."[74] The defense scored well on its first objective, and this set back the anti-evolution movement. Initial reports flooded the national media from Dayton proclaiming the ACLU gospel. *The Nation* reported on "the intolerance, bigotry, and arrogance" behind the prosecution. An editorial cartoon showing monkeys replacing men in the *Scopes* jury box appeared in the *Literary Digest*. The *New Republic* dismissed the law as "foolish." H. L. Mencken relentlessly ridiculed Bryan and anti-evolutionists in widely reprinted *Baltimore Sun* editorials. A *New York Times* magazine article reached precisely the verdict sought by the defense, concluding that "although Scopes was found guilty of a misdemeanor for teaching evolution, and was fined $100, Bryan was beaten and beaten badly."[75]

American historians came to accept this verdict on *Scopes*, thereby reinforcing its impact toward achieving the defense's first objective of discrediting the anti-evolution movement.

Paxton Hibben began the trend with his debunking 1929 Bryan biography, *The Peerless Leader,* which concluded that Darrow made "hash" of the Commoner at Dayton.[76] At midcentury, the influential historian Richard Hofstadter carried this verdict to a generation of scholars and students. In his classic treatises and popular history textbooks, Hofstadter maintained that the *Scopes* trial turned the tide against the anti-evolution movement by ridiculing the cause.[77] Two books appearing in 1958 echoed this interpretation. In a chapter entitled "To the Loser Belongs the Spoils," Ray Ginger's study of the trial asserted "that the Scopes trial was crucial for rallying the opposition to Fundamentalism and repression."[78] *The Perils of Prosperity,* William E. Leuchtenburg's widely read history of the twenties, agreed that "Scopes had lost, but, in another sense, Scopes had won" due to the reportedly fatal ridicule heaped on the anti-evolution movement.[79]

In a supreme testimony to the success of the ACLU at molding public perceptions through Scopes, Leuchtenburg described the anti-evolution movement as a southern rural phenomenon defeated by growing "cosmopolitanism."[80] In marked contrast to this image, which the ACLU had carefully cultivated at Dayton, many anti-evolution and fundamentalist leaders hailed from northern cities. Riley, for example, lived in Minneapolis and Straton in New York. Dwight L. Moody, a key late nineteenth-century figure in the rise of Fundamentalism, and his influential Bible institute that adopted the anti-evolution crusade in the twenties, both operated from Chicago. In addition, Boston's J. C. Massee and Toronto's T. T. Shields led key fundamentalist organizations about the time of the *Scopes* trial. Even the midwestern Bryan gained significant, albeit minority, support from the urban North for his blatantly evangelical presidential races. But the image proved self-fulfilling, as the anti-evolution movement and Fundamentalism shifted increasingly southward after *Scopes.*[81]

Many recent histories also presented *Scopes* as a mortal defeat for the anti-evolution movement. Lawrence W. Levine's sympathetic 1965 Bryan biography stressed the importance of the trial in "helping to check the spread of the anti-evolution movement."[82] Six years later, Louis W. Koenig's biography of the Commoner did the same.[83] "Scopes was found guilty of teaching evolution," George M. Marsden added in his 1980 history of Fundamentalism. "But in the trial of public opinion and the press, it was clear that the twentieth century, the cities, and the universities had won a resounding victory, and that the country, the South, and the fundamentalists were guilty as charged."[84] The image of Darrow slaying Bryan and routing the anti-evolution movement was further stamped on the public consciousness by the popular 1950s play about the trial, *Inherit the Wind*, which was made into an award-winning movie in 1960. More recently, a one-man touring show and television special about Darrow carried the same theme.

The media and historiographic presentation of the *Scopes* trial offer support for Malone's claim of victory at Dayton.[85] But a closer analysis, made in light of Malone's stated trial objectives, reveals an incomplete victory at best. Success at achieving the first objective of ridiculing opposition to evolutionary teaching was negligible in the South, perhaps because Southerners were the butt of the joke.[86] Beyond this, failure to attain the second objective of having the Tennessee law declared unconstitutional left states free to enact similar measures should prevailing popular opinion so warrant.

A few historians recognized this regional eddy within the main current of response to *Scopes*. Ray Ginger and George M. Marsden reported a short-lived southern spurt in anti-evolution activism quickened by the Commoner's death. A 1971 Bryan biography by Paolo E. Coletta noted a more enduring anti-evolution movement in the South "[s]timulated by the 'martyrdom' of Bryan." Ronald L. Numbers went even further in a 1982 article uncovering continued nationwide creationist activities linking Bryan's anti-evolution crusade to current creationism. Ferenc M. Szasz took another step in his 1982 history of American Protestantism. "The Scopes trial is often seen as the high point of the Fundamentalist controversy," Szasz noted, "but instead of being the apex, it was really just the beginning of the concerted antievolution agitation. The trial proved that an antievolution law could be passed and upheld, and pressure on many of the legislatures increased after 1925 until the peak year, 1927," with reduced "agitation" continuing to the present.[87]

The bewildering disparity in opinion about the impact of *Scopes* on the anti-evolution movement—from the immediate verdict for the defense in the eastern press to Szasz's recent verdict for the prosecution—highlights the unexpected resilience of this cause despite its pounding at Dayton. This is revealed in the legal actions following the *Scopes* trial and Bryan's death. During the months following Bryan's death, dozens of evangelical leaders rushed to pick up the fallen mantle, loosing a frenzy of uncoordinated and often localized legal activity against evolutionary teaching.[88] Three days after Bryan died, anti-evolution legislation was introduced in Georgia, one of the few states where the legislature remained in session. In 1926, three of the nine state assemblies meeting that year faced such bills, a record number for a legislative off-year. When the bulk of state legislatures next convened in the spring of 1927, eighteen different anti-evolution bills appeared in fourteen widely scattered states, an all-time high in both categories. A final introduction two years later in Texas rounded out the decade.[89]

Supplementing this legislative activity, some state and local educational boards took the initiative in moving against evolutionary teaching. A year before the *Scopes* trial, the state Board of Education in California had directed teachers to present Darwinism "as a theory only" while the North Carolina Board had barred state high schools from using biology textbooks that "in any way intimate an origin of the human race other than that contained in the Bible."[90] A few months after *Scopes*, the Texas Textbook Commission, acting at the insistence of Governor Miriam Ferguson, ordered the deletion of evolution from all public school texts. The Louisiana Superintendent of Education took similar steps the following year. Scattered local restrictions against evolutionary teaching also cropped up across America during the late twenties. Despite these administrative successes, legislative relief remained the primary legal objective for anti-evolution crusaders during the first few years after the *Scopes* trial.[91]

Only two of the legislative seeds scattered after *Scopes* fell on good soil and bore fruit. The first occurred in Mississippi, where local evangelist and Bryan-pretender T. T. Martin led the charge. He faced a remarkably homogeneous and potentially friendly legislature. During the twenties, Mississippi was the most rural, and perhaps the most Democratic, state in the Union. About seven-eighths of all Mississippians lived in the country, and none of them lived in a city having more than 25,000 residents. Further, Republicans had been few and far between in the state since the Grand Army of the Republic returned north following Reconstruction. Accordingly, the Mississippi legislature was entirely composed of rural Democrat lawmakers typically loyal to the ideals of their former standard bearer, William Jennings Bryan.[92] An anti-evolution bill gave them an opportunity to display that loyalty.

The Mississippi legislation followed the Tennessee law in making it a misdemeanor for any public school teacher "to teach that mankind ascended or descended from a lower order of animals." The new bill conspicuously omitted the Tennessee language stating that the proscribed theory denied the biblical account of human creation, presumably to avoid the interpretation of that account again becoming a legal issue at trial. The Mississippi bill also added provisions outlawing the selection or use of evolutionary textbooks and requiring the dismissal of any teacher or textbook commissioner violating the statute.[93]

Little fanfare greeted the introduction of the anti-evolution bill into the Mississippi House of Representatives in early January 1926, and the measure appeared dead following an adverse committee report. But this was before Martin descended on the state capital from his base in Blue Mountain, Mississippi. A fervent tent revivalist with a national ministry, Martin had railed against evolutionary teaching for nearly a decade, called the curious at Dayton to repentance from a street booth during the *Scopes* trial, and formed the Bible Crusaders of America to continue the fight against evolution after Bryan's death. Capturing the tone of his appeal, Martin's leading tract likened evolutionary teachers to German soldiers who were said to have poisoned French children during the First World War. "Ramming poison down the throats of our children is nothing compared to damning their souls with the teaching of evolution," Martin proclaimed.[94] Now he set his sights on his home state legislature, and he would not be denied.

Martin's lobbying efforts centered on demonstrating popular

support for the measure, beginning with a series of mass meetings in Jackson during the first week of February. Addressing a joint legislative session at midweek, Martin taunted members, "It is claimed that the law will bring on Mississippi the ridicule and abuse from the North that has been heaped on Tennessee. Shall the legislature of Mississippi barter the faith of the children of Mississippi in God's word and the Savior for the fulsome praise of a paganized press?"

Petitions were offered from around the state to support Martin's claim that "every man, woman, and child in the place wants an antievolution law passed."[95] After these efforts persuaded House leaders take up the bill, Martin called his largest rally for the day before the vote and packed the House galleries with supporters.[96] The longest, most heated debate of the session ensued, as the House ground through opposition amendments, arguments, and delaying tactics.[97]

The prime sponsor of the bill, a rural Church of God minister, opened the floor debate by warning, "Let this tommyrot be taught in the schools of Mississippi and the whole system of state and Christianity will be undermined." A co-sponsor added that "if the evolutionists want to teach this theory, let them build their own schools just as the Baptists, the Methodists, and the Catholics. Defeat of the bill will be a compromise with the devil."

"I am a firm believer in the 'old time religion,' but this kind of legislation is not proper," responded one legislator. "We should not attempt to say that the schools shall teach the truth or denial of any theory."

Meeting this plea for academic freedom with a countervailing cry for parental rights reminiscent of Martin's bombast, a proponent exclaimed that "we don't want evolution theory rammed down the throats of our children."

The greater danger, an opponent shot back, is not this ramming "iron hand, but the wooden head" that refuses to accept evolution. Charges of ignorance and bigotry were then exchanged all around, coupled with offsetting defenses of theistic evolution and biblical creationism. But the claim that "90 per cent" of the people favored the bill could not be challenged, and the bill passed the House on a vote of 76 to 32. One disgruntled representative explained, "I knew then, as I know now, that a majority of the members of the House are conscientiously opposed to the passage of the bill. But I also knew that, when forced to cast a record vote on this measure, conscience would give way to public opinion." With all the members serving as Democrats from rural districts, voting patterns cannot disclose any partisan or demographic divisions in this public opinion.

The drama was then re-enacted in the Senate. Again confronted with a negative committee report, Martin and his followers pressured the upper chamber into bringing the bill to the floor on a special order. There, a spirited, three-hour debate pierced to the heart of the matter.[98]

"I do not believe in legislation relating to religion," a leading opponent affirmed in opening debate. "If this legislature had been in session several centuries ago, we would have been called upon to consider a bill prohibiting the teaching that the earth revolves around the sun. If such an act had been passed, we would not be here today as a progressive people. To stop the study of science is to stop progress."

This eloquent plea against religious restrictions on academic freedom immediately forced proponents back to their basal position that school children need protection from evolutionary ideas even if those ideas are true. Capturing this position in a phrase, one senator declared that "though I am an evolutionist of a certain sort, I am going to vote for the bill in order to save our boys and girls from materialism." Building on this, another supporter added, "Great scientists look at all things as material and they frequently lose sight of the spiritual. I'd rather have the leadership of one Christian mother than of all the scientists in the world."

As the ensuing debate drifted over the familiar topics of theistic evolution versus biblical literalism and educational neutrality through silence on the subject of origins versus the legitimacy of evolutionary teaching, nothing really added to the initial exchange of pleas for academic freedom and protecting the faith of children. Claims that evolutionary teaching did not destroy faith fell on deaf ears, as did assurances that the bill did not interfere with freedom of thought or speech because it only applied to teachers during classtime. In the end, the rural, Democrat senators chose between these concerns. Faith won by nearly a two to one margin. The local paper gave full credit to the popular pressure generated by Martin's Bible Crusaders.[99] When the fundamentalist governor of Mississippi signed the bill on March 11th, popular opposition to evolutionary teaching gained another triumph.[100]

The most blatant example of popular opinion seeking to control public science occurred in Arkansas two years later. There, after the legislature narrowly defeated an anti-evolution bill, the editors of two state denominational journals, Ben M. Bogard of the *Baptist and Commoner* and J. S. Compere of the *Baptist Advance*, launched a campaign to enact an initiative act identical to the Mississippi law. With the help of Bogard's Missionary Baptist State Convention and Compere's state Southern Baptist Convention, a petition drive succeeded in placing the measure on the November 1928 ballot as Initiative Act No. 1. An evolutionary scientist's nightmare appeared in the offing. During the *Scopes* trial, one prosecutor had jokingly suggested a vote on evolution. "No, no, we are talking about scientific things," Darrow tersely replied.[101] Now, for the first time, a vote tested popular sentiment regarding evolutionary teaching.

National attention was diverted from the election, however, by the concurrent supercharged presidential race pitting the wet, Catholic, Democrat Al Smith against a dry, Protestant, Republican Herbert Hoover. Excitement over the presidential race in dry, Protestant, but Democratic Arkansas, coupled with the presence of Arkansas Senator Joseph Robinson on the ticket as Smith's vice presidential candidate, drew much local attention away from the initiative campaign as well.[102] With two chief evangelical bugaboos of a Catholic President and the repeal of prohibition at stake, even Bogard and other anti-evolutionists split their energies between supporting the initiative and opposing Smith.[103] Yet, like a local sideshow to the main event, the initiative campaign went on.

The people of Arkansas heard America laughing. They knew that the eastern press had pilloried Tennessee for the *Scopes* trial. Many of them surely read *Elmer Gantry*, Sinclair Lewis's best-selling 1927 satire whose benighted main character was modeled partially on the anti-evolution leader John Roach Straton.

Whether Arkansas would be tarred with the same brush became a major campaign issue. "To vindicate the Arkansas of the Twentieth century before the nation every man and woman who loves his state and loves intellectual and educational freedom should vote against this ill-conceived measure," editorialized the largest newspaper in the state, the *Arkansas Gazette*.[104] "Evolution may be true or false, but a popular vote to show that it is false can do nothing but arouse the pity and contempt of most civilized people," University of Arkansas Dean Vergil L. Jones told the press.[105] An opposition newspaper advertisement signed by scores of prominent state residents put it even more bluntly, pleading, "save our state from ridicule."[106]

Striking back against these charges, Bogard declared that "those who make such a silly statement fail to mention that Tennessee has taken on new life since the evolution bill became law. People of the right sort want to live in a state where the faith of their children will not be attacked in the free schools."[107] This bare statement, made without citing any supporting evidence, is reminiscent of Bogard's earlier claims that the greatest living scientists opposed evolution. When challenged, Bogard could name only Howard A. Kelly, but added that "God and Dr. Kelly are a majority."[108] It is a puzzle to compute how much Kelly added in this calculation.

Under the banner "The Bible or Atheism, Which?," proponents starkly stated their case in a small newspaper advertisement placed in the *Arkansas Gazette*. "If you agree with atheism vote against Act No. 1. If you agree with the Bible vote for Act No. 1." The ad went on to explain, "The bill does not prohibit free speech, it does not seek to help the church. It simply forbids the state attacking the church by having evolution taught in the schools at taxpayer's expense. Should concerned church members be forced to pay taxes to support teachers to teach evolution which will undermine the faith of their children?" Addressing the opposition's main theme, the ad closed with the rhetorical question, "The Gazette and Russian Bolsheviks laughed at Tennessee. True, and that sort will laugh at Arkansas. Who cares?"[109]

A much larger opposing ad in the same paper cut to the core of the issue, observing that "it is not the theory of evolution that is on trial, but the people of Arkansas."[110] As it turned out, those people showed their overwhelming opposition to evolutionary teaching by giving the initiative nearly two-thirds of the statewide vote. Political scientist Virginia Gray's quantitative analysis of this Arkansas vote found broad-based support for the meausre. She reported that "anti-evolution sentiment, as manifested by voting for Initiated Act 1, was not strongly associated with preference for Hoover, illiteracy, or the percent of Baptist church membership and was moderately associated with ruralism among the white populace." These characteristics of the stereotypical southern fundamentalist, taken either separately or together, fail statistically to account for the Arkansas results.[111] Opposition to evolutionary teaching reached far beyond any stereotype to a solid majority of the people. Now, through the democratic initiative process, that majority sought direct control over public science.

Two differences possibly attributable to the intervening *Scopes* trial emerge from comparing the Mississippi and Arkansas legislative actions with those occurring earlier in Oklahoma, Florida, and Tennessee. One of the main arguments raised against enacting anti-evolution legislation after *Scopes* was the risk of adverse national publicity. That argument had not appeared earlier. Beyond this, no cleavage was detectable between rural and urban legislators on the issue before *Scopes*. Afterwards, the only state legislature passing an anti-evolution statute was composed entirely of rural lawmakers, and Gray's analysis of the Arkansas initiative vote found a rural tilt in support for the measure. This evidence suggests increased media and urban opposition to anti-evolution laws following *Scopes*. Both shifts perfectly accorded with the ACLU's goals for that trial.

Uneasy Truce

Quiet fell over the battlefield after enactment of the Arkansas law in 1928. Both the anti-evolution movement and opposition efforts by the ACLU and other organizations died down. The sides entered a thirty-year truce.

On the one hand, anti-evolution legal activity slowed considerably. Only one anti-evolution bill surfaced the year following the Arkansas victory, and thereafter none appeared anywhere until 1959. Further, no indictments were filed during the hiatus under the three existing anti-evolution laws. Tennessee prosecutors, taking a cue from the state supreme court's recommendation not to prosecute Scopes, did not actively enforce their law. In 1927 the Mississippi attorney general refused to give his law an enforceable interpretation, seeing no violation if teachers "will in the future as in the past teach your pupils to look through nature up to nature's god."[112] The attorney general of Arkansas adopted a similar molifying approach in 1929, when he officially interpreted his state law as permitting all evolutionary instruction except the "teaching that man was ever anything but man."[113]

On the other hand, the opposition also reduced their activities during the period. Periodic legislative efforts to repeal the existing laws failed miserably.[114] At first, the ACLU eagerly sought new court challenges to all three laws, but lost interest after failing to find either willing litigants or active enforcement of the law. Several months after passage of the Mississippi law in 1926, the ACLU's publicity director reported that we "volunteered to assist the suit of any Mississippi taxpayer to enjoin expenditure of public funds for enforcement. Similar offers were made to Mississippi members of the American Association of University Professors. As yet no Mississippian, professional or lay, has responded."[115]

The Union broadened this search to cover Tennessee after the *Scopes* litigation reached a dead end in 1927, and on to Arkansas after the 1928 initiative passed, but still without success. "Circular letters and public offers of legal services brought interested inquires, but nobody willing to make the sacrifice," the ACLU reported in 1931. "The Fundamentalist drive on the teaching of evolution has somewhat let up; the laws are not effective in the state universities; and our counsels are divided as to the wisdom of taking the issue to the Supreme Court of the United States. But we intend to do so if a teacher for a test case is found." Finally willing to let a sleeping dog lie, the ACLU announced in its 1932 annual report that the Union was dropping the issue.[116] A pair of legal complaints challenging the constitutionality of anti-evolution laws, one filed with the

Knoxville federal court in 1925 by a state taxpayer opposed to the Tennessee statute and the other mailed into a Little Rock state court in 1929 by a New Yorker against the Arkansas law, were withdrawn without further litigation. Stillness returned after a decade of feverish fighting. Despite some threats, no other suits were filled until the landmark *Epperson* case in 1965.[117]

Historians have offered varying explanations for this decline in anti-evolution activism. Some simply attributed it to the public ridicule associated with the *Scopes* trial, dismissing the burst of activity after the trial as insignificant. Richard Hofstadter, Ray Ginger, and Lawrence Levine fit into this camp.[118] Willard Gatewood viewed the entire movement as ending when fundamentalists shifted their attention to defeating Al Smith in 1928. "A single personality came to replace a scientific theory as the focus of their socio-economic and religious prejudices," Gatewood claimed.[119] Yet Arkansas fundamentalists somehow focused their alleged prejudices on defeating both evolution and Smith in 1928, and Gatewood offered no explanation for their inability to refocus on evolution after the Happy Warrior was struck down. Arthur Link and Kenneth Bailey appear on stronger ground when they attributed the end of the drive for anti-evolution laws to the string of legislative defeats suffered in the late 1920s, especially in 1927 when eighteen bills went down in all parts of the country.[120] Most of these bills died in committee without ever receiving floor consideration.

Although this last explanation does not explain why the 1928 Arkansas victory failed to revive the drive, it provides a basis for understanding the lull in anti-evolution legal activity—especially if combined with the view attributing that lull to the impact of *Scopes* on popular opinion. George Marsden pointed out that the rural, southern image of the anti-evolution movement popularized by *Scopes* became self-fulfilling. Thereafter, statewide victories were confined to the South.[121] By 1929, most states of the old Confederacy had imposed restrictions against evolutionary teaching by law, legislative resolution, or administrative ruling. The widespread defeats of 1927 showed little to gain from carrying the battle to enact anti-evolution laws north. This futility was shown when the Rhode Island legislature referred its post-*Scopes* anti-evolution bill to the Committee on Fish and Game. At the same time, the Tennessee Supreme Court ruling in *Scopes,* the unwillingness of other litigants to challenge the laws, and the failure of all repeal measures showed, in the words of a 1932 ACLU report, "stubborn Southern hostility against Northern conceptions of science and faith."[122] With each side occupying its territory as delineated by prevailing popular opinion, an uneasy truce descended until battle conditions changed. During the ensuing three decades, further restrictions against evolutionary teaching were left to local school districts.

The terms of the truce decidedly favored anti-evolution forces because existing restrictions and fears of further controversy led commercial publishers to de-emphasize evolution in their high-school textbooks. As early as 1923, Ginn and Company, publishers of an evolutionary text already encountering opposition, sought peace with Bryan by guaranteeing to present evolution as a "theory" rather than "dogma."[123] Bryan responded favorably, although cautioning, "It would take a great deal in the way of elimination and addition to make it clear that evolution is presented only as a hypothesis, unproven, but an hypothesis that educated people should understand."[124] The crusade unleashed by Bryan on its own momentum rushed past this point of compromise, however, as statutes and administrative rulings soon prohibited the teaching of human evolution altogether. "Naturally we want to sell our books," the Ginn letter confessed to Bryan, but added, "It is exceedingly difficult . . . to avoid the use of the word 'evolution.' "[125] Faced with a complete ban on evolutionary teaching in much of the southern market and scattered controversy elsewhere, publishers soon surmounted this difficulty.

Anti-evolutionists focused their fire on George W. Hunter's *A Civic Biology*, the most popular high school biology textbook and the one used by Scopes.[126] "It could not be more objectionable," Bryan observed. "It does not refer to evolution as a hypothesis but presents it as if it were an established fact."[127] Riley agreed, specifically identifying the text as "not sound."[128] In 1926, the Louisiana Superintendent of Education went so far as to demand the removal of six pages on evolution from the Hunter text.[129] The author and his publisher, the huge American Book Company, readily complied by issuing *A New Civic Botany* in 1927 to replace the older version nationwide. The pages identified by the Louisiana official were rewritten, deleting the introductory title "The Doctrine of Evolution," two charts depicting evolutionary development, and every explicit reference to evolution. Man remained classified as a mammal in the surviving copy, but with the biblically orthodox addition, "Man is the only creature that has moral and religious instincts."[130]

Similar changes appeared throughout Hunter's new book. A paragraph on natural selection remined, but with all conclusions expressly identified as scientific suggestions rather than facts. A brief biography of Darwin still appeared with those of other leading biologists, but no longer identified him as "the grand old man of biology." References to the evolution of man and statements praising Darwin's theory completely disappeared from this biography. The phrase, "His wonderful discovery of the doctrine of evolution," now read, "His interpretation of the way in which all life changes." Equivocation and qualification replaced praise and dogma. The very word "evolution" disappeared from the book altogether, replaced where needed by the word "development."[131]

Other textbooks fell into line and stayed in line throughout the thirty-year lull in anti-evolution activity. "Strong pressure has been brought by Fundamentalists on publishers and authors of textbooks," pro-evolution science popularizer Maynard Shipley reported in 1930. "Many publishers have instructed their authors to omit all discussion of evolution or even to omit the word altogether." Shipley estimated that, largely as a result of this "emasculation of textbooks," 70 percent of public high schools omitted teaching evolution.[132] Corroborating this estimate, a 1932 Columbia University analysis of the eleven most widely used high-school textbooks found only two texts presenting the relationship between hereditary and environment—the key concept in evolution. Although all eleven tests presented at least some of the evidence for evolution and nearly three-fourths of them included biographical references to Darwin, only one text presented theories of the origin of life.[133] A decade later, a Carnegie Foundation-funded survey of American high-school biology teachers found slightly less than half of those responding taught evolution as "the principle underlying plant, animal and human origin."[134]

This trend continued through 1959. About that time, two leading biologists marked the centenary of *Origin of Species* by giving separate addesses, both entitled "One Hundred Years Without Darwinism Are Enough," decrying the inadequate treatment of evolution in high-school biology textbooks. In the earlier of these speeches, Indiana University zoologist Hermann J. Muller laid the blame for this treatment on a "vicious circle" of legal restrictions against evolutionary teaching throughout the South and in some local communities elsewhere giving textbook authors and publishers an economic incentive to de-emphisize the theory. "Can we afford to let the profit system destroy us?," Muller asked. "Here is where intervention by government, by the general public, and by the professional groups most concerned—those of teachers and scientists—is in order to break the vicious cycle."[135] Dr. Muller's prescription was taken during the sixties. In the later speech, Harvard paleontologist George Gaylord Simpson complained that the treatment of evolution in textbooks effectively blocked evolutionary teaching in high schools. "Some biology texts do omit evolution," Simpson observed. "Most of them relegate evolution to a single section, preferably in the back of the book, which need not be assigned."[136]

The *Origin* centennial was marked by another event testifying to the treatment of Darwinism in high-school textbooks. The last old-fashioned anti-evolution bill ever offered in America appeared in the Missouri House of Representatives that year.[137] The chief sponsor, an Ozark County schoolteacher, explained his reason for offering the bill with the observation that the doctrine of human evolution had already infiltrated college textbooks and was "creeping into the high school texts too." Coming from a legislator who was also a teacher, this comment testified to the omission of the doctrine from earlier high-school texts, suggested that the omission contributed to the lull in anti-evolution activity, and foreshadowed a hostile response to a return of evolution into those texts. The action also reflected several ongoing trends. Continuing the shift of anti-evolutionism toward the rural South and anticipating growing Republican support for the cause, the bill was sponsored by four Republican representatives from rural southern Missouri. Other members of the overwhelmingly Democratic legislature of that heavily urbanized border state ridiculed the measure, leading the chief sponsor to vow, "They might treat it as a joke. But when it comes to time for a roll call, the joke will be on them." That roll call never came because the bill died in committee, but the effort pointed toward a new dawn for creationist legal activity. For present purposes, however, the chief sponsor's comments primarily offered further first-hand evidence of the omission of evolution from high-school texts during the lull in anti-evolution legal activity.

Two retrospective surveys of high-school biology textbooks confirmed this point. Gerald Skoog's quantitative analysis of representative texts found only about 3 percent of the words in texts published between 1930 and 1959 dealt with evolutionary topics, compared with over 8 percent in texts published during the sixties after evolution generally returned to the classroom. The most sensitive evolutionary topics, including the origin of life and the evolution of man, rarely appeared at all. Less than half of the texts even used the word "evolution."[138] A parallel qualitative analysis by Judith V. Grabner and Peter D. Miller concluded that textbooks "downgraded their treatment of evolution" during the twenties. "Not until 1960," the authors observed, "was the treatment of evolution in the most widely used high school texts substantially improved over that found before the Scopes trial."[139]

Both studies cited Truman Moon's *Biology for Beginners* as a case in point. Under various titles and with different co-authors, Moon published new editions of his popular text about every five years from 1921 to 1963. Moon's initial text carried a picture of Darwin as the frontispiece, opened with the affirmation that biology was "based on the fundamental idea of evolution," and stated that "both man and ape are descended from a common ancestor." Three chapters of this edition ran afoul of the 1925 Texas restrictions on evolutionary textbook material and were omitted by the publisher from volumes delivered to that state. The 1926 edition dropped Darwin's picture and replaced the word "evolution" with "development" in the opening. Some religious quotations were added to the otherwise unchanged chapters on evolution. Seven years later, those chapters underwent a substantial overhaul, with passages about the evolution of man and natural selection deleted. Succeeding revisions during the forties and fifties further downgraded evolution, with the term itself finally disappearing. Grabner and Miller found that Moon's text became more popular as it became less evolutionary, until it "dominated the market" during the 1950s.[140]

Lamenting this situation, Grabner and Miller found "the greatest culpability in the scientific community itself, for the large-scale failure to pay attention to the teaching of science in the high schools."[141] To support this accusation, the authors observed that only two professional biologists authored high-school texts from 1925 to 1960, whereas teams of biologists joined in writing the texts that reintroduced evolution into the classroom during the sixties. Further evidence could be offered from the nineteenth century, when scientists Asa Gray, James Dwight Dana, and Joseph LeConte led the way in originally introducing evolution into high-school science texts. But the argument failed to note that biology is an interdisciplinary field created around the turn of the present century for educational rather than scientific purposes. Educators dominated the biology textbook market from the start.[142] Biologists did not abandon the field after *Scopes;* they simply did not enter it until 1960. Further, even if their entrance turned the tide during the sixties, their presence earlier might not have had the same effect. Public receptiveness to scientific opinion increased during the lull in anti-evolution activity. More than anything else, this change paved the way for evolution to re-enter the classroom.

Although public esteem for scientific opinion defies simple measurement, it was never strong enough during the twenties to intimidate anti-evolution crusaders. Bryan attacked scientific opinion head on, arguing in his last public address that society should not defer to it on evolutionary teaching and other moral issues. "Science is a magnificent material force, but it is not a teacher of morals. It can perfect machinery, but it adds no moral restraints to protect society from the misuse of the machine." By undermining Scripture, evolutionary teaching wrongly robbed society of the Christian moral restraint of brotherly love, Bryan reasoned, and therefore should be stopped regardless of scientific opinion.[143] Prosecutor Thomas Stewart, who later served in the United States Senate, expressed similar sentiments at the *Scopes* trial, arguing that when evolutionary teaching invaded religious grounds, "I say, bar the door, and not allow science to enter."[144] A state senator explaining his vote for the Mississippi anti-evolution law similarly declared, "If science could not be taught without teaching evolution, it should not be taught."[145] The state appellate brief in *Scopes* captured this defiant spirit. The "Fact" that " 'Scientists' Believe that a Certain Thing or Theory is True," the brief stated in a long headline, "Does Not to Any Degree Prevent the State Legislature, in the Exercise of the Police Power of the State, from Forbidding the Teaching or Practicing of Such Thing or Theory."[146]

In such a milieu, scientists could exert little influence against anti-evolution sentiment. Their loud pleas against anti-evolution legislation in Tennessee, Mississippi, and Arkansas went unheeded, their expert testimony was barred from the *Scopes* trial, and the *Scopes* appellate brief of the Tennessee Academy of Science had no appreciable effect on the state supreme court. Scientists did speak up for evolutionary teaching in the twenties, but few people listened. Darrow "says that evolution is an established fact, and there are a lot of them in this country" that believe it, a *Scopes* prosecutor argued to the Rhea County court in Dayton. "But I tell you one thing, no great number of them grow on the mountain sides in the valleys in Rhea."[147]

This disregard for scientific opinion changed somewhat as the American scientific community gained size and public support during the thirty-five years following *Scopes*. Bryan found it easy to bully the small American scientific community of the twenties. Estimating a total of only "5000 real scientists in the country"—half of the membership of the American Association for the Advancement of Science—the Commoner sarcastically dismissed their support for evolutionary teaching with the observation, "Strange that the wisdom of so great a people should reside in so small a number."[148] Pro-evolution partisan Maynard Shipley recognized this as well, observing in 1927 that "millions of organized voters can wipe out the few feeble ballots of the scientists and friends of science."[149] Although the precise number of American scientists has never been counted, that figure undoubtedly increased sharply during the lull in anti-evolution activity. Using Bryan's method of estimating it, the number increased over sixfold between 1925 and 1960, to about 31,000 "real scientists." More reliable estimates for 1960 placed the total number of American scientists approximately ten times higher than this, but suggested a similar relative increase during the preceding years.[150] More scientist were present to complain about anti-evolution restrictions in the sixties than in the twenties, and complain they would.

Although the number of scientists still remained small compared to the total population in 1960, they commanded a rapidly increasing share of public resources. This provides one quantitative indicator of the growing public appreciation of the value of science and scientific opinion. At the height of the anti-evolution crusade in 1927, combined federal and state expenditures for scientific research and development stood at $17,119,000, less than .02 percent of the gross national product.[151] In that year, Secretary of Commerce Herbert Hoover became so concerned about the low level of funding for science that he founded a National Research Fund to support pure science. A privately raised endowment of $20,000,000 was sought for the Fund, but despite a vigorous campaign by first Secretary and then President Hoover, aided by a committee that included famed physicist Robert A. Millikan and financier Andrew Mellon, less than 2 percent of the goal was collected and the contributions were returned.[152]

Governmental financial support for science mounted steadily during the Depression and exploded during World War Two and the ensuing Cold War. By 1960, federal expenditures for scientific research and development topped seven and a half billion dollars annually, or about 1.5 percent of the gross national product.[153] Where Hoover had estimated that the total public and private funds spent for pure science during the 1920s was less than $10,000,000 a year, that figure approached two billion dollars by the 1960s.[154]

This federal largess began spilling over into high-school science education during the 1950s, reflecting growing public concern for better scientific training in schools. The federally funded National Science Foundation, established in 1950 to "promote the progress of science," led the way in financing early programs to improve high-school science instruction, including the acclaimed Physical Science Study Committee in 1956. This Committee of leading physicists took on the task of revamping secondary-school physics textbooks, and its success made it a model for improving other subjects. According to a Congressional study, the public concern fueling these early efforts focused on the fear "that the Soviet Union rapidly was overtaking the United States in its training of technical manpower."[155] Soviet development of an atomic bomb in 1949 and the first hydrogen bomb in 1954 created this fear, but the real shock came in 1957, when the Soviet Union launched the first satellite.

Sputnik captured the attention of the American people, creating widespread support for improving science education. In response, President Eisenhower requested a "billion dollar, four year program to strengthen and improve science education and research," leading to the enactment of the massive National Defense Education Act in 1958.[156] That year, a Gallup survey found that a majority of interviewed high-school principals were changing their science programs in response to Sputnik.[157] Fear of Soviet science drove the American public to heed scientific opinion in reforming domestic science education. These reforms included the biological sciences, especially after the National Science Foundation began funding the Biological Science Curriculum Study (BSCS) in 1959. Like its counterpart for physics, the BSCS set about rewriting high-school textbooks, and the leading biologists serving on the Study (which included Hermann Muller) boldly embraced evolution.[158] The appearance of the BSCS texts in the early sixties shattered the thirty-year truce in legal activities enveloping the anti-evolution issue.

Even as the scientific community grew in size, support, and influence during the period from 1930 to 1960, creationists fortified their own position. Although the WCFA disappeared during the period, an even larger National Association of Evangelicals appeared in its place and the percentage of Americans attending and joining evangelical churches steadily increased.[159] At the same time that the government was pouring money into improving science education to meet the Soviet threat in the late 1950s, a Gallup public-opinion poll showed over four-fifths of Americans surveyed believed "that religion can answer all or most of today's problems." Nearly as many thought that "religion as a whole is increasing its influence on American life."[160] Evolution may have dropped into the background as an issue with evangelicals, but concern remained. Demonstrating the breadth of this concern, best-selling books by the leading liberal evangelical author of the post-World War II period, Oxford literary scholar C. S. Lewis, regularly raised the specter of modern science undermining Christian values. Even though Lewis accepted limited theistic evolution, he feared whenever "Darwin starts monkeying with the ancestry of Man."[161]

In a society increasingly deferential to scientific opinion, some conservative evangelicals acted to keep creationism alive by seeking scientific evidence for the Genesis account. These evangelicals, who typically possessed some training in engineering or science, laid the foundation for modern scientific creationism during the lull in public anti-evolution activity. Reviewing these activities, historian Ronald L. Numbers concluded that scientific creationists "turned their energies inward and began creating an institutional basis of their own. Deprived of the popular press and unable to publish their views in organs controlled by orthodox scientists, they determined to organize their own societies and edit their own journals."[162] Henry M. Morris, the chairman of the civil engineering department at Virginia Polytechnic Institute, emerged from this period of institution building as the leading voice for scientific creationism when he jointly authored, with John C. Whitcomb, *The Genesis Flood* in 1961. By presenting scientific evidence for a literal interpretation of the biblical creation account, this book bolstered creationists just as the BSCS textbooks resurrected the issue of evolutionary teaching. Creationists faced a rear-guard action, however. A new environment of heightened popular responsiveness to scientific opinion and judicial sensitivity to religious freedom gave pro-evolution partisans a decided edge in this renewed conflict.

4

Legalizing Evolution

1961–1970

The Bill of Rights begins by guaranteeing that "Congress shall make no laws respecting an establishment of religion, or prohibiting the free exercise thereof." During the past two decades, the legal controversies surrounding the teaching of evolution and creation in public schools have focused on the interpretation of these two clauses of the U.S. Constitution, with the Establishment Clause becoming a bulwark for evolutionary teaching, and the Free Exercise Clause invoked for teaching creationism. That neither clause figured prominently earlier bespeaks a changing interpretation of the Constitution.

The Establishment Clause has undergone a complete reinterpretation by the Supreme Court in the past forty years. During the heyday of the anti-evolution crusade in the twenties, no court would have seriously considered a legal argument that state anti-evolution statutes violated the Establishment Clause.[1] The clause traditionally barred only an American state church, like the Anglican Church in England. "The real object of the amendment was, not to countenance, much less to advance Mahometanism, or Judaism, or infidelity, by prostrating Christianity," the influential nineteenth-century Supreme Court Justice Joseph Story advised, "but to exclude all rivalry among Christian sects, and to prevent any national ecclesiastical establishment, which should give to an hierarchy the exclusive patronage of the national government."[2] Since the federal government never established a state church, the Supreme Court did not directly encounter the clause until the *Everson* case questioned the constitutionality of providing public transportation for parochial school students in 1947, and it did so then only by interpreting the clause to preclude aiding religion generally rather than simply establishing a particular denomination.

Even more ominous for the anti-evolution statutes, the *Everson* decision, written by Justice Hugo Black, applied this newly recognized constitutional "wall of separation" between religion and government to the states.[3] The Establishment Clause expressly limited only federal action—states were left free to establish state churches, and many states did so during the first half-century of the Republic. The Fourteenth Amendment to the Constitution, added in connection with ending slavery in the 1860s, barred states from depriving "any person of life, liberty, or property, without due process of law." Over the years, the Supreme Court gradually incorporated many of the federal rights contained in the Bill of Rights into the "liberty" protected from state interference by the Fourteenth Amendment. The Court first used this mechanism to apply the Free Exercise Clause to the states in 1940, followed by the Establishment Clause seven years later in *Everson*.[4] Only then were the constitutional principles in place for the federal judiciary to address the issue of evolutionary teaching, but the full impact of that new interpretation of the Constitution did not become apparent until the early 1960s.

Public education first felt the effect of the Establishment Clause in 1948, when the Supreme Court struck down a school program providing classroom religious instruction by local churches. "Here not only are the state's tax supported public school buildings used for the dissemination of religious doctrine," Black wrote for the Court. "The State also affords sectarian groups an invaluable aid in that it helps to provide pupils for their religion classes through use of the state's compulsory public school machinery. This is not separation of Church and State."[5]

The Court carried this principle a step further in 1962, when it outlawed state-sponsored prayer in school. At the time, eighteen widely scattered states authorized classroom prayer. Yet the Court, again speaking through Justice Black, found even the non-denominational and non-compulsory New York State school prayer "wholly inconsistent with the Establishment Clause."[6] A year later, the Court in *Abington School District v. Schempp* overturned statutes and practices mandating the reading of Bible verses and the Lord's Prayer in public school classrooms. In his majority opinion, Justice Tom C. Clark wrote "that to withstand the strictures of the Establishment Clause there must be a secular legislative purpose and a primary effect that neither advances or inhibits religion."[7] This became the test applied against the anti-evolution statutes. The ACLU, which participated in bringing these ground-breaking cases, pressed for more. Alerting "its 33 local affiliates throughout the nation to review religious practices in their public schools," the 1963 ACLU annual report declared "we are confident that when more sectarian religious practices are brought to the Court's attention, they likewise will be declared unconstitutional."[8] The anti-evolution statutes hung ripe for the picking.

Ironically, creationists grasped at these decisions before their opponents. Responding to charges that the first school-prayer ruling reflected hostility to religion, the *Schempp* decision asserted a goal of "neutrality" on religious matters in public education. While such neutrality prohibited promoting religion through prayers and Bible study, the *Schempp* Court added, "We agree of course that the States may not establish a 'religion of secularism' in the sense of affirmatively opposing or showing hostility to religion, thus 'preferring those who believe in no religion over those who do believe.'"[9] This was Bryan's plea exactly. The Commoner viewed evolutionary teaching as anti-religious. Assuming that biblical creationism could not be taught in public schools, Bryan sought neutrality through silence on the subject of biological origins by excluding evolutionary teaching as well. Alternatively, he suggested neutrality through presenting both theories.[10] His anti-evolution crusade achieved the first form of neutrality in that biology textbooks de-emphasized evolution after *Scopes* while continuing to exclude creationism.[11]

This form of neutrality ended when the BSCS texts successfully reintroduced evolution as the central concept in biology instruction during the early 1960s. Despite significant state and local opposition to their evolutionary content, the three tenth-grade BSCS texts quickly gained and held half the biology textbook market.[12] Explaining their success, one of the BSCS authors, biologist John A. Moore, observed that the federally funded BSCS organization, "unlike an individual author, carried sufficient clout to insist that evolution be included in its texts even though sales would suffer."

The BSCS then called the bluff of school boards demanding alterations. "Subsequent events showed that nearly every objecting school board ended up adopting the books—evolution, sex, and all," Moore reported. "Word was spreading that BSCS biology was the 'new thing,' and there were community pressures on school boards to be up to date, even if a little wicked, rather than behind the times and fully virtuous. Once this situation was understood, nearly every newly published biology book included an explicit discussion of evolution."[13] After this reintroduction of evolution ended the so-called neutrality based on silence, creationists pursued neutrality through presenting creationism along with evolution. To anyone convinced that evolutionary teaching affirmatively opposed religious belief, the Schempp decision offered strong legal support for teaching creationism along with evolution. Nell Segraves was such a person.

The Schempp case inspired Segraves, a southern California suburban housewife and mother. Schempp was in part brought by a professed atheist, Madalyn Murray, who complained that school Bible reading violated her son's freedom to disbelieve. When the Court agreed and professed support for educational neutrality on religious matters, Segraves claimed a similar right to protect her son Kelly's freedom to believe from violation by evolutionary teaching. "Do Christian children have equal rights with atheist and unbelieving children under the law in tax supported schools?" Segraves asked. Concluding that they do and that evolutionary teaching promotes atheism, Segraves argued that "a neutral position can be achieved in the school by . . . the objective presentation of both points of view regarding origins." She added, "To restrict the teaching concerning origins to a single theory, that of organic evolution, violates the Constitutional prohibition against the teaching of sectarian religious views just as clearly as if the teaching concerning origins were restricted to the Book of Genesis."[14]

Driven by this conviction, Segraves and her friend Jean Sumrall first petitioned the California Board of Education for relief in 1963, touching off persistent legal controversies in that state. The newly established Creation Research Society, an association of scientifically and technologically trained creationists co-founded by Henry Morris, assisted Segraves and Sumrall in preparing this petition. California creationists drew first blood that same year when the elected state Superintendent of Public Instruction Max Rafferty, a popular, conservative Republican educator and politician, responded to the petition by ordering that textbooks identify evolution as a theory. He based this order on a vague state Department of Justice opinion concluding that public schools could not constitutionally prescribe irreligious teaching. Segraves and other California creationists were far from satisfied. With Rafferty's active encouragement, they continued agitating throughout the decade for a state Board of Education order mandating the addition of creationism to the public-school biology curriculum.[15]

These efforts slowly spread and multiplied. In both 1964 and 1965, state legislators in neighboring Arizona responded to marked local resistance to the use of the BSCS texts in Phoenix by introducing measures requiring that public schools give "equal time and emphasis to the presentation of the doctrine of divine creation, where such schools conduct a course which teaches the theory of evolution."[16] These bills drew little attention, dying in committee without a hearing, and no similar bills appeared elsewhere during the decade. Nevertheless, the idea of applying the equal-time concept to the study of origins was planted and gradually took root.

The concept apparently was borrowed from broadcasting law, which had long required equal time for opposing political candidates and a "reasonable opportunity for the presentation of contrasting viewpoints on controversial issues of public importance." These broadcasting rules, officially called the Fairness and Equal Opportunities doctrines, received added public attention during 1964 due to the presidential election and the publication of a new federal regulation restating the requirement.[17] Applying these concepts to creationist instruction struck a more responsive chord in the American populace during the years to come than the older notion of banning evolutionary teaching—but further creationist victories did not come until later. During the last half of the 1960s, while creationists continued laying a foundation on *Schempp* for introducing creationism into public education, some evolutionists appealed to that decision and its precursors to overturn the surviving legal restrictions against evolutionary teaching.

"A Mouse in a Maze"

The new evolutionary biology textbooks reached the Little Rock, Arkansas, public school system in 1965. In the spring of that year, a committee of local biology teachers, including a young, first-year instructor named Susan Epperson, selected *Modern Biology* by James H. Otto and Albert Towle as the assigned text for the following school year. In accordance with school district procedures, the Little Rock Board of Education supplied the text to all its high schools.[18]

The Otto and Towle text was the 1965 edition in the popular line of high-school biologies begun by Truman Moon in 1921, and appeared as the first edition not identifying Moon as at least a co-author. Moon had deleted all references to human evolution from his text after the 1926 edition, but, following the lead of the BSCS, Otto and Towle reintroduced the concept into the 1965 edition.[19] "In 1871 the English biologist Charles Darwin published his famous book entitled The Descent of Man," read the new edition. "Darwin proposed that the same forces operating to bring about changes in plants and animals could also effect man and his development." The text then discussed fossil evidence for human evolution. After several pages, the passage concluded, "It is believed by many anthropologists that, although man evolved along separate lines from the primates, the two forms may have had a common, generalized ancestor in the remote past."[20] With these additions, *Modern Biology* remained the most widely used single biology textbook during the 1965–66 school year.[21] The addition, however, brought the text into direct conflict with the never enforced Arkansas law that barred teaching "the theory of doctrine that mankind ascended or descended from a lower order of animals."

The Arkansas Education Association (AEA), a professional

teachers' organization affilitated with the National Education Association (NEA), grew increasingly restive about the anti-evolution statute during the early sixties. On December 4, 1965, after the evolutionary *Modern Biology* was in use but before teachers reached the illegal chapter, the AEA Board of Directors authorized "using the judicial process for determining the constitutionality of the law." The AEA leadership immediately asked Epperson to stand as its plaintiff in a declaratory judgment action against the statute. Epperson made an ideal plaintiff. She was born in Arkansas, held an undergraduate degree from a local church-related college and a master's degree in zoology from the University of Illinois, was married to a young Air Force officer with top-security clearance, and would leave the state when her husband was transferred. With nothing to lose and seeing the action as "my responsibility both as a teacher of biology and as an American citizen," Epperson agreed to bring the test case.[22]

Epperson's complaint, filed December 6th, asserted that the anti-evolution statute violated her freedom of speech and other constitutional rights.[23] The AEA's Assistant Executive Secretary Hubert H. Blanchard, Jr., joined the lawsuit as the parent of school-age children allegedly denied their constitutionally protected freedom to learn by the statute.[24] Local AEA counsel Eugene R. Warren handled the case for both plaintiffs. Arkansas Attorney General Bruce Bennett, a conservative Democratic politician best known for fighting Court-ordered desegregation decided to argue the case himself for the state.

The high ground had shifted during the forty years since the *Scopes* trial. Both the law and the court's view of evolutionary teaching favored the state in *Scopes*. Accordingly, the *Scopes* prosecution simply asserted Tennessee's legal authority to regulate state teachers and fended off defense efforts to prove the statute constitutionally unreasonable. Four decades later, the law and the court's view of evolutionary teaching favored Epperson. The trial judge made no secret of his contempt for the old statute—he even scheduled the trial for April Fools' Day, allowing the case only one day rather than the two weeks requested by the state for presenting scientific arguments against evolution.[25] Exploiting his advantages, Warren simply asserted

Epperson's constitutional right to teach evolution and moved to silence defense arguments about the reasonableness of the statute. The tactical positions of the parties for and against evolution in *Epperson* were thus exactly the reverse of their positions in *Scopes*, owing to both the intervening decisions applying expanded First Amendment rights to the states and the greater acceptance of evolutionary teaching. This became apparent even before trial.

Unlike the *Scopes* defense, Warren did not use the case to promote popular acceptance of evolution—on the contrary, he assumed that acceptance. The complaint commencing the lawsuit simply alleged Epperson's duty as a science teacher to acquaint her students with "various and sundry scientific theories and hypotheses," including the concept "that man ascended from a lower form of animal life."[26] Similarly, Hubert Blanchard, in his opening petition, alleged that "to deny his sons the right to be informed of all scientific theories and hypotheses is to deny them equal access to a complete education."[27] In a request reminiscent of Bryan's strategy at Dayton, Warren moved before trial to "exclude the testimony of scientific and religious witnesses" and to confine the triable issues to the status of the plaintiffs as teacher and parent plus the textual material that they wanted taught.[28] With the Constitution and the judge on his side, Warren did not want any distractions from what he saw as a purely legal question of First Amendment freedom.[29] This pre-trial strategy left one major gap: it did not distinguish an anti-evolution statute from any other restriction on teaching.

The state took advantage of this opening, and in doing so inevitably raised the larger questions about the reasonableness of the anti-evolution statute. Recognizing that constitutional law no longer permitted a religious justification for the statute, Bennett, in his pre-trial pleadings, committed the state to defend the law as a simple exercise of administrative control over curriculum content. Here the state exploited the plaintiffs' unlimited claims for academic freedom. To Epperson's plea for freedom to teach various and sundry scientific theories, the state replied that "she wants to teach the Darwin Theory only when in fact there are dozens of other off-beat theories that other teachers might want to explain to their students. Someone has to administer the schools."[30] If Blanchard's plea for his sons' freedom to learn all scientific theories prevailed, the state warned that "then the public schools of the State of Arkansas must of necessity open its doors to the haranguing of every soap box orator with a crack pot theory on the premise that 'it is scientific knowledge' which the students would have explained."[31] Clearly, the plaintiffs needed a limiting definition of science, but their decision to forgo expert witnesses frustrated this.

The state's *reductio ad absurdum* argument, however, placed it in the vulnerable position of equating Darwinism with any and all allegedly scientific theories. Science, under this argument, was whatever anyone said that it was. The state continually claimed that "there must be some uniform school curriculum"; Epperson could not freely "substitute her judgment for that of her employer."[32] But undermining this legal position as a defense for the anti-evolution statute only required distinguishing that law from reasonable, non-religious restrictions on teaching. The trial began doing just that.

Presentation of the plaintiffs' case took only a few minutes. First Epperson testified, "I brought this law suit because I have a Text Book which includes the theory about the origin or the descent or the ascent of man from a lower form of animals. This seemed to be a widely accepted theory and I feel it is my responsibility to acquaint my students with it." Subsequent testimony identified this textbook as the official school text, Otto and Towles's *Modern Biology*.[33] Later Blanchard added that he wanted his sons "exposed to the material that is in the text" and other evolutionary biology books that his sons needed to know for college.[34] With this, the plaintiffs rested. The original plea for unfettered academic freedom thus narrowed to claiming a right to teach the evolutionary material in the assigned text. Darrow could have made the same argument on Scopes's behalf, but viewed it then as inadequate. Now, Warren relied on intervening Supreme Court decisions applied in an atmosphere of greater popular acceptance of evolutionary teaching to win the case. He had no intention of repeating the scene at Dayton that promoted Darwinism while leaving the anti-evolution statute intact.

Attorney General Bennett also recognized the need for an original trial strategy. Where the *Scopes* prosecution had opposed any testimony on the merits of evolutionary teaching, the state now raised just such issues in defense of the statute. Maintaining at trial that the "sole question of the law suit is whether or not the statute is reasonable," Bennett sought to raise all the traditional objections to evolutionary teaching.[35] He pushed hardest on the lack of proof for evolution, persistently questioning Epperson about various weaknesses in the theory—including conflicts among evolutionary scientists, the missing links in the fossil record, the contrivance of Java Man from slight evidence, and the Piltdown Man hoax. "Mrs. Epperson," Bennett asked in conclusion, "if the theory of Darwin is a false theory, is it still reasonable to teach it?" Warren's objection foreclosed an answer.[36]

Beyond trying to supply a rationale for excluding evolutionary teaching, the state defended its role in imposing the restriction. "There must be some uniform system of conducting the schools," Bennett asserted as he peppered the plaintiffs with questions aimed at fixing that responsibility with the state. "So, you are going to trust your judgment only as to what the students should be taught?" he asked Epperson. "And it is your assertion to this Court that one parent's wish should control over the great majority of the rest of the people of the State of Arkansas?" he fired at Blanchard.[37] In both cases, timely objections prevented any reply. The state concluded its case by presenting a string of local school administrators testifying that no one ever objected to them about the anti-evolution restriction.[38]

The state found itself limited throughout the trial by the same straitjacket that bound Darrow from probing the merits of evolutionary teaching at Dayton. "[T]he question before this Court is not whether the theory of evolution is true or false, or what anyone thinks about it," trial judge Marray O. Reed explained as he repeatedly limited questioning by the state.[39] Just as in *Scopes*, this ruling presupposed that the issue was purely a matter of the state's authority over its employees versus the constitutional rights of those employees. Treating this as the issue allowed the court to profess neutrality on matters of scientific and religious opinion, a favored position for the judiciary. "The spectacle, if any," reported a local newspaper, "was in observing the Arkansas attorney general grope to maintain a line of questioning, seeking at every turn—like a mouse in a maze—to find the opening that would allow him to put on a parade of witnesses questioning the validity of the Darwin evolution theory itself. Repeatedly, Bennett tried to elicit witnesses' opinions of the act itself; repeatedly Warren objected and consistently Judge Reed sustained him."[40] In the end the trial took little more than two hours. Even though the judge did not rule for nearly two months, a dejected local pastor left the courthouse saying, "They've rejected Creation."[41]

Whether or not the judge rejected creation, he did reject the anti-evolution statute for violating various undefined federal constitutional rights applied to the states since *Scopes*. A close reading of his written opinion suggests that increased public acceptance of evolutionary teaching also played a role in the ruling. "This Court is of the opinion," Judge Reed decreed, "that a chapter in a biology book, adopted by the school administrative authorities, stating that a specific theory has been advanced by an individual that man ascended or descended from a lower form of animal life, does not constitute such a hazard to the safety, health and morals of the community that the constitutional freedoms may justifiably be suppressed by the state." The decision skirted the issue of whether evolution could be taught as fact and strongly suggested that biblical creationism could be taught along with evolution, but it stood firm on the central issue. "In the Court's opinion the unconstitutionality of the statute under consideration is not subject to doubt, irrespective of the motives of those who secured its passage."[42]

Four decades after Bryan's emotional crusade publicized the dangers of evolutionary teaching, Reed did not see a sufficient public hazard to justify the ban. This stood in sharp contrast to the *Scopes* court's fear for the cause of public education should the unpopular doctrine be taught. The quiet atmosphere surrounding the *Epperson* trial, especially when compared with the carnival at Dayton, contributed to this sense of reduced popular opposition to evolutionary teaching.[43] Even as the state appealed to the Arkansas Supreme Court, Tennessee again took center stage as a flurry of legal activity engulfed its long-dormant anti-evolution statute.

Legal attacks against the Tennessee anti-evolution statute began on both judicial and legislative fronts early in 1967. Inspired in part by Epperson's victory, a Knoxville lawyer sued on behalf of his school-age son for a state-court order voiding the statute. His complaint, filed January 13th, alleged that the statute violated his son's constitutional rights and wrongly established "Protestant Fundamentalism as a State religion."[44] The state's attorney moved to dismiss the suit on March 1st. Bills repealing the anti-evolution statute surfaced in both chambers of the state legislature on the same day, and the judge deferred further consideration of the suit pending a legislative solution.

Repeal legislation stood a better chance of passage than ever before. Thanks to intervention by the United States Supreme Court, the first fairly apportioned Tennessee legislature since long before *Scopes* convened in 1967. Six decades of urbanization without redistricting had given the Tennessee legislature such a grossly rural bias that the U.S. Supreme Court rejected established precedent to command court-ordered reapportionment in 1962. This landmark decision first applied the constitutional concept of one-man, one-vote to the states, and eventually revolutionized state democracy throughout America.[45] Foot-dragging kept Tennessee from full compliance until 1967, when urbanization finally caught up with the 44-year-old anti-evolution statute.

Following the unanimous recommendation of its Judiciary Committee, the lower house easily passed the repealer on April 12th.[46] The sponsor of the measure, a 28-year-old Harvard-trained lawyer from Memphis, opened debate by simply describing the anti-evolution statute as "a bad law which should be repealed." Capturing the easy confidence on his side of the issue, a fellow supporter of repeal then presented him with a live monkey carrying a sign reading "Hello Daddy-o." As the monkey watched from the well of the House, only two representatives defended the law.

"We will bring chaos to the hearts and minds of the young if they believe they are just another type of animal," maintained a 65-year-old rural lawmaker in a plea reminiscent of the twenties. "It is the go-ahead word to teach as fact that you came from a wiggle-tailed something."

Arguing that "my child might be misled by the zeal of some educators," a Knoxville representative added, "I must cling to faith."

Discounting this risk to children, a Nashville legislator responded, "We don't want to stop with the answer that God created life. We want to go further. Let's don't stifle any quests for truth. Our kids are pretty smart; they can separate what is true from what is false."

Obeying the legislative maxim of not talking when you have the votes, supporters pressed for a vote after only a half-hour of floor debate. The measure passed by a two-to-one margin, 58 aye to 27 nay. Although representatives from both urban and rural counties voted heavily in favor of repeal, the strongest vote came from urban lawmakers. But an ominous eddy appeared within the main current of urban support. Paralleling the suburban Republican creationist stirrings in California, ten of the thirteen representatives from urban counties voting against the measure were suburban Republicans. When coupled with the ten rural Republican no votes, this left the minority party voting against repeal, 16 aye to 20 nay, while only 7 out of 49 Democrats opposed the measure.

This partisan and demographic split stood in sharp contrast to the uniform support for the statute in 1925 when the anti-evolution bill swept through the Tennessee House on a vote of 71 to 5. The rural shift continued a trend in anti-evolution lawmaking apparent since *Scopes*. Historian of religion George M. Marsden has detected a parallel shift in Fundamentalism generally, which he has attributed to a self-fulfilling public perception of an association between that religious viewpoint and rural areas stemming from publicity of the showdown at Dayton.[47] The disproportionate support for the cause displayed by suburban Republicans represented a newer phenomenon than the rural shift, but bore greater potential significance due to the growing political strength of this element of the electorate. Both trends would reappear in the seventies.

Publicity surrounding the House vote apparently reminded

some people about the anti-evolution statute. On the following day, the rural Campbell County School Board, in the first official application of the law, invoked it in firing a young temporary teacher. The teacher, Gary L. Scott, was hired midway through the 1966–67 school year to teach physics and general science courses at the small county high school. He planned on returning to graduate school the following fall. The board acted after parents complained that Scott described the Bible as "a bunch of fairy tales." Scott admitted only defining evolution in class and telling students that some Bible stories "cannot be taken literally." When the local ACLU chapter offered legal and financial assistance, Scott agreed to challenge his dismissal in court. "We need the money," his wife explained.[48]

The importance of this pending suit increased when the Tennessee Senate surprisingly defeated the repealer a week later.[49] In its place, the Senate proposed amending the existing statute to outlaw only teaching evolution as a fact. The passionate, two-hour Senate debate before network television cameras juxtaposed professions of faith with pleas for academic freedom. Opposition from senators representing rural counties proved decisive. The bill failed on a 16 to 16 tie vote. Rural senators split 7 to 10 against the repealer, exactly offsetting the 9 to 6 affirmative vote by urban senators. Republicans also played a key role, with seven of the eight minority party senators voting against repeal. Under the state Senate rules, however, the measure still had a chance because the body could reconsider tie votes.[50]

The Senate action focused added attention on Scott's pending lawsuit.[51] A highly skilled and flamboyant defender of radical causes, William M. Kunstler, signed on as Scott's attorney. The national ACLU and the National Science Teachers Association (NSTA), a department of the NEA affiliated with the American Association for the Advancement of Science, pledged their legal and financial help. Clearly overawed, the Campbell County School Board reinstated Scott with full back pay on May 11th. On the same day, the state Senate scheduled a second vote on the repealer for the following Tuesday. To keep the pressure on, Scott's attorneys on Monday filed a federal class action on behalf of state teachers against the anti-evolution statute. The

NSTA and sixty Tennessee professors joined Scott as named plaintiffs in the suit, alleging that the law "violates fundamental freedoms guaranteed by the U.S. Constitution." Scott's attorneys then publicly offered to dismiss the action if the Senate repealed the offending statute.

The Tennessee Senate capitulated without a word of debate.[52] "Everyone is ready to vote on this, and I will make no speech," the leading proponent of the measure simply announced in moving for final passage. With network television cameras again rolling, the measure passed easily. Two senators from rural counties switched their votes, along with one urban lawmaker. A rural senator who previously abstained, now voted for passage. Only one of these converts was a Republican, however, leaving the minority party still voting heavily against repeal. The governor promptly signed the measure into law without comment, and Scott dropped his lawsuit. From Shreveport, Louisiana, Scopes expressed his happiness with the turn of events.[53] Touching all the bases, historian of science Judith V. Grabiner, in an article jointly written with high-school math-teacher Peter D. Miller, attributed this repeal to "the new public interest in improving high-school science teaching; the large body of legal precedents limiting religious influence in the schools; and the increasing urbanization and educational level of the people of the south." The interaction of these social and legal "major historical changes" burst the fetters on evolutionary teaching.[54]

Just when the anti-evolution statutes appeared routed, the Arkansas Supreme Court, acting without the benefit of oral argument, revived its state law by reversing the initial *Epperson* ruling on June 5, 1967. The bizarre, two-sentence, unsigned opinion offered little clue to the justices' motives.[55] As if nothing had changed during the preceding four decades, the court simply followed *Scopes* in holding the law "a valid exercise of the state's power to specify the curriculum in its public schools." Although states generally possess such power, the decision avoided discussing the specific constitutional objections against an anti-evolution statute. Compounding the confusion, the decision strangely added, "The court expresses no opinion on the question whether the Act prohibits any explanation of the theory of evolution or merely prohibits teaching that the theory is true." [56]

United States Supreme Court Justice John M. Harlan knew precisely what this decision meant. "With all respects," Harlan wrote in an early draft of his opinion on the matter, "the court's handling of the case savors of a studied effort to avoid coming to grips with this politically controversial statute and to 'pass the buck' for dealing with it to us." [57] At least in Arkansas, enough popular opinion still supported the statute to influence the elected state supreme court. Apparently the elected trial judge did not feel such pressure in urban Little Rock, and certainly the appointed federal bench in Washington would not. So the issue rose to the United States Supreme Court when the High Court accepted Epperson's appeal early in 1968.

"Quixotic Prohibition"

The anti-evolution statute reached the Supreme Court during an era of widespread political radicalism. The civil-rights and anti-war movements were tearing America apart. Much of the tumult centered in the schools, where students demanded, and received, greater individual freedom of speech and action. At a time when radical student groups protesting the military draft and social injustice threatened to destroy some of the finest universities in America, an unenforced law barring evolutionary teaching in Arkansas public schools and colleges seemed strange indeed. Reinforcing this impression for the liberal Supreme Court, still led by the controversial Chief Justice Earl Warren, the school where Epperson taught—Little Rock Central High—was also the infamous battleground where federal troops enforced the landmark Warren Court order for school desegregation in *Brown v. Board of Education*. Once again, Mr. Warren's Court faced a case alleging the abridgement of constitutional rights at Central High.

Epperson's attorney Eugene Warren knew that in such a climate and before such a Court, the anti-evolution statute must be unconstitutional, but he never figured out why. "It is the contention of appellants that the intent and meaning of the First and Fourteenth Amendments to the Constitution of the United

States, as originally adopted, and as considered in the light of the meaning and purpose of 20th Century living in the United States, require the free exchange of all scientific theory," Warren wrote in his petition appealing for Supreme Court review. "The Arkansas statute here considered, if permitted to stand in the face of these constitutional guaranties, makes all of them meaningless."[58]

Eugene Warren painted with a broad brush. The First Amendment expressly guarantees freedom of religion and speech in addition to barring the establishment of religion. Existing case law suggested that these rights implied broader individual liberties such as the freedom to learn, to teach, and to think. Warren invoked all these individual rights in Epperson's trial, and the lower court referred to each in overturning the statute.[59] Warren appealed to all of them again in his arguments to the U.S. Supreme Court and added new allegations as well. Touching on the points raised in his written briefs, Warren began his oral argument by stating that "the act violated and collided with the first amendment freedoms, the freedom of speech, the freedom to speak and to learn, and the question of the freedom of religion, the question of the establishment clause of the first amendment."[60] He then devoted the rest of his time to advancing the new allegation, first raised in his Supreme Court briefs, that the statute violated the Fourteenth Amendment guarantee of due legal process by being too vague to enforce fairly.

Arkansas teachers do not know, Warren argued, whether the law prohibited only teaching human evolution as true, or also barred discussing the theory with students, or, at the most extreme, outlawed even using books mentioning evolution. Erecting the third interpretation as a straw man, Warren claimed the statute banned the school use of all biology textbooks, dictionaries, and general reference works. "That is just plain ridiculous," he asserted. "That is book burning at its worst." Noting the effect of this in light of the general acceptance of evolutionary texts, Warren added that "there simply is no biology textbooks that simply doesn't have some reference or some explanation of the theory of the evolution of man." In response to questioning by Justice Black, Warren admitted that the statute had never been so applied or, for that matter, enforced in any way. Brushing this aside, Warren concluded his oral argument, "We say that the act is clearly vague, clearly unconstitutional."[61]

Supreme Court litigants customarily have friendly organizations with particular credibility on an issue submit written arguments relating to that issue. In this case, two such briefs proved decisive.

Epperson's plea for academic freedom appeared in a brief submitted by the National Science Teachers Association and its parent organization, the NEA. "The Darwinian Theory of evolution is commonly recognized as a fundamental scientific principle," this brief stated. "It is clearly an infringement of academic freedom to deny the teaching of so commonly and popularly accepted a theory as this." To prove this point, the brief here quoted from a statement signed by 179 leading biologists affirming that organic evolution is "accepted into man's general body of knowledge by scientists and by other reasonable persons who have familiarized themselves with the evidence."[62] The biologists' statement went on, "There is no hypothesis, alternative to the principle of evolution with its 'tree of life,' that any competent biologist of today takes seriously. Moreover, the principle is so important for an understanding of the world we live in and of ourselves that the public in general, including students taking biology in high school, should be made aware of it, and of the fact that it is firmly established even as the rotundity of the earth is firmly established."[63]

Carrying this argument to its logical conclusion, the NSTA brief asserted that "theories within the area of recognized academic or scientific standards could not be omitted from the curriculum."[64] Anticipating the counterargument that the religious overtones of evolutionary teaching justified the restriction despite the common acceptance of evolution, the brief added that Darwinism "is purely a scientific theory, neither atheistic or theistic in scope."[65] Under this approach, the bounds of popularly accepted science determined the public-school curriculum, and scientists fixed those bounds.

Epperson's alternative plea that the anti-evolution statute constituted an unconstitutional establishment of religion was left

to the ACLU, which submitted a written brief jointly with the
American Jewish Congress. "We submit that the sole purpose
of the Arkansas law is to use the State's coercive power to protect and aid those sects that adhere to a literal interpretation of
Genesis," the ACLU brief argued without citing historical evidence. Appealing to the Court's recent interpretation of the Establishment Clause, the brief then simply asserted that this
purpose "alone requires invalidation under the *Schempp* test."[66]
The ACLU enjoyed its new position of strength and admitted
as much in its brief. "The Union, having been intimately associated with *Scopes v. Tennessee* 40 years ago, when the issue first
arose in the courts, looks forward to its final resolution in this
case."[67]

Arkansas offered scant opposition. The Anglo-American ad-
versarial judicial process relies on each opposing side presenting the facts and legal theories supporting its case. Courts then
distill the truth from these one-sided presentations. This process worked in *Scopes* and the *Epperson* trial because both sides
tried their best. But, after an urban-led progressive tide swept
Attorney General Bennett and other segregationists from office
in the 1966 elections, Arkansas shirked its adversial responsibilities before the Supreme Court. The Assistant Attorney General defending the statute, Don Langston, began his oral argument by disassociating the new state Attorney General from
Bennett's earlier vigorous efforts on behalf of the law. Then, after
suggesting that the statute was probably unconstitutional,
Langston gave a fatally repressive interpretation to the law. In
his opinion, it barred any mention of human evolution by public school teachers at all levels from kindergarten through graduate school. During this presentation, one Justice was moved
to comment that "your administration doesn't like the statute."[68]

Arkansas raised only two points in defense of the statute. "We
feel that the state has a right to set the curriculum in its schools,"
Langston stated. "This is our main point, Your Honor."[69]
Fleshing this out in a written brief, the state noted, "We submit
that the American people have never abandoned to anyone the
sole responsibility for selecting the course of study in our school.
. . . [M]any individuals, teachers included, espouse a philos-

ophy which is not representative of the beliefs of the people as a whole, nor conducive to the welfare of the Nation as a whole. In a democracy, the majority rules, and the people have it within their power to enact the laws whereby they should be governed, regardless of whether one or more educators approve of them."[70] Beyond this, Langston tentatively added in his oral presentation, "Another point that could be made here is that we say that this is a religious neutrality act here. It could keep the discussion of the Darwin Case versus the Bible story out of the teaching in the public schools."[71] Here, the state's attorney fumbled toward Bryan's justification for the statute, which assumed that the Bible could not be taught in public schools. Under further questioning, however, Langston undermined this argument by saying that teaching the Genesis account was permitted.[72]

Justice Black aptly characterized the defense argument as "palled, unenthusiastic, even apologetic."[73] The fire had gone out since Dayton. The state's attorney did not understand the once popular arguments for an anti-evolution statute, and clearly felt uncomfortable defending the restriction before the Supreme Court. Representing the people of Arkansas and ultimately answerable to state voters, he never once questioned the truth of evolution or suggested any harm from evolutionary teaching. Although his predecessor's vigorous defense of the anti-evolution statute never became a campaign issue, the new Arkansas Attorney General was elected without significant rural support and apparently felt free to abandon the statute.[74] Perhaps popular opinion—or at least the popular opinion that counted—had finally shifted against the restriction even in Arkansas. A leading Little Rock newspaper, in blasting the state supreme court decision reviving the statute, editorialized that the survival of the law was based on the contemptuous assumption "that the educational level of the people has not improved over the nearly 40 years in which the Darwin Law has been on the books." The editorialist predicted that the U.S. Supreme Court would know better.[75]

This prediction proved accurate. Liberal Justice Abe Fortas, writing for the Court in a decision issued November 12, 1968, began his legal analysis by describing the statute as a "curiosity" and noting "the discomfort which the statute's quixotic prohibition necessarily engenders in the modern mind." Through footnotes, Fortas compared the anti-evolution law with restrci-tions against teaching that the earth is round or revolves on its axis and suggested Darwin's critics exhibited phylogenetic snobbery. The concurring conservative Justice John M. Harlan referred to the statute as "anachronistic," reflecting a belief that any justifiable concern about evolutionary teaching had long passed. In his separate opinion, moderate Justice Potter Stew-art compared human evolution to higher mathematics and as-tronomy, calling each "an entire system of respected thought."[76] Clearly, the United States Supreme Court of 1968 believed in human evolution and assumed most modern Americans did too. The justices were not about to let the quixotic prohibition stand. Quixotry, however, is not an express constitutional basis for voiding a statute.

After casting about among the constitutional challenges to the statute raised on Epperson's behalf, the Court settled on reli-gious establishment. This conclusion was far from automatic. The lively conference where the nine-member Court privately reviewed the case following the oral argument was deeply split. The Chief Justice and three associate justices initially favored voiding the law for vagueness. Three other justices, including Fortas, saw only an Establishment Clause violation. Justice Stewart, in contrast, primarily criticized the law for limiting the free speech of teachers. These eight justices agreed, however, that the law must go. Only Black expressed a reluctance to strike the statute, claiming, "There is no case or controversy here" because the law is not enforced.[77] Despite this division, Warren assigned the task of writing the majority opinion to Fortas—who clearly wanted that privilege.

Fortas welcomed the opportunity to strike down the anti-evolution statute from the start. The Supreme Court appeal process begins with a petition to the Court requesting review of a lower court decision. The full merits of a case are con-sidered only if the appeal is accepted. Convinced that the *Ep-person* case lacked substance because the challenged statute had never been enforced, Fortas's law clerk advised his boss to vote against accepting the appeal. "Unfortunately," the clerk concluded in a memorandum to Fortas, "this case is not the proper vehicle for the Court to elevate the monkey to his proper position." Across the top of this memo, Fortas scrawled, "maybe you're right—but I'd rather see us knock this out + [the] Sup[reme] C[our]t seems to be playing games."[78]

Fortas's interest in the issue probably stretched back to his youth in Memphis where he was a public high-school student from a Jewish family when the Tennessee anti-evolution statute was enacted and the *Scopes* drama occurred.[79] Later, after graduating at the top of his Yale Law School class, Fortas became a leading Washington lawyer with an active civil-liberties practice and close ties to both the liberal wing of the Democratic party and the ACLU. President Johnson appointed Fortas to the Court in 1965, but Johnson's subsequent effort to elevate his old friend to the post of Chief Justice failed three years later against aroused conservative opposition in the Senate. Warren then stayed on as Chief Justice pending the choice of a new successor and, in the meantime, assigned writing responsibility for *Epperson* to his embattled associate. This became the first majority opinion authored by Fortas since his nomination as Chief was withdrawn, and would be one of his last before a new controversy over his personal finances forced Fortas off the bench altogether. Fortas took advantage of this respite in his public ordeal to strike the anti-evolution statute.

Sticking close to the position Fortas had taken in conference, his majority opinion overturned the law solely for violating the Establishment Clause. In reaching this result, Fortas's decision expressly passed over the primary objections raised by other justices in conference, undue vagueness and interference with free speech. "Today's problem is capable of resolution in the narrower terms of the First Amendment's prohibition of laws respecting the establishment of religion," Fortas wrote. The 1963 *Schempp* decision against school Bible reading interpreted the Establishment Clause as barring any statute having solely a religious purpose or primarily a religious effect. Invoking the religious-purpose part of this test for the first time to void a statute, Fortas concluded, "The overriding fact is that Arkansas' law selects from the body of knowledge a particular segment which it proscribes for the sole reason that it is seemed to conflict with a particular religious doctrine."[80]

Although religious purposes unquestionably contributed to the passage of the Arkansas statute, Fortas exaggerated their actual importance. In launching the crusade that generated the Arkansas law, Bryan was concerned about preventing war, labor exploitation, and the other social consequences he saw following from a belief in the Darwinian struggle for survival. Further challenging a purely fundamentalist religious purpose for the Arkansas statute, Virginia Gray's later analysis of the anti-evolution initiative election found that fundamentalists did not disproportionately vote for the law.[81] Fortas's opinion suggested none of this. In his defense, judges rely on what litigants tell them, and the state in this case never provided adequate information about the purposes behind the statute.[82] Instead, Fortas assigned a law clerk to research the point. "It is a matter of common knowledge that the fundamentalists were behind the movement for anti-evolution statutes," the clerk concluded. "Most articles that I have seen don't bother to prove this, but simply assume it to be true."

Relying heavily on his clerk's research, Fortas provided scant documentation for his bold conclusion about the original purpose of the law. The only historical works cited in Fortas's opinion were autobiographies by Darrow and Scopes, a 1937 ACLU report entitled "The Gag on Teaching," and a history of American academic freedom by Richard Hofstadter and Walter P. Metzger. These works constituted an obviously biased sample of the available literature, but were the only ones identified by the clerk. Making use of the best direct evidence supplied by his clerk, Fortas quoted at length from the *Arkansas Gazette* advertisement exhorting voters, "If you agree with the Bible vote for" the anti-evolution initiative. Yet, again accepting his clerk's research at face value, Fortas described this ad as "typical of the public appeal," when in fact it was an obscure, two-column advertisement that appeared only twice in the Little Rock daily newspapers during the two-week period preceding the election.[83]

Beyond this, Fortas used ellipses to delete two central sentences from the ad. Curiously, Fortas made this deletion after circulating the first draft of his opinion among his colleagues.[84] In the original ad and draft opinion, those sentences noted, "The bill does not prohibit free speech, it does not seek to help the church. It simply forbids the state attacking the church by having evolution taught in the schools at taxpayers' expense."[85] This was Bryan's express "religious purpose" for restricting evolutionary teaching. It assumed biblical creationism could not be taught in public schools and sought neutrality by also removing evolution.

Immediately after deleting this significant evidence to the contrary, Fortas wrote that "Arkansas' law can not be defended as an act of religious neutrality. . . . The law's effort was confined to an attempt to blot out a particular theory because of its supposed conflict with the Biblical account, literally read."[86] Bryan's stated religious purpose for the law—neutrality—was not nearly so sinister, though perhaps still unconstitutional if it had been the sole purpose for the law. Other solid constitutional grounds existed for voiding the statute, including the vagueness challenge pressed by Epperson's attorney and still accepted by two justices in their separate opinions. But the nine-member Supreme Court rules by majority vote, and Fortas's view prevailed. "Your opinion suits me exactly, and I am happy to join it," Chief Justice Warren informed Fortas.[87] Justice William J. Brennan, Jr. added, "I am happy to join your excellent opinion."[88] Four other justices also agreed with Fortas's Establishment Clause analysis, and his opinion became law.

Without other considerations, the Supreme Court probably would not have stuck down the statute on religious purpose grounds alone. In his separate opinion Justice Black complained that "this Court has consistently held that it is not for us to invalidate a statute because of our views that the 'motives' behind its passage were improper; it is simply too difficult to determine what those motives were."[89] As a case in point, the Warren Court had already upheld laws requiring business to close on Sunday. Those so-called "blue laws" seemingly reflected the same attempt to enforce biblical orthodoxy through statute as the anti-evolution laws, yet the Court went out of its way to hypothesize a non-religious purpose for them.[90] But, despite the actual existence of other motives, the Court saw only a religious purpose for the Arkansas anti-evolution statute. This blindness to any alternative purpose betrayed a belief that the statute lacked any non-religious justification whatsoever. Further, the justices' descriptions of the statute as anachronistic and quixotic, terms implying that the statute was outdated rather than patently wrong, suggested a view that changes over time had undermined the restriction.

Increasing popular acceptance of evolutionary teaching helped turned the tide. Forty years earlier, the Tennessee Supreme Court in *Scopes*, although accepting evolution as "established by a preponderance of scientific thought," gave the legislature the benefit of the doubt as to whether, "by reason of popular prejudice," forbidding evolutionary teaching promoted science. The *Scopes* court perceived that popular opposition to evolutionary teaching was strong enough that "the cause of education and the study of science generally" could be harmed by including evolution in the public-school curriculum.[91] This did not concern the *Epperson* Court. Indeed, along with describing the statute as discomforting to "the modern mind," the majority opinion declared it was "much too late" to defend such a restriction.[92] After reading these comments, Black added to his separate opinion the pointed observation that "this Court is prepared to simply write off as pure nonsense the views of those who consider evolution an anti-religious doctrine."[93] The *Epperson* Court apparently perceived less popular prejudice against evolutionary teaching in 1968 than the *Scopes* court had in 1927. As Justice Stewart bluntly stated in his *Epperson* opinion, the theory of human evolution simply was too highly "respected" to permit its continued expulsion from public schools.[94] Changing public opinion left anti-evolution statutes unconstitutional.

Black's separate opinion underscored this central role played by shifting popular opinion. Although "reluctantly" acquiescing in the Court's result, Black disagreed with his brethren's view of Darwinism. Despite the statement of 179 biologists submitted to the Court affirming the theory of human evolution, Black wrote, "Certainly the Darwinian theory precisely like the Genesis story of creation of man is not above challenge." As the only justice to question the truth of evolution, Black also was the only justice to perceive a non-religious purpose for the anti-evolution statutes. "It may be," Black suggested, "that the people's motive was merely that it would be best to remove this controversial subject from its schools; there is no reason I can imagine why a State is without power to withdraw from its curriculum any subject deemed too emotional and controversial for its public schools." Accordingly, Black proposed remanding the case back to the Arkansas Supreme Court to clarify whether the law unconstitutionally favored biblical creationism or simply prohibited "all teaching of human development."[95] *Scopes* upheld the Tennessee law on this very basis, and Black was willing to do the same. Behind this similar legal analysis lay a similar perception of popular opinion forged in the crucible of the anti-evolution crusade.

Black's *Epperson* opinion, like the majority opinion in *Scopes*, betrayed a keen awareness of popular anti-evolution sentiment. Given Black's background, this is not surprising. At eighty-two, Black was the Court's oldest member. He was reared by devout Baptist parents in rural Alabama, where he received a public elementary education during the 1890s followed by two years at a local private secondary school, one year of medical school in Birmingham, and two years of law school in Tuscaloosa. After law school, Black became active in the populist wing of the Democratic party, which put him in the same camp as Bryan when the Great Commoner was crusading against evolution. On the same day that the people of Arkansas enacted their anti-evolution statute by initiative, the people of nearby Alabama elected Black to the U.S. Senate, replacing Bryan's archrival Oscar Underwood. Black was elected with active support from the Ku Klux Klan, at a time when the Klan opposed evolutionary teaching.[96]

Once in Washington, Black began an ambitious self-education program focusing on the classics that continued for the rest of his life. At the time of his death, Black's personal library contained nearly 1000 volumes, excluding reference and law books. This collection did not contain any scientific works, other than those included within Black's set of *The Harvard Classics*; and the two volumes in that set by Darwin, *Origin of Species* and *The Voyage of the Beagle*, did not contain any of the markings that

appeared in many of Black's books.[97] Nothing here suggested that Black possessed any particular appreciation of current scientific opinion. At the same time, Black's political activities during the heart of the anti-evolution crusade and his evangelical heritage assured his awareness of the early twentieth-century popular prejudice against evolutionary teaching.

Attuned more to historical opposition to evolutionary teaching than to current social or scientific acceptance of the theory, Black believed that anti-evolution laws could be constitutional as measures designed to protect public education from harmful controversy. Indeed, his separate opinion ranged even farther into the past to justify the law by reviving Bryan's neutrality argument. "Since there is no indication that the literal Biblical doctrine of the origin of man is included in the curriculum of Arkansas schools," Black asked, "does not the removal of the subject of evolution leave the State in a neutral position toward these supposedly competing religious and anti-religious doctrines?"[98]

In contrast, Black's brethren, whose *Epperson* opinions never question the popular or scientific acceptance of evolutionary theory, only saw an antiquated religious purpose for the anti-evolution statutes. This difference cannot be attributed to an insensitivity on Black's part to Establishment Clause violations. More than any other justice, Black crafted the Court's strict separationist interpretation of the Establishment Clause and, five years before *Epperson*, he wrote the landmark decision outlawing prayer from public schools. But he had a different view of public opinion of evolution from the rest of the Court, and that difference resulted in differing readings of the constitutionality of anti-evolution laws. Black's view, which had prevailed in *Scopes*, was now a minority voice in *Epperson*. In each instance, however, perceptions of popular opinion helped determine the constitutionality of anti-evolution statutes.

The Final Purge

The national popular press, agreeing with the Court's view of modern public opinion, greeted the *Epperson* decision as a curious but welcome victory over the dead hand of a bygone era.

Time magazine suggested that the matter "seemed to come from another era, a benighted past."[99] Attributing the ruling to "the evolution of the U.S." since *Scopes*, *Newsweek* reported that "finally last week, 43 years after Scopes's conviction, the Supreme Court struck down one of the monkey laws."[100] A sarcastic "Special Report" in *Life* magazine expressed surprise that "in this year of our Lord 1968, even as Apollo 7 twinkled in space, the possibility of there being some monkeys in the woodpile would come up for discussion in no less august a body than the United States Supreme Court." The "Report" ridiculed the stand of "Arkansas against the onrush of the 20th Century," and rejoiced "that the human freedom to think, to formulate ideas and spread them about, unpleasant as they may sometimes be, extends to Arkansas and, who knows, possibly even to Mississippi, where the country's last anti-Ev law remains in effect."[101] The Magnolia state, however, proved a surprisingly tough nut to crack even though the *Epperson* decision almost certainly doomed its statute as well.

The legal drive against the Mississippi anti-evolution statute began late in 1969, when Mrs. Arthur G. Smith of Jackson filed suit in state court complaining that the law both improperly denied her school-age daughter's freedom to learn and violated the Establishment Clause of the federal Constitution. Smith's suit was hampered by the lack of state declaratory judgment procedures, forcing her to seek an injunction against enforcement rather than a declaration of unconstitutionality. The state moved before trial for a dismissal, claiming that the absence of any actual or threatened enforcement precluded an injunction. By as much as admitting that the statute could never by enforced, the state thus conceded the substance of the law to save the form. Beyond this, by interpreting the Mississippi anti-evolution statute to bar only teaching Darwinism as fact, the state claimed that its law differed from the voided Arkansas statute, even though the two measures contained nearly identical language.[102] With this pre-trial motion pending, a declaratory judgment suit against the Mississippi law was filed in federal district court, but the federal judge deferred any action until the state courts reached a final decision.[103]

The dismissal motion remained undecided when the legisla-

ture tried its hand at the issue in January.[104] Soon after the 1970 Mississippi House of Representatives convened, a Jackson legislator introduced the first anti-evolution repealer offered in Mississippi since the twenties. Guided by a friendly Judiciary Committee chairman, the measure raced through committee and appeared before the full House on January 21st.

The Chairman opened the floor debate by describing the old statute as "a restriction on man's mind, thoughts, and beliefs which the state should not abrogate to itself." But his call for repeal met entrenched resistance.

Denouncing Darwin as an atheist who "wanted to give you a reason why we were here," a rural lawmaker sounded Bryan's cry for educational neutrality. "Since it is against the law to teach religion, it should be against the law to teach atheism."

"Let's hold the line as a Christian state," another opponent of repeal added in a plea going beyond neutrality to religious establishment. "This is another attempt to chip away at religion."

A Biloxi supporter of repeal framed the issue quite differently. "I believe God created man and how He did it does not matter," he affirmed. "[S]ubmit it to students and let them decide." Another legislator then expressed even stronger support for evolution by arguing that any law "that infringes and abridges the teaching of truth is wrong—it's time we repealed this."

Much like the scene nearly a half-century earlier, however, the Mississippi House debate generated more heat than light. Abuse hurled against "the silly restriction" met charges that repeal would "make a monkey out of God." At least in Mississippi, little had apparently changed since 1926. The 42 to 70 vote against the repealer nearly mirrored the earlier vote for the statute. This overwhelmingly negative vote masked two subtle changes already apparent in the successful Tennessee repeal effort. Although the 1970 Mississippi House had a much smaller urban delegation than the 1967 Tennessee legislature, and no Republican members, the seventeen Democratic representatives from urban counties mimicked their Tennessee counterparts in disproportionately supporting repeal, 9 aye to 8 nay.[105]

Further, both legislatures acted in the shadow of the federal courts. In Tennessee, this shadow spurred Senate action. But the Mississippi legislature was fed up with the federal courts. Even as the House debated repeal, the Jackson public schools were closed pending court-ordered racial desegregation. Similar decrees wrenched other schools throughout the state, leading the 1970 state legislature to enact several constitutionally suspicious laws supporting private education. Reflecting this ornery mood, one legislator stubbornly declared during the anti-evolution debate, "If this law is to be repealed, let it be done by a federal judge—not by this legislature." So the issue remained in the courts. Two weeks later, the state trial court hearing Smith's challenge displayed similar defiance to federal constitutional law by granting the pre-trial motion to dismiss the case.[106] The issue then rose to the Mississippi Supreme Court on appeal.

The state high court accepted the inevitable. "In determining this question," the court announced on December 21, 1970, "we are constrained to follow the decisions of the Supreme Court of the United States." After quoting at length from *Epperson*, the Mississippi justices unanimously concluded, "It is clear to us from what was said in *Epperson* that the Supreme Court of the United States has for all practical purposes already held that our anti-evolution statutes are unconstitutional." Without independently analyzing the constitutional issues involved, the Mississippi Supreme Court mechanically ruled America's last anti-evolution statute "void and of no effect." The *Smith* court offered some consolation to creationists by pointedly commenting that biblical creationism "certainly" could be taught in public schools along with evolution.[107] Creationists were already moving in this direction.

Even as the *Smith* court performed the final purge of statutory legacy from the anti-evolution crusade, the creationist counterattack gained strength. While the Mississippi courts wrestled with Smith's challenge, a half-decade of work by California creationists paid off. The state Board of Education incorporated into its 1969 *Science Framework for California Public Schools* the affirmation, "All scientific evidence to date concerning the origin of life implies at least a dualism or the necessity to use several theories to fully explain relationships between established data points." Identifying creation and evolution as historical scientific theories, the *Framework* noted, "Some of the scientific data, (e.g., the regular absence of transitional forms) may be best explained by a creation theory, while other data (e.g., transmutation of species) substantiates a process of evolution."[108] This document gave California creationists authority for demanding the inclusion of their views in science teaching during the seventies. The authority, however, extended only to natural, rather than supernatural, evidence for creation. Creationists came to call this body of evidence either "scientific creationism" or "creation science" to distinguish it from biblical creationism.

Recognizing a need for new textbooks to implement this demand, Nell and Kelly Segraves in 1970 joined with Henry Morris in forming the Creation-Science Research Center to prepare teaching materials appropriate for presenting scientific creationism in public schools. This organization was founded as an arm of the Christian Heritage College, a new church school near San Diego created by the Rev. Tim LaHaye, a prominent fundamentalist spokesman deeply concerned about the effect of evolutionary beliefs on moral values.[109] About this same time, Morris's older Creation Research Society also responded to the need for a creationist biology text by issuing *Biology: A Search for Order in Complexity*. In his preface to the book, Morris described it as "a textbook of biological *science*" but added that "it is explicit throughout the text that the most reasonable explanation for the actual facts of biology as they are known scientifically is that of Biblical creationism."[110] Despite Morris's expressed hope that the book would "be of interest to public school systems desiring to develop a genuine scientific attitude in their students," public use of the text was mired in legal controversy throughout the seventies.

Halfway across the country from California, Texas creationists were also pressing for relief from evolutionary teaching. The controversy began with the first appearance of the BSCS texts in the early sixties, and grew from there. Responding to complaints vigorously pressed by Mel Gabler, a conservative Longview oil-company clerk, and his wife, the elected state Board of Education acted in 1969 to remove two BSCS works from the list of biology textbooks approved for use by Texas public schools and, a year later, proclaimed that all evolutionary texts must identify evolution as a thoery.[111] One month before the *Smith* court issued its decision striking down the last anti-evolution statute, a Houston mother filed suit on behalf of her school-age daughter, Rita Wright, to enjoin her local public schools from teaching evolution at all. Wright alleged that evolutionary teaching unconstitutionally inhibited the free exercise of her creationist religion while establishing a "religion of secularism."[112] These charges touched a raw nerve during the early seventies, as the case wound its way through the courts. The suit also represented a new tactic for creationists. After years of being on the defensive in court, *Wright* marked the first time creationists instituted a judicial action. Following a decade of legal triumph for evolutionary teaching, creationists began probing the perimeter.

5

Legislating Equal Time

1970–1981

"And after World War I there was a period much like the period today, where there was a sense of general unease for the progress of American civilization," historian George Marsden testified at the 1982 trial against a new Arkansas creationism law. "There was a sense that something had gone wrong; a rather indefinite sense, not a real disaster, much like the 1980s, it seems to me. And in that context, that saying evolution is a problem was something that became convincing to a wide variety of people." Marsden added that fundamentalists, then as now, turned to a literal reading of the Bible as a source for truth during times of uncertainty. With this testimony, Marsden became one of the first historians to attempt placing the current creationism movement in historical perspective. He described the original anti-evolution crusade as a reaction against First World War German "barbarism," which at the time was widely attributed to the acceptance of a Nietzschean evolutionary philosophy. According to Marsden, similar concern for the progress of civilization fed the revived creationism movement. Yet Marsden did not identify a source for that renewed concern equivalent to the traumatic and seemingly meaningless carnage of World War One.[1]

Historian Ronald L. Numbers offered a different view of modern creationism by finding a continuum of anti-evolution concern linking the twenties to the present. Following the twenties, Numbers wrote in a ground-breaking 1982 article on the entire movement, "contrary to appearances, the creationists were simply changing tactics, not giving up. Instead of lobbying state legislatures, they shifted their attack to local communities." So long as these tactics succeeded in keeping evolution out of high-school textbooks, creationists could afford to maintain a low profile. According to Numbers, the return of evolution to the classroom following the publication of the BSCS texts prompted the apparent "creationist revival" beginning in the sixties. This view accords with evidence revealing a steady growth of both evangelical church membership and creationist scientific activities during the entire period since the First World War.[2] Marsden and Numbers agreed, however, in recognizing a current burst of creationist legal activity comparable only to the anti-evolution crusade of the twenties.

Following the skirmishes in California and Texas during the sixties, creationist legal activities rapidly spread during the seventies and early eighties. In 1974, only a decade after one historian of the anti-evolution crusade suggested that "a renaissance of the movement is most unlikely," University of Tennessee law professor Frederic S. Le Clercq warned of "a second consumption" of "monkey laws."[3] Reviewing early creationist legislation and lawsuits, Le Clercq wrote that "creationists hope to dilute the theory of evolution to the level of hypothesis or speculation and to win equal time for the doctrine of special creation. Recent events suggest that the creationist movement is both potent and truly national in scope." This early analysis correctly identified the emerging two-prong attack on evolutionary teaching and recognized the broad support for the movement. "Ultimately," Le Clercq predicted, "the issues raised in the controversy over science teaching and textbooks will probably have to be resolved in the courts."[4]

Le Clercq's analysis proved accurate. In 1980, creationist Henry Morris described the seventies as the "Decade of Creation" and predicted that the term "may well apply even more to the decade of the eighties."[5] That same year, Republican presidential nominee Ronald Reagan blessed both prongs of the creationism offensive by describing evolution as a "theory only" and endorsing public-school instruction in biblical creationism wherever evolution is taught.[6] By then, as Le Clercq earlier predicted, the creation-evolution controversy was back in the courts, with creationists trying both to qualify evolutionary teaching and to secure a place for creationist concepts while evolutionists sought to oust creationism from the science classroom once and for all. The *Epperson* decision left these three issues unresolved. That decision simply ruled that a state could not "prevent its teachers from discussing the theory of evolution"—it did not address either restrictions on the nature of such discussion or the constitutionality of teaching creationism.[7] Some partisans on both sides leaped at these openings with a religious fervor.

Creationists struck first on both legislative and judicial fronts. Cornell University sociologist Dorothy Nelkin gave her explanation of these events in testimony against creationism laws at the 1982 Arkansas trial. "I found that one of the reasons underlying the whole of their activities were concerns about the growing secularism in society and a concern that this was going to cut down on the[ir] constituency [and] would destroy the values of their young," Nelkin testified. Responding to this concern, she noted, creationists were "using science as a kind of political resource to legitimize and give credibility to their own views concerning the literal interpretation of the Bible." Nelkin went on to explain, "They want people to believe their definition of reality. And in order to do that, they really felt it was incumbent upon them in today's age to call into question scientific ideas and to give their own ideas a sense of scientific credibility." She offered Henry Morris as a case in point.[8] Morris both believed in the literal truth of the Genesis account and viewed creationist instruction as a "ministry" for leading students to Christianity. This quite naturally led him vigorously to advocate teaching creation science in public schools.[9] At the same time, less ambitious creationists focused on simply qualifying evolutionary teaching.

Some evolutionists displayed similar missionary zeal toward outlawing creation-science teaching. George Gaylord Simpson offered a prime example. From his pulpit as a well-known Harvard University paleontologist, Simpson decried restrictions against teaching evolution in a 1963 book proclaiming his evolutionary philosophy of life. Hailing such teaching as "supremely important," Simpson argued, "It is evolution that can provide answers, so far as answers can be reached rationally and from objective evidence, to some of those big and universal questions" about how to live and to act.[10] When the move for creation-science teaching spread a decade later, Simpson joined in sponsoring an American Humanist Association statement denouncing measures "that would require creationist views of origins be given equal treatment and emphasis in public-school biology classes and text materials." The statement was signed by nearly 150 leading scholars, published in *The Humanist* magazine, and distributed to school districts throughout the country. Henry Morris later described this 1977 statement as the "first significant salvo" in the evolutionists' assault against creation science.[11]

Such quasi-religious enthusiasm for evolution was duly noted by the defense at the Arkansas creationism trial. Under cross-examination by the state at the 1982 trial, University of Chicago theologian Langdon Gilkey agreed that some religious humanists "have taken evolution from its original scientific state and adopted it as a part of their belief system."[12] In a follow-up article, Gilkey added, "Many scientists share with the fundamentalists the confused notion that so-called religious knowledge and scientific knowledge exist on the same level and that, as science advances, scientific knowledge simply replaces and dissolves religious myth. . . . One encounters this view of science as dissolving religious truth in the writings of Julian Huxley, Gaylord Simpson, Jacob Bronowski, and Carl Sagan."[13] All these men strongly advocated evolutionary teaching. With partisans such as Morris and Simpson involved, both sides of the renewed creation-evolution legal controversy were egged on by zealots.

As the controversy grew during the years of the 1970s, dozens of organizations took sides in the dispute, with many becoming directly involved in legal efforts. On the creationist side, the two organizations that Morris played a part in founding during the sixties, the Creation Research Society (CRS) and the Creation-Science Research Center (C-SRC), continued to promote creationist teaching. The Center split in 1972, however, with the Segraves keeping the C-SRC name and some textbook-publishing activities while Morris founded the Institute for Creation Research (ICR) to carry on creation-science research at the Christian Heritage College. After producing a set of creationist teaching materials, C-SRC became increasingly involved in administrative and judicial activities to secure and to defend their use in public schools. "In the course of these activities," Center promotional literature claimed during the early eighties, "C-SRC has become a leading center of knowledge and expertise in the application of constitutional and legal principles for the restriction and protection of constitutional rights of Christian citizens in the public sector."[14] Meanwhile, ICR grew to include over two dozen scientists and science educators either on staff or serving in an advisory capacity. Although never initiating legislation or lawsuits, ICR offered to assist such efforts with "scientific and legal consultation, service as expert witness, etc."[15]

In addition to these core bodies, two small creationist organizations joined the legal fray during the seventies. The Gablers formed the Educational Research Analysis in 1973 to finance their expanding efforts against allegedly anti-American textbooks. Through this organization, the Gablers continued lobbying educational agencies for the removal of objectional textual material, including passages presenting evolution as a fact.[16] A few years later, respiratory therapist Paul Ellwanger of Anderson, South Carolina, founded a similar organization, called the Citizens for Fairness in Education, which drafted and distributed creationist legislation while fighting evolutionary teaching in the local schools.[17] Behind these associations directly involved in creationist legal activities stood a much larger number of religious, professional, and public organizations more or less promoting creationist doctrines.

In the period 1970–1980, an increasing array of prominent organizations opposed creationists' efforts. The American Civil Liberties Union, the National Education Association, the National Science Teachers Association, and the American Jewish Congress continued their courtroom and lobbying activities. In 1972 the two most prestigious scientific societies in the country, the American Association for the Advancement of Science and the National Academy of Sciences, began actively opposing measures to require creation-science teaching in public schools.[18] About the same time and despite stubborn internal dissent, the National Association of Biology Teachers (NABT) launched an aggressive nationwide legal effort against creationism and later helped form state-based "Committees of Correspondence on Evolution" to monitor and to resist creationist efforts at the local level.[19]

A variety of organizations with ties to organized religion also stood up against creation-science laws during the seventies, including two respected legal organizations committed to religious freedom, the American Jewish Committee and the predominantly Baptist and Adventist Americans United for Separation of Church and State. Finally, several secular, politically liberal organizations were formed in reaction to growing conservative political activity by evangelicals. Two of these new organizations, the People for the American Way established in 1980 by prominent cultural leaders and the NEA-related National Coalition for Public Education and Religious Liberty, took a special interest in opposing creationism laws. Through lobbying and litigation, these varied organizations have battled the creationists at every turn during recent years.

Faced with this formidable elite opposition, creationists appealed to popular opinion. Even though the 1977 American Humanist Association statement signed by scores of leading scientists, educators, and liberal religious leaders claimed that evolution is "accepted into humanity's general body of knowledge by scientists and other reasonable persons who have familiarized themselves with the evidence," public opinion surveys during the period consistently found at least as many Americans believing in creation as in evolution.[20] Most of these surveys were amateur local polls conducted by creationists to boost their cause, but a 1979 survey by the Gallup polling organization confirmed these results by finding that "[h]alf of the adults in the U.S. believe God created Adam and Eve to start the human race."[21]

Beyond this, polls typically found even more people favored the teaching of creationism than believed in the doctrine, presumably because this seemed only fair where evolution was already taught.[22] These polls did not indicate how deeply people cared about the issue or how closely they had studied it. None-theless, creationists appealed to this popular sentiment and de-cried the closed-mindedness of their opponents. "A nation-wide poll commissioned by the Associated Press and NBC News late in 1981 showed that over 86% of the people favored having creationism taught in the schools," an IRC book co-authored by Henry Morris noted. "Nevertheless, creationists only request *fair* treatment, not favored treatment, in the schools. The attitude of the liberal humanistic establishment in science and educa-tion, in trying to maintain an exclusive indoctrination in evo-lutionary humanism, seems incredibly intolerant and arrogant in a free country."[23] Brandishing such arguments, creationists took their cause to the people, to the people's elected represen-tatives, and, in a few unsuccessful instances, to the courts. For the most part, their opponents relied on the courts to check any advances.

Double Jeopardy

Creationist efforts to qualify evolutionary teaching, begun dur-ing the sixties in response to the BSCS texts, continued into the next decade. With creation scientists still building an adequate institutional structure for advancing their views, these initial efforts focused more on defending biblical creationism than on promoting creation science. The hapless *Wright* case, which languished in the Houston federal courts from 1970 to 1972 while the lead plaintiff unsuccessfully struggled to retain an attorney, showed the limits of this approach. The *Wright* case began when the mother of Rita Wright, a Houston public-school student, challenged the constitutionality of teaching the theory of evo-lution as a fact in public schools "without critical analysis and without reference to other theories which purport to explain the origin of the human species."[24] According to her complaint, such teaching represented a direct attack on creationist "religious beliefs" in violation of the Free Exercise Clause and lent "offi-cial support to a 'religion of secularism' " in violation of the Es-tablishment Clause.[25]

The case never got to trial. Without looking beyond the base allegations, Judge Woodrow Seals dismissed the complaint for failing to state a claim upon which relief could be granted. Dismissal on this severe procedural ground is highly unusual, occurring only when the complaint itself demonstrates no possible basis for a judicial remedy under any conceivable facts.[26] Wright's unusual allegations only made this dismissal more telling. The controlling court rule provided "that the more extreme or even far-fetched is the asserted theory of liability, the more important it is that the conceptual legal theories be explored and assessed in the light of actual facts, not a pleader's suppositions."[27] Yet the judge found Wright's allegations too far-fetched to survive even this least restrictive standard. It was not that the judge doubted the motives behind the case. Indeed, he described the principal protagonist, Wright's mother, as "an obviously sincere and concerned parent." But he totally rejected her cause.

"Plaintiffs' case must ultimately fail," Seals ruled, "because the proposed solutions are more onerous than the problem they purport to alleviate." First, Seals rejected as "decidedly totalitarian" the solution earlier suggested in Justice Black's *Epperson* opinion of barring all instruction in human origins. "Science and religion necessarily deal with many of the same questions, and they may frequently provide conflicting answers," the judge reasoned. "Teachers of science in the public schools should not be expected to avoid the discussion of every scientific issue on which some religions claim expertise." Seals came down just as hard against requiring " 'equal time' for all theories regarding human origins" on the grounds that there were too many such theories. "This Court is hardly qualified to select from among the available theories those which merit attention in a public school biology class." He mentioned the defendant's willingness to exempt creationist students from evolutionary instruction as a possible compromise, but noted that the plaintiffs objected to this as exposing exempted students to undue peer pressure. Foreseeing no acceptable remedy, Seals dismissed the complaint.

In a brief, unsigned opinion issued a year later, a federal appellate court affirmed Seals's decision on all points. When the U.S. Supreme Court refused to review this ruling in 1974, Wright and her fellow plaintiffs were left without a direct judicial remedy.[28] The first appeal by creationists to the courts was an utter failure. At every level, the judiciary refused even to hear creationist arguments for restricting evolutionary teaching. Scientific opinion could determine science teaching even if that teaching offended religious beliefs. Subsequent cases simply reaffirmed the *Wright* ruling.

Creationists returned to the courts twice during the seventies to challenge different aspects of governmental support for evolutionary instruction. In 1972, William T. Willoughby, the religion editor of the conservative *Washington Star-News*, filed suit against the National Science Foundation for funding the BSCS textbooks. Two years later, Dale Crowley of the rightist National Foundation for Fairness in Education instituted a similar action against evolutionary educational exhibits at the Smithsonian Institution. Both actions alleged that federal support for one-sided evolutionary presentations unconstitutionally inhibited the free exercise of creationist religions and established a religion of secular humanism. Each sought either to stop the offending activity or to secure equal support for creationist presentations.[29]

Neither case ever made it to trial. The federal district court in Washington, where both actions were filed, handed down pretrial judgments against both plaintiffs. The federal appellate court for the District of Columbia affirmed these decisions and the Supreme Court refused further review.[30] Summing up its approach to both actions, the *Crowley* appellate court observed that "this case necessarily requires a balance between appellants' freedom to practice and propagate their religious beliefs in creation without suffering governmental competition or interference and appellees' right to disseminate, and the public's right to receive, knowledge from government, through schools and other institutions." Reflecting the high cultural status accorded science, the court continued, "This balance was long ago struck in favor of diffusion of knowledge based on responsible scientific foundations, and against special constitutional protection of religious believers from the competition generated by such knowledge diffusion."[31]

This approach effectively precluded a courtroom trial for religious challenges to evolutionary teaching. Trials are for deciding factual disputes, but creationism loses under any facts so long as the courts automatically deferred to scientific opinion over religious belief in questions involving science instruction. Creationists' only hope lay in undermining the scientific status of evolution and then basing their legal claims for equal time on this anti-evolutionary science. As early as 1975, Morris told his followers just this, but with only a limited initial impact.[32]

Building a credible scientific challenge against a century-long tradition of evolutionary science took time, and many believers could not wait. Confident of popular support for their cause, eager creationists reopened a legislative front in their battle to qualify evolutionary teaching. During the seventies, dozens of bills spontaneously appeared in state legislatures across America to require the classroom presentation of creationist religious concepts as a foil to evolutionary teaching.[33] These bills recognized the judicial restrictions against banning evolutionary teaching altogether, but typically did not fully appreciate either the established limits on religious instruction or the emerging claims of scientific creationism. Once again, Tennessee provided the first breakthrough.

The new Tennessee creationism bill was introduced on March 26, 1973, by a bipartisan coalition of five senators, four of whom represented rural districts. All five were members of the 1967 legislature that repealed the old anti-evolution statute—but none of them then voted for repeal. Now they struck back.[34] The legislation required that all public-school textbooks presenting a theory of human origins identify the concept as a theory "not represented as a scientific fact." The bill also mandated that texts presenting any such theory give "equal space" to other theories "including, but not limited to, the Genesis account in the Bible."[35] The measure neither banned evolutionary teaching nor specifically promoted scientific creationism; rather it aimed at defending creationist religious beliefs by qualifying the treatment of evolution in textbooks.

The idea for the bill came from Russell Artist, a biology professor at a small, church-affiliated Tennessee college. As a member of the Creation Research Society, Artist co-authored the 1970 creationist textbook, *Biology: A Search for Order in Complex-*

ity. After failing to get the text approved by the State Textbook Commission for use in Tennessee public schools, Artist sought a legislative restriction against using purely evolutionary texts and offered the CRS book as a model of balanced treatment. "What's the matter with the evolutionists that they can't stand a scrutiny by honest scientists? We're not telling them not to teach it—let them teach it all they want," Artist declared. "Now is that being prejudiced? No, it's simply asking that we should have the same amount of time to present our creation point of view."[36] Wrapped in such basic notions of fairness, the creationism bill swept through the Tennessee Senate barely three weeks after its introduction. Partisan affiliation and district demographics made little difference as the predominantly Democratic upper house approved the measure with only one dissenting vote. Even the eight surviving Senators who voted to repeal the old anti-evolution statute now voted to give equal time to biblical creationism.[37] Clearly, the new approach enjoyed broad appeal.

The only drama during the Senate action came from the presence of network-news cameras.[38] Although the creationism bill obviously had local popular support, senators feared that national public opinion condemned it. To avoid network-television coverage reinforcing the *Scopes* stereotype, the Senate acted without floor debate. In a flash, lawmakers approved friendly amendments specifying that alternative theories of origins receive equal emphasis rather than equal space in state textbooks and then passed the bill without comment. Before the vote, media representatives asked the one black member of the Senate to denounce the bill during floor debate for network coverage. Instead, that senator rose after the vote to hail the measure as extending "freedom" by acquainting students with all sides of the issue. Southern politicians and the national media clearly perceived an equal-time statute quite differently—and the split would widen.

The Tennessee House of Representatives, acting even more swiftly than the Senate, brought the bill up for floor action a week after receiving it.[39] This time the television cameras got some footage as the House vigorously debated and amended the bill for over an hour. Its action, however, only further demonstrated the popular support for creationism and the equal-time concept.

"The plain facts of the situation are that these people who want to teach a theory like Darwinism and can't prove it want to say 'Let us teach the children what we want them to know and the hell with everything else,' " a proponent charged. "I think they want to brainwash our children."

Even opponents of the measure avoided questioning creationism during the floor debate. Quite the contrary, they mostly attacked the bill for requiring the presentation of all explanations of human origins, including the Genesis account, as mere theories. Calling the bill "a sacrilege to my religion," the leading opponent of the measure proclaimed, "I believe the Biblical account is fact, not theory." Belying the sincerity of this claim, however, was the speaker's 1967 vote to repeal the anti-evolution statute. But the allegation hit home, and the House amended the bill to exempt "the Holy Bible" from carrying the disclaimer required for textbooks.

Critics also charged that the legislation would crowd textbooks with "hundreds of strange and weird theories about the creation." One glib opponent, who had also voted to repeal the *Scopes* law in 1967, now went so far as to profess that the bill mandated teaching creation theories propounded by "draft evaders who fled this country during its hour of need to engage in a marijuana smoking party." In response, the floor manager for the measure assured House members that the bill only required teaching the Genesis account along with evolution. To be safe, however, another House amendment added that "teaching of all occult or satanic beliefs of human origins is expressly excluded from this act." Further amendments reduced the burden of compliance by limiting application of the measure to biology textbooks and allowing the presentation of alternative theories though supplementary materials.

These House amendments carried through the popular intent behind the bill of defending the Genesis account from dogmatic evolutionary teaching. The Speaker of the House reported receiving "about 500 letters on the proposal, only one of which was unfavorable." Another representative, after stating his personal distaste for the measure, voted for it because of constituent pressure. Riding the crest of popular opinion, the creationism bill passed the House by a margin of 69 votes for to 16 against. Although representatives from urban districts cast thirteen of the no votes, most urban lawmakers joined their country cousins in supporting the measure. Democrats and Republicans showed almost equal support. Three of the seven surviving representatives who voted to lift the earlier ban on evolutionary teaching now joined in supporting the equal-time legislation.[40] The Senate overwhelmingly approved the House amendments on April 30th.[41] The bill automatically became law a week later when Governor Winfield Dunn refused either to sign or veto the popular measure.[42]

Judicial challenges to the Tennessee creationism law quickly sprang up. University of Tennessee law professor Frederic S. Le Clercq began plotting a federal court attack almost immediately, and soon asked support from the National Association of Biology Teachers. That organization agreed and, with Le Clercq serving as counsel, filed suit against the law in federal district court on behalf of itself and three local members, Joseph Daniel, Arthur Jones, and Larry Wilder. Alleging that the law violated "the prohibition against the Establishment of Religion and the rights of all citizens to the free exercise of religion, freedom of speech, and freedom of the press," the NABT sought to have the statute declared unconstitutional.[43]

Before the state answered the *Daniel* complaint, Americans United for Separation of Church and State, along with three of its local members including Harold Steele, challenged the statute in state court. Claiming that the "law is intended to aid or oppose religious points of view," the *Steele* complaint attacked the law for violating both state and federal constitutional prohibitions against the establishment of religion.[44] When the *Daniel* trial court decided to defer further action pending the resolution of the state court action, the NABT both intervened as an additional plaintiff in *Steele* and appealed to continue its federal court action. With the two actions running in tandem, the Tennessee attorney general faced double jeopardy in his efforts to defend the statute as providing "textbook fairness."[45]

While the state courts struggled to unravel the issue by considering legal arguments for and against the Tennessee statute, the federal court of appeals cut the Gordian knot with surprising ease. Without hearing any substantive arguments, the *Daniel* appellate court declared the law "patently unconstitutional" early in 1975.[46] This decision represented a repudiation of creationist legal theories as radical as the earlier dismissal of Wright's complaint for failing to state a cause of action. The *Daniel* trial court had never considered the merits of the statute. For the appellate court to overturn the law at this point rather than to direct the trial court to proceed with the case required determining that the statute was unquestionably unconstitutional—indeed, that any claims to the contrary were so "essentially fictitious" and "obviously frivolous" as not to merit any review. Typically, this procedure is reserved for direct violations of established constitutional principles.[47]

Applying this standard to the Tennessee creationism law, the court identified two portions of the law as clear-cut violations of the Establishment Clause. First, exempting the Genesis account from carrying a disclaimer wrongly gave a "preferential position for the Biblical view of creation as opposed to any account of the development of man based on scientific research and reasoning." Second, expressly excluding satanic theories from protection under the law improperly embroiled the state in identifying and censoring particular religious or anti-religious views. "We deem the two constitutional violations," the court concluded, "to be patent and obvious on the face of the statute and impossible for any state interpretation to cure."[48] After the attorney general decided not to appeal this decision, the Tennessee Supreme Court issued a brief concurring opinion in *Steele*.[49] The first equal-time statute was doubly dead.

Incredibly, some creationists were encouraged by these decisions. They interpreted the blanket *Daniel* condemnation as merely identifying a couple of technical problems with the law when, at the most, the court simply saw those problems as egregious enough to obviate further review of the law. In a comment typical of this viewpoint, a Vanderbilt University law professor who had helped defend the statute in court told a conclave of Tennessee creationists, "The word 'Genesis' and the whole bit about devil and satanic cults should never have been drafted." He then assured them that, if such pitfalls were avoided, the state could constitutionally provide equal time for their views.[50] An Adventist journal concluded its 1975 report on the "adverse" Tennessee rulings with the prediction, "Since creationists, who pay for public education, are discriminated against by current practice in public schools, the issue will probably arise again."[51] In fact, it arose concurrently in several states as creationists continued to grope for ways to qualify evolutionary teaching.

The Middle Way

While the courts were still dealing with the Tennessee statute, the Gablers' ongoing efforts bore fruit in Texas when the state Board of Education formalized its 1970 proclamation that textbooks should present evolution as a theory. Following that earlier victory, the Gablers had pressed the Board either to provide equal space for creationism in biology textbooks or to delete all evolutionary dogma from such texts. In mid-1974, the Board adopted a compromise resolution acceptable to the Gablers.[52] "Textbooks that treat the theory of evolution should identify it as only one of several explanations of the origins of humankind and avoid limiting young people in their search for meanings of their human existence," the Board ruled. "Textbooks presented for adoption which treat the subject of evolution substantially in explaining the historical origins of man shall be edited, if necessary, to clarify that the treatment is theoretical rather than factually verifiable. Furthermore, each textbook must carry a statement on an introductory page that any material on evolution included in the book is clearly presented as theory rather than verified."[53] Applying this new regulation, the Board then rejected all three versions of the BSCS texts. Mel Gabler described this compromise as a "middle way" between dogmatic evolutionary teaching and mandatory equal time for creationism.[54] Given the fate of the Tennessee statute, such a middle way appeared as the creationists' best hope. At least it did not raise serious legal challenges for nearly a decade.

The California Board of Education also edged toward this middle way during the early seventies as evolutionists railed against its 1970 *Science Framework.* That *Framework* gave equal recognition to creationism and evolution, and provided authority for demanding that textbooks do the same. In 1972, however, when the time first arrived for approving biology textbooks under the new *Framework*, the Board was deluged with protests from scientists and scientific organizations opposed to including creationism in the texts. According to one of the protesters, University of California-Riverside biologist John A. Moore, "the board could no longer continue to believe, as apparently some of its members had, that professional scientists who had studied the origins and diversity of life were seriously divided on the question."[55]

Instead of including creationism in the new texts, the Board adopted an policy requiring that "dogmatism be changed to conditional statements where speculation is offered as explanation for origins." In this respect, the policy statement added, "science should emphasize 'how' and not 'ultimate cause' for origins."[56] The resulting textual changes were modest and generally acceptable to protesting scientists.[57] In response to further creationist demands, the California board voted in 1973 to include creationism in social-science textbooks, but revoked this too before ever applying it. The creationist affirmations were formally dropped from the *Science Framework* in 1974, leaving the 1972 anti-dogmatism policy as the only relic of the stormy California creationism controversy. After flirting with the equal-time approach, the California Board of Education had moved to the middle way.

California creationists promptly challenged this retrenchment by their Board of Education. Two conservative Republican legislators from suburban Southern California districts asked the state attorney general to review the matter. Was the so-called constitutional requirement of neutrality "satisfied by making the textbook treatment of evolution 'less dogmatic,' " they asked, "or is there an affirmative, legal obligation of the State Board of Education to adopt textbooks which present 'both sides'—that is, both evolution and creation?"[58] In a sweeping repudiation of the creationist legal claims, California's Attorney General Evelle J. Younger in 1975 vindicated the actions of the Board. Even if evolutionary teaching wrongly promoted atheism,

Younger observed, "the state could not repair its entrance into the sectarian arena by balancing its 'religious' treatment of evolution with a 'religious' treatment of creation." Instead, the proper remedy would be to exclude both views. But, Younger added, "It is unlikely to the point of improbable that a court would find that a scientific treatment of evolution in science textbooks is, directly or indirectly, the advancement of an agnostic or atheistic belief."

Younger then discussed proper considerations for determining the content of public science instruction. "Essentially," he opined, "such considerations turn upon the degree of scientific certainty as perceived by contemporary society." Not what science accepted, mind you, but what the public perceived that science accepted. Popular opinion in this way controlled public science. In an observation that encapsulated the entire history of the creation-evolution legal controversy, Younger then added, "Ultimately, the question of whether a particular body of social or scientific knowledge should be part of a public school textbook depends upon its contemporary support in the community including its scientific and academic segments."

At one time, this standard permitted the exclusion of evolutionary teaching in many parts of the country. Since 1960, however, it led first to the reintroduction of evolution into public schools and then toward the expulsion of creationism. At least according to the California attorney general, the middle way of an anti-dogmatism policy was the most the Board could offer creationists. Constitutionally invalid religious considerations aside, creationism did not possess adequate public status as science to enter the classroom.[59] A California trial judge reached a similar result in 1979, when he rejected a petition from the Segraves's Creation-Science Research Center to enjoin implementation of the new *Science Framework* for violating creationists' religious rights.[60]

Two years later, a California court issued a curious confirmation of this middle way in the closest thing to a courtroom victory for creationists since *Scopes*. By this time, Kelly Segraves had children of his own in public school. Very much his mother's son, Segraves objected to the evolutionary teaching that his sons received in class. Fresh from the unsuccessful 1979 challenge of the theoretical *Science Framework*, Segraves filed suit against the allegedly dogmatic way that evolution was actually presented in California public schools. Segraves's complaint feigned a broad attack on evolutionary teaching replete with demands for giving equal time to creationism, but he executed a planned retreat at trial.[61] Describing the only issue as religious freedom, Segraves's attorney demanded in his opening statement only that "they must stop posing the theory that man and all life on earth developed from a common ancestor, as a fact, in the schools of this State." Putting this issue in its best light, he pleaded that "at the very least, we might expect that the government not affirmatively tell my clients' children in the public schools that their beliefs are wrong."[62]

This approach of seeking state accommodation for personal beliefs appealed to the liberal, Jewish trial judge. When the state moved for the customary dismissal on the grounds that science teaching cannot infringe on religious freedom because science is neutral on religious matters, the judge expressed skepticism and bid the trial proceed. Segraves's new approach forced the state to drop its plan to discredit scientific creationism through the testimony of over a dozen leading scientists and scholars. Instead, the parties fought for days over whether or not the wording of state-approved textbooks and teaching guidelines unduly infringed on religious freedom. In the end, the judge was most impressed by the 1972 anti-dogmatism policy and testimony from a Board member that the policy still applied.[63] Kelly Segraves later recalled the judge explaining that since the state Board of Education accepted this policy, "I thought I'd hang them with it."[64]

The decision itself represented a studied compromise. The state had not infringed on religious freedom through evolutionary teaching, the judge ruled. "To the contrary, defendant State Board of Education has had for a number of years and currently has [an anti-dogmatism] policy." Finding this policy "an appropriate compromise" between state science teaching and individual religious beliefs, the judge concluded, "If such policy were not disseminated . . . an appropriate accommodation would not be made as guaranteed by the First and Fourteenth Amendments to the Constitution."[65] Accordingly, the judge ordered the Board to distribute the anti-dogmatism policy statement to school officials, science teachers, and textbook publishers, and to include the policy in all future state *Science Frameworks*.[66]

Both sides claimed victory. The letter from the Board distributing the policy stated that the court "upheld the validity of the State Board's 1978 Science Framework against a legal action" by creationists. The letter went on to state that equal time should not be given to creationism.[67] Meanwhile, in a letter to his supporters, Segraves emphasized the court-mandated anti-dogmatism policy and announced plans to apply "the court injunction to state approved textbooks for science."[68] He stressed that, according to the court, the Free Exercise Clause requires that science teaching accommodate religious beliefs regardless of the scientific validity of those beliefs. "We made science irrelevant to our decision," Kelly Segraves later gloated.[69]

As California moved toward this middle way, the Kentucky state legislature enacted an entirely different approach for accommodating evolutionary teaching to personal religious beliefs. At the commencement of the 1976 legislative session, a fundamentalist minister serving as a state senator from a rural Appalachian district introduced legislation giving teachers the option of presenting biblical creationism along with evolution. This alternative instruction would come directly from the Bible without stressing any particular denominational beliefs. Students "receiving such instruction, and who accept the Bible theory of creation," could receive academic credit for correctly learning the biblical account.[70]

This accommodation struck a responsive chord in a state legislature that had never bowed to creationists. Over a half-century earlier, a bitterly divided Kentucky legislature had defeated the first anti-evolution bill in America. In 1974, legislation similar to the Tennessee equal-time law died in a Kentucky House committee. But the new bill sailed through both chambers with almost no legislative debate or public comment.[71] The Senate placed the measure on the consent calendar for non-controversial legislation and approved it on a vote of 32 to 3. The House added its overwhelming approval during a hectic afternoon meeting devoted to clearing away a backlog of popular bills. The measure became law on March 30, 1967. By neither imposing restrictions on either students or teachers nor challenging the scientific status of evolution, this statute has escaped the legal and political controversies that have dogged all other creationism laws.

At the same time that Kentucky legislators forged this pacific compromise, a different approach toward accommodating creationist beliefs ran amok just across the Ohio River in Indiana, in the suburbs of Louisville, Kentucky. It began innocently enough the previous December, when the Indiana Textbook Commission adopted the creationist text, *Biology: A Search for Order in Complexity*, as one of seven biology textbooks approved for use by public schools within the state. Since all of the other texts presented a traditional evolutionary perspective, the Commission viewed the creationist alternative as a fair way "to inculcate in the student an open and questioning mind on all subjects of inquiry."[72] But what seemed a fair accommodation at the state level and in the five local school districts adopting *A Search for Order* along with one of the other approved texts became a flagrant violation of the constitutional right to teach evolution established by *Epperson* when the West Clark Community Schools adopted only the creationist textbook in the spring of 1976.[73]

After the Commission rejected ensuing demands to withdraw approval for the creationist text, the Indiana ACLU filed suit the following February against both the Commission and the West Clark schools on behalf of a local student named Jon Hendren. In a notable recognition of the principle of religious accommodation, the *Hendren* complaint differentiated sharply between the local decision to use only the creationist textbook and the Commission approval for that text along with several evolutionary books. Both acts allegedly violated a state law against sectarian textbooks but only the local action was challenged as unconstitutional.[74]

Pursuant to normal administrative-law procedures, the complaint was then referred to the Commission for a hearing on the ACLU demands in prelude to judicial review. At that hearing, the ACLU presented a string of Indiana biologists and theologians who uniformly described the textbook as a sectarian presentation of fundamentalist Christian beliefs. Despite this testimony, the Commission reaffirmed its earlier decision. "What the school board of Clark County has done is not the Commission's fault," one steadfast commissioner sighed in support of the original compromise. "We solely adopted the book, and what the actions of the school board has done is something outside the matter of this hearing."[75] Frustrated, the ACLU returned to court alleging that the Commission action violated both state law and the Establishment Clause.

After reviewing the challenged text, Indianapolis trial court judge Michael T. Dugan rejected any public school use of the book—either alone or in conjunction with evolutionary materials. Finding the text a transparent attempt to clothe the Genesis account in scientific garb, Dugan asked, "The question is whether a text obviously designed to present *only* the view of Biblical Creationism in a favorable light is constitutionally acceptable in the public schools of Indiana. Two hundred years of constitutional government demand the answer be *no*." Implicitly rejecting any scientific basis for creationism, Dugan added, "The attempt to present Biblical Creationism as the only accepted scientific theory, while novel, does not rehabilitate the constitutional violation." State approval of the textbook unconstitutionally "advanced particular religious preferences and entangled the state with religion."[76]

Arguments that teaching creationism represented a fair accommodation of alternative beliefs and promoted the free expression of ideas made little impression on the judge. According to Dugan, these concerns were addressed by "the constitutional rights of individuals to substitute private and parochial schools to exercise dissent and independent views."[77] Public schools should not provide religious instruction under any circumstances. In this respect, *Hendren* blended the *Epperson* bar against suppressing evolutionary teaching with the *Daniel* prohibition against teaching religious creationism. The decision did not reach the issues raised by the Texas and California antidogmatic policies. Indeed, Dugan objected to *Search for Order* precisely because of its dogmatic presentation of creationism.[78] At most, Dugan narrowed the middle way, he did not close it.

Although the Indiana Textbook Commission dropped the

creationist text from its approved list without seeking an appeal, the issue did not go away. The Commission's trial court brief captured this spirit: "The State of Indiana may well survive the destruction of a book, but can its people or its courts countenance the destruction of an idea?"[79] Certainly, many people would not. Throughout the seventies, creationists in many parts of the country secured official recognition for their educational demands. Events at the state level in Tennessee, Texas, California, Kentucky, and Indiana were only the tip of an iceberg—a tip made visible by the legal controversies that they generated. Below the surface, several other states, numerous local school boards, and countless individual teachers either restricted evolutionary teaching or promoted creationist instruction in a multitude of legal and extralegal ways.[80]

Court decisions and constitutional principles have only a limited effect on actual school practices, as shown by the widespread disregard for the Supreme Court rulings against school prayer. Nearly a decade after *Schempp* supposedly settled the school prayer issue, political scientists Kenneth M. Dolbeare and Phillip E. Hammond found that one-third of the schools conducting morning prayers before the Court ruled still readily acknowledged doing so. On closer examination of one midwestern state, Dolbeare and Hammond concluded that even these figures overstated the impact of the Court decisions. "Despite questionnaire responses indicating full compliance with the Court's rulings," they reported, "wherever we examined actual practice, we found prayers or Bible reading or other religious observances clearly proscribed by the Court."[81] Finding little local public concern about the issue, they concluded that the most important reason for non-compliance was the desire of local school officials to avoid conflict. "Although in most cases," they noted, "key members of the local power structures only marginally favor schoolhouse religion on its merits, and acknowledge the abstract duty to obey the Court, they are unanimous in wanting to avoid public airing of the issue and hence are entirely committed to maintaining the status quo of religious practices."[82]

Dolbeare and Hammond's findings probably applied to creationist instruction as well, especially since the judicial decisions in that area were less well-known and definitive than the absolute Supreme Court ban against school prayer. The Establishment Clause protects minority rights, but even the smallest minority must include at least one person, and in many places no one actively opposed creationism in the classroom.

Sheep's Clothing

Shortly after the *Hendren* decision, a top Yale Law School student and avowed creationist named Wendell Bird took time out from his studies to devise a legal strategy for the creationism movement. He was motivated by personal experience. Because of high-school evolutionary teaching, Bird later recalled, "he came to believe in 'theistic evolution,' because he did not realize that the Bible taught anything different or that any scientists held any other viewpoint." Once set straight, he longed to protect other students from a similar fate by securing a place for creationism in the classroom.[83] In January 1978 he published his legal strategy as a long student note in the influential *Yale Law Journal*, and won a school prize for his efforts. Civil War historian Bruce Catton once observed that great soldiers (he was referring to Robert E. Lee at the time) plan in terms of complete victory whenever they have the slightest warrant for doing so.[84] Bird, an American history buff from Atlanta and an admirer of General Lee, did just this by leavening the unbroken string of courtroom defeats suffered by creationists since *Epperson* with a handful of religious free-exercise rulings to concoct a constitutional mandate for teaching scientific creationism.

Starting from the proposition that several religious denominations "affirm divine creation as a cardinal tenet of faith," Bird revived the well-worn argument that teaching only evolution violated the free exercise of such religions by compelling public-school students from those denominations to receive instruction in heretical views or to forgo biology training.[85] By appealing to three reasons given in earlier Supreme Court decisions interpreting the Free Exercise Clause to exempt Amish children from compulsory attendance at high school and Jehovah's Witnesses from classroom flag ceremonies, Bird argued that evolutionary teaching unconstitutionally undermined creationist beliefs, infringed on religious principles of separation from unholy doctrines, and compelled responses by students contrary to their personal beliefs. Applying the constitutional principle that the government may not restrict individual rights more than necessary in achieving its objectives, Bird then proposed that when furthering the goal of biology instruction schools should "neutralize" their curriculum by teaching both scientific creationism and evolution.[86]

Using past creationist defeats to help justify this conclusion, Bird read *Daniel* and *Hendren* as prohibiting only the teaching of religious creationism and *Epperson* as overturning religiously motivated restrictions aimed solely at evolutionary teaching. "Incorporation of scientific creationism to neutralize public school instruction in the origin of the universe and life would not have the primary effect of advancing some religions," Bird asserted. Primarily citing the work of Henry Morris and his colleagues at the Institute for Creation Research, Bird maintained that a model of creationism and critique of evolution "could be constructed from scientific discussion of empirical evidence divorced from theological reasoning and terminology."[87] This, then, was the cornerstone of Bird's argument—scientific creationism was science, not religion, and teaching it did not violate the constitutional restrictions against religious instruction, while not teaching it violated the free-exercise rights of creationist students. To complete the task of distinguishing earlier judicial decisions, Bird dismissed *Wright* and *Willoughby* for not recognizing the coercion against religious freedom caused by evolutionary instruction and claimed that "Clarence Darrow of *Scopes* trial fame remarked that it is 'bigotry for public schools to teach only one theory of origins.' "[88]

Bird's legal analysis relied on a series of factual assumptions. These included the centrality of creationism to widely held religious beliefs, the insupportable burden placed on those beliefs by evolutionary teaching, the appropriateness of parallels drawn from constitutional protections for the Amish and Jehovah's Witnesses, the suitability of protecting creationist students from evolutionary ideas by balancing those ideas with creationist alternatives, and, most critically, the non-religious basis of scientific creationism. Although these assumptions may appear self-evident to an avid creationist like Bird, others could easily question them. Indeed, the judicial law clerk for the 1982 Arkansas creationism trial concluded, "Bird's assumptions are incredible."[89] To fellow believers, however, Bird offered a legal theory that, when combined with Morris's scientific theories, provided a hope for a complete victory. Better than simply presenting evolution as a theory, exempting creationist students from attendance, or even banning all instruction in origins, schools would teach creationism as science! By offering this hope, Bird and Morris together influenced the course of creationist legal efforts more than any individuals since Bryan sounded the original call for anti-evolution laws.

After finishing law school, Bird joined Morris at the Institute for Creation Research, serving as a legal adviser and, for a time, as staff attorney. One of his first tasks was to update the ICR model equal-time resolution. This resolution, first written by Morris in the early seventies, was designed for adoption by school boards wishing to include scientific creationism in their curriculum.[90]

Bird's new resolution began by summarizing the key points of his journal article to provide an express constitutional justification for the measure. In a strident litany of creationist affirmation, this summary hammered home the dialectic that creationism was as scientific as evolutionary theory, and evolutionary theory was as religious as creationism. Reaching a crescendo, the resolution affirmed that, although teaching only evolution violated religious freedom, the presentation of "both the theory of evolution and the theory of scientific creationism would not . . . because it would involve presenting of the scientific evidence for each theory rather than any religious doctrine." In a remarkable appeal to the authority of public opinion, the resolution then declared, "Most citizens, whether they personally believe in evolution or creation, favor balanced treatment in public schools of alternative scientific theories of origins." Based on these affirmative findings, the resolution then directed schools to give "balanced treatment" to both theories in classroom lectures, textbooks, library materials, and other educational programs. As if wishing it could make it so, the resolution concluded by requiring that the treatment of both theories "must be limited to scientific evidence and must not include religious doctrine."[91]

The Institute for Creation Research distributed this draft resolution by the thousands to supporters throughout the country in mid-1979. Each copy carried the disclaimer, "Please note that this is a suggested *resolution*, to be adopted by boards of education, not *legislation* proposed for enactment as law. ICR has always taken the position that the route of education and persuasion on this issue is more fruitful in the long run than that of coercion."[92] Scientific creationists at ICR retained the hope that their views could prevail through public education. This placed the scientific creationism submovement squarely in the third stage of Goodwyn's model of reform movement development. Beginning in the sixties, Morris and other visionaries built an organizational base at ICR and elsewhere. From this base, they recruited a core of scientists and supporters to the cause and proceeded to spread the word that scientific evidence supported creationism. This new approach offered the hope of voluntarily restoring orthodoxy to public science without the need for coercion.

As a scion of anti-evolutionism, however, the scientific creationism submovement fed into an older cause and its work product was regularly appropriated by anti-evolutionists long accustomed to coercing reform by legal means. Paul Ellwanger, a private citizen who had battled evolutionary teaching in his own state of South Carolina for years, almost immediately transformed Bird's resolution into model legislation for introduction into his home state legislature and for distribution to fellow believers throughout the country.[93] Although the measure failed in South Carolina, similar bills surfaced in eight state legislatures during 1980 and fifteen such assemblies in 1981.[94] Ellwanger sent one copy of his proposal to the Rev. A. A. Blount in suburban North Little Rock, Arkansas. Early in 1981, when a local biology teacher was challenged for teaching creationism, Blount remembered the bill and passed it on to his state senator, James L. Holsted. "You know the rest of the story," Blount wrote to Ellwanger in May of 1981. "The idea swept through the Legislature and to the Governor's desk, and as I watched the progress I said simply to myself and to others, 'This is an idea whose time has come.' "[95]

The Arkansas creationism bill closely followed the Ellwanger draft of Bird's resolution. The only significant change in the Holsted-Ellwanger bill from Bird's original resolution involved renaming and expressly defining the two opposing theories. " 'Creation-science,' " the bill stated, "means the scientific evidence for creation and inferences from those scientific evidences." These inferences were identified to include the biblical concepts of the "[s]udden creation of the universe, energy, and life from nothing," the special creation of basic biological "kinds" including man, a world-wide flood, and the "relatively recent inception of the earth and living kinds." In contrast, "evolution-science" was defined to mean the scientific evidence for evolution and related inferences, including the "emergence of life from non-life," the naturalistic evolution of man and all other "present living kinds" from "simple earlier kinds," strict geological uniformitarianism, and a long earth history.[96]

Just as in Bird's resolution, the bill then mandated the balanced treatment for both theories in all public elementary and secondary schools teaching either concept. Bird's litany of creationist affirmations appeared as legislative findings of fact. In introducing this bill, Holsted adopted the Ellwanger draft as his own, confident that it "represents my beliefs and the beliefs of the majority of my constituents."[97] Apparently most of Holsted's colleagues felt the same, because they accepted the bill without even considering any amendments.

With final adjournment less than a week away, the Senate moved quickly to pass the bill on Friday, March 13th. In a procedure commonly afforded non-controversial bills by that body during the closing days of a session, the Arkansas Senate leadership brought up the measure for final consideration without either a prior committee hearing or any advance public notice. After fifteen minutes of floor debate disclosed no active opposition, senators from all parts of the state joined in passing the bill by a vote of 22 to 2.[98]

The state House of Representatives hastily followed suit only one day before final adjournment. After a ten-minute, pro-forma committee hearing earlier in the day, cheering House members passed the bill by a margin of 69 to 18 on March 17th. In the press of last-minute business, efforts to amend or to debate the bill on the House floor were ruled out of order. Although both rural and urban legislators voted heavily in favor of the bill, opposition increased somewhat among representatives from the more urbanized districts. Six out of the fifteen House members from the only truly urban county in Arkansas (the one including Little Rock) opposed the bill while only five of nineteen representatives from counties having 75,000 to 100,000 people voted no—along with 7 of the 66 members from counties with fewer than 75,000 persons. To some extent, popular support for the equal-time concept bloated the final tally. "This is a terrible bill," one member from a mid-size county lamented shortly after voting for it, "but it's worded so cleverly that none of us can vote against it if we want to come back up here."[99]

Arkansas Governor Frank White signed the bill into law as Act 590 two days after the House vote. "If we're going to teach evolution in the public school system, why not teach scientific creationism?" he concluded. "Both of them are theories." Painting the issue as a purely scientific dispute, White added, "I don't think this is addressing a law on religion itself. I think this is equal treatment of two theories and that's the way it should be approached."[100]

Approaching the anti-evolution issue this way indeed found favor in Arkansas. The entire legislative process, from initial Senate consideration to the Governor's approval, took less than a week. In the waning days of the session when even the slightest hesitation could prove fatal, the vast majority of legislators in both chambers uncritically embraced the proposal without change or comment. Probably few of these lawmakers fully understood the bill and even the Governor admitted having not read it before adding his signature, but they liked the concept. Even partisanship was never a factor: the state legislature that overwhelmingly passed the bill was composed almost entirely of Democrats, while the governor was a Republican. This new, equal-time approach to the old anti-evolution issue, an approach made tenable by Morris's scientific claims and Bird's legal theories, finally fulfilled its promise. Equal time for scientific creationism was now the law in "The Land of Opportunity."

Traditional opponents of the anti-evolution movement saw a wolf beneath this sheep's clothing, however, and reacted swiftly. Even before the governor affixed his signature to the bill; the ACLU vowed to challenge the new law in court as violating the separation of church and state.[101] Yet even as the ACLU prepared for battle, Louisiana lawmakers joined their Arkansas neighbors in legislating equal time for scientific creationism.

The Louisiana legislature acted much more deliberately than its Arkansas counterpart. Disturbed by evolutionary teaching in his local public schools, Senator Bill Keith of Shreveport first introduced a home-brewed scientific-creationism bill in 1980.[102] The extensive committee hearings on this bill caught the eye of Ellwanger, who sent Keith a copy of his model legislation, ICR creationism materials, and tactical advice about stressing scientific rather than religious objections to evolution. After his initial bill died in committee, Keith introduced Ellwanger's proposal on the opening day of the 1981 session.

Following another series of hearings, the Senate Education Committee amended Keith's new bill so that it merely allowed balanced treatment for scientific creationism as a local option. The committee also dropped Bird's creationist findings of fact, the list of inferences from the two theories, and the bar against referring to religious doctrine. Balanced treatment was defined to mean simply that instruction needed "to provide insight into both theories" rather than actual equal time. A further committee amendment authorized local schools to develop creation-science teaching skills and resources with the aid of seven Louisiana creation scientists to be named by the governor. These changes transformed Keith's radical mandate into a compromise bill somewhat similar to the non-controversial Kentucky law permitting teachers to temper evolutionary teaching with creationist concepts. On this basis, the measure sailed through the Senate with little comment or dissent in early June. But the House soon upset this compromise and brought Louisiana into the creationism legal controversy for the first time.

Louisiana House members knew just what they were doing.[103] After a lengthy public hearing, the House Education Committee restored the mandate for balanced treatment to the bill while leaving the other Senate amendments intact. The committee then added provisions to require teaching both evolution and creation as unproven theories and to prohibit public schools and universities from discriminating against creationist teachers. These committee amendments generated a storm when they reached the House floor on July 6th.

Creationism is "pure science," the floor manager for the bill argued as Keith distributed ICR literature to House members, "It has no missing links in it." Noting that he once taught evolution as an education professor at Northeast Louisiana University, the floor manager added, "I came to feel like there was another side of it, and it's a side that has been avoided for many years." He then assured his colleagues, "Creationism has a religious basis, but it would be taught in schools on a scientific basis."

"I don't know what's scientific about creationism," the chief opponent shot back, "there's nothing factual about it." He then drew on his training as a civil engineer to refute the creationists' scientific arguments. "I don't want my children to be subjected to an absolute lie," he concluded. "Let religion stay in the churches."

After listening to this exchange and defeating amendments to weaken the bill, the full House approved the committee's handiwork by a healthy margin of 71 to 19. The bill then returned to the Senate, where Keith moved to concur in the House amendments two days later.[104]

"Evolution is no more than a fairy tale about a frog that turns into a prince," Keith declared in the renewed Senate debate. "We force our children to go to school, and when they get there we teach them man came from monkeys."

"I don't believe we ought to require teachers to teach or not teach anything," replied the Senate Education Committee chairman who had twice held back the tide. But this time he failed, as 26 out of 38 senators voted to accept the House amendments.

With this vote, the Louisiana legislature became the first preponderately urban state assembly to approve an anti-evolution measure. Over 60 percent of the state lawmakers represented counties having more than 100,000 people, and those urban legislators voted for the bill in substantially the same ratio as their rural colleagues.[105] At least in Louisiana, and to a lesser extent in Arkansas and Tennessee, the stereotype of creationism emanating from the rural backwaters of American civilization simply did not hold up. Most urban legislators in all three states voted for their equal-time laws. Partisanship was never a factor either because of the overwhelmingly Democratic composition of the legislatures in all three states. The only remaining obstacle for the Louisiana bill was that state's Republican Governor David C. Treen, who had expressed his doubts about the whole idea.[106]

Not wanting to veto such a popular measure, Treen reluctantly signed the bill into law after two weeks of indecision. He searched hard for ways to justify this decision. Finding a glitch where the House forgot to change back one of the Senate amendments making the bill permissive, Treen argued that the bill "simply 'permits' competing theories to be covered, rather than mandating that one be covered if the other is included." Even if that dubious interpretation failed, he claimed that balanced treatment required only a brief explanation of creationist beliefs, not equal emphasis for both theories. Finally, Treen added, "Academic freedom can scarcely be harmed by inclusion. It can be harmed by exclusion."[107] Treen was right to an extent. The surviving Senate amendments toned down the law from the radical Ellwanger draft enacted by Arkansas. But some sort of balanced treatment for creationism still appeared mandatory under the Louisiana law and the ACLU was not the least bit mollified. Roger Baldwin, the 97-year-old founding executive director of the Union and last survivor of the *Scopes* battle, commented, "It is a strange feeling. Here's where I came in, and here's where the ACLU goes out to another battle to defend the same principle of freedom."[108]

6

Outlawing Creation

Legal Developments Since 1981

"The average American gives rhetorical assent to the strict separation of church and state, yet frequently approves of policies which involve considerable cooperation between church and state," University of Virginia sociologist James Davison Hunter concluded in analyzing a comprehensive 1987 survey of American popular opinion on religion in public life. "Nowhere is this more clearly seen than in the conflict over public education. In this context the particular and inviolable rights of parents to see that their children are taught within the value system of their own choosing (usually religious in nature) are pitted against the needs of the state for a universal system of education."[1] In this manner, Hunter sought to explain the seemingly self-contradictory findings of the survey. A clear majority of those polled favored the concept, "There should be a high wall of separation between church and state," over the concept, "The government should take special steps to protect the Judeo-Christian heritage." Yet, by even larger majorities, the survey found widespread support for public schools to set aside daily moments of silence for student prayer, to allow meetings by student religious groups, and to begin sporting events with public prayer.[2]

These responses did not reflect support for erecting a high wall of separation between church and state in the case of specific school events. At the very least, they indicated a desire for public schools to accommodate students' religious views. Beyond this, they suggested support for using schools to protect or promote religion in disregard of the prevailing interpretation of the Establishment Clause. "A significant portion of the country's population do not understand the Establishment Clause of the 1st Amendment—or if they understand it—they don't want the courts to enforce it," Judge William R. Overton concluded based on the mail generated by his ruling on the Arkansas creationism law.[3]

The survey revealed that this attitude applied to the teaching of origins. Out of every ten persons polled, seven thought that public schools should teach both evolution and "the Bible's account of the creation of life on earth," while one each either favored only evolutionary teaching, favored only creationist instruction, or expressed no opinion. The survey found similar divisions of opinion on this issue to exist in all regions of the country and among all age groups, including high-school students. Solid support (in at least the sixtieth percentile) for teaching both views was expressed by men and women; by business executives, newspaper editors and broadcast news directors, and government leaders; and among people of all education levels from less than high school to college graduate. In the only clear break from the overall pattern, nearly one-third of the evangelicals and fundamentalists polled favored teaching only the biblical account, while approximately two-thirds of the surveyed college professors thought that only evolution should be taught.[4] Although the question did not expressly inquire about the teaching of scientific (as opposed to biblical) creationism, the response at least revealed broad support for accommodating a creationist viewpoint in public education.

Arkansas and Louisiana legislators had responded to such popular sentiment by enacting creationism laws in 1981. Indeed, those Southern legislators did not simply represent a constituency that favored teaching both evolution and creation: they represented a region where belief in biblical creationism ran deep. When releasing an opinion survey conducted shortly after passage of the two creationism laws, pollster George Gallup observed, "Debate over the origin of man is as alive today as it was at the time of the famous Scopes trial in 1925, with the public now about evenly divided between those who believe in the biblical account of creation and those who believe either in a strict interpretation of evolution or in an evolutionary process involving God." Looking only at the responses from the South, Gallup found 49 percent accepted creation, 34 percent believed in theistic evolution, and only 6 percent accepted atheistic evolution.[5] Given such beliefs, many observers assumed that the new statutes aimed as much at discouraging evolutionary teaching as at encouraging creationist instruction, because the law could be obeyed either by a Bryanesque silence on the subject of origins or by offsetting "evolution-science" with "creation-science."[6] Even though two generations of secular commentators had pronounced efforts to outlaw evolutionary teaching as dead in the aftermath of *Scopes*, popular opinion had revived them.[7]

The issue now passed to the courts, when the national ACLU stepped forward to challenge the new creationism laws as promptly as it once moved against the Tennessee anti-evolution statute. But the forum changed. No longer would an obscure county court, presided over by an elected judge applying state law, be the site of such a confrontation. In the thirty-odd years since the U.S. Supreme Court had assumed final authority for state-level disputes involving religious freedom, a comprehensive body of federal constitutional law had developed to deal with the subject. This change was widely accepted. The 1987 survey, which had found strong support for including creationist instruction in public education, reported overwhelming agreement with the statement, "The Supreme Court is the best place to decide controversies about the separation of church and state." Curiously, respondents also tended to agree that the ACLU "files too many law suits regarding religion."[8] Yet it was those ACLU lawsuits that often allowed the Supreme Court to address the thorniest Establishment Clause disputes, including those raised by the new creationism laws. As the ultimate responsibility for resolving those disputes moved from elected state legislators and judges to the appointed federal judiciary, persistent popular support for accommodating creationism in public education would still influence the law, but its impact became subtler.

The Constitution and Common Sense

Marshalling its considerable resources for a battle royal against scientific creationism following enactment of the two equal-time statutes, the ACLU moved first against the more vulnerable Arkansas law. In doing so, the ACLU generated the most dramatic creation-evolution legal confrontation since *Scopes*. Dozens of scientists, theologians, and scholars assembled in Little Rock to testify at the two weeks' long trial. Seventy-five news media organizations from across the country and as far away as London registered with the court to cover the proceedings. A team of nine New York attorneys for the ACLU and three local lawyers pressed the case against the embattled Arkansas attorney general's office.

Yet nothing akin to the profound social experiences of *Scopes* emerged. Too many differences separated the two cases. Two world views clashed at Dayton as leading protagonists for each side debated the reasonableness of evolutionary teaching, which was then the central constitutional issue. New constitutional principles against religion in public education now refocused the debate. "Our strategy from the beginning of the case through the trial was to avoid challenging the scientific merits of the creationists claims," lead ACLU counsel Jack D. Novik later explained. "It was our position, not that creationism was bad science, but that it was not science at all. Rather, we argued, it was religious apologetics, and a particular religious view at that." One of the attorneys assisting Novik noted, "Since the seminal case interpreting the Establishment Clause of the First Amendment (*Everson v. Board of Education*), it has been the law that, to survive constitutional challenge, legislation must have a secular purpose and have a 'primary effect' that neither advances nor inhibits religion."[9] Accordingly, the Little Rock trial focused on the religious purpose and effect of the Arkansas statue rather than on the reasonableness of evolution and creation.

Further, the sensation of Darrow confronting Bryan gave way to careful legal arguments advanced by skilled but mostly faceless attorneys. The only chance of changing this died when the court refused to let Wendell Bird intervene in the lawsuit on behalf of four creationist organizations and fifteen like-minded individuals. The state "Attorney General will defend the suit with adequate vigor and diligence" without outside help, the court ruled in rejecting Bird's petition. Finally, even the type of action lessened the glamour. A civil action argued to a judge on the constitutional infirmities of adding creationism to the curriculum simply lacked the high drama of a teacher in the dock before a jury of his peers for presenting evolution. "I don't believe Hollywood could ever make a sequel to *Inherit the Wind* out of the transcript," trial judge Overton observed afterward.[10]

Press accounts generally critical of the Arkansas statue and the creation-science movement poured out of Little Rock during the trial, but they seldom got the prominence once given reports from Dayton. Indeed, these articles relied heavily on the continued fascination in *Scopes* to get what attention they did for the event billed as "Scopes II." After reviewing the news media coverage for the trial, science-journalist Marcel C. La Follette concluded that "if the readers learned anything, we may assume it is the details of the Scopes trial."[11]

Nonetheless, the ACLU presented quite a case in Little Rock. The Union began by assembling a remarkable collection of plaintiffs to bring the suit. Highlighting the deep rift between Arkansas Christians over the law, these plaintiffs were led off by the Rev. Bill McLean of Little Rock and included the local bishop or principal officer of the United Methodist, Episcopal, Roman Catholic, African Methodist Episcopal, and Presbyterian churches. A variety of national Jewish groups and professional teachers' associations joined as organizational plaintiffs. Their complaint alleged that the equal-time statute unconstitutionally promoted religion, violated academic freedom, and imposed overly vague demands on teachers. This complaint was filed in May with the federal district court at Little Rock, and the matter proceeded to trial in December before William R. Overton, the young, liberal jurist "plucked from obscurity," as he later put it, to hear the case.[12]

Concentrating their assault on the Establishment Clause questions, the ACLU gathered an impressive array of leading experts to testify that the Arkansas statute had a purely religious purpose and effect. "Consistent with this approach," one of the plaintiff's lawyers explained, "the expert testimony at the trial was intended to offer the trial judge an understanding of the history and social context of the 'creation-science' movement, of the consideration and conclusions of the scientific and philosophical communities regarding the status of 'creation-science' as science, of the relationship of the 'two-model approach' enshrined in the Act and the history and theology of Christian Fundamentalism, and of the impact of Act 590 on the educational system within Arkansas."[13]

The plaintiffs' ten expert witnesses were divided into two teams. "The ACLU first presented expert witnesses from their 'religious team,'" reported one of those witnesses, Cornell University sociologist Dorothy Nelkin. "These witnesses argued that, historically, philosophically, and sociologically, creationism is a religious movement of fundamentalists who base their beliefs on the inerrancy of the Bible and that creation science is no more than religious apologetics." Nelkin went on, "The ACLU then presented its 'scientific team'; a geneticist, a paleontologist, a geologist, and a biophysicist. They documented the absence of scientific evidence for the creationist beliefs" and the affirmative case for evolution. "Here then is the significance of science in the case," ACLU attorney Jack Novik explained. "For if, as we contended, creationism was not science at all, then whatever else the Arkansas legislature thought it was doing, meaningful science education could not provide a legitimate secular purpose for enacting the creationism statute." The plaintiffs' case closed with local teachers and school administrators discussing their inability to implement the statute without teaching religious doctrine.[14] At last, expert testimony on the creation-evolution controversy had made it into court.

According to the plaintiffs' counsel this use of expert witnesses had two purposes. First, it allowed the judge to rely on experts rather than having to determine any scientific facts for himself. Second, it presented "the assertion in the legal forum of the legitimate, and indeed superior, claims of the specialized communities of scientists and educators to determine issues bearing directly on their particular competence."[15] At the very least, this approach asked the judge to use expert testimony in determining whether scientific creationism was primarily a religious doctrine. Pushed further, it flowed into the plaintiffs' alternative pleas for academic freedom. In violation of the so-called "Constitutional doctrine of academic freedom," the plaintiffs' argued; "the Arkansas legislature has overridden the professional judgment of teachers, scientists and educators, that 'creation-science' lacks recognized educational value, thereby giving this subject matter a most peculiar and privileged place in the curriculum."[16] Under this view of academic freedom, popular opinion acting through elected officials loses any direct control over public science. The plaintiffs' final, and weakest, plea claimed that the statute was fatally vague because it forced teachers to surmise "the meaning of 'balanced treatment' while their jobs and livelihood remain the penalty for an incorrect guess."[17]

Struggling to deflect this assault, Arkansas Attorney General Steve Clark adopted the basic line of argument presented in Bird's law-journal article. This argument centered on defending creation science as a scientific, non-religious theory of origins constitutionally worthy of equal treatment with evolution. "Rather than advancing religion, Act 590 advances both scientific inquiry and academic freedom," Clark's trial brief asserted. "Scientific inquiry is advanced by providing students with an alternative scientific theory to evolution-science. The proof will show that many competent scientists believe that the scientific data on origins best supports creation-science. Act 590 has the primary effect of furthering academic freedom in that a controversial scientific theory should not be squelched or censored based on one small segment of society's political, philosophical, or religious opposition to the theory."[18] The state here rested its defense squarely on showing that competent scientists accepted creationism as good science.

The difficulty lay in finding recognized scientists who could testify on behalf of creationism without being discredited for their religious presuppositions. Obviously Henry Morris and his colleagues at ICR were out of the question because they readily admitted a religious purpose and effect for their scientific activities, and that was just what the statute could not have. From the court's viewpoint, however, the best that the state pro-

duced were scientists who questioned evolution without necessarily accepting creation science or creationists whose science
was influenced by their religious beliefs. Fitting the first mold,
respected British astrophysicist Chandra N. Wickramasinghe
testified that the mathematical probability of chance chemical
combinations producing life from non-life was essentially nil,
but then totally rejected the basic tenets of creation science and
added his own views that life was seeded on earth by comets.
In the second mold, creationist chemist Donald Chittich refused to acknowledge whether he could ever accept any scientific result at odds with a literal reading of Scripture.[19] In a fu-
tile effort to bolster his case, Clark advanced the argument that
creationist instruction served the constitutionally valid purpose
of neutralizing evolutionary teaching and presented evidence of
the overwhelming public support for such equal time for the
two views.[20]

In a decision issued on January 5, 1982, Judge Overton rang
in the new year with a resounding repudiation of the Arkansas
statute. Just as the *Epperson* Court once ruled regarding the old
anti-evolution laws, Overton now found that the new equal-time
statute had an unconstitutional religious purpose. In reaching
this conclusion, Overton relied heavily on the proclaimed religious motivations of the creation-science movement and of the
individuals involved in drafting, sponsoring, and promoting the
legislation. "The State failed to produce any evidence which
would warrant an inference or conclusion that at any point in
the process anyone considered the legitimate educational value
of the Act," Overton wrote. "It was simply and purely an effort to introduce the Biblical version of creation into the public
school curricula."[21]

Although this finding alone was enough to overturn the statute, Overton pushed on to condemn its sectarian effect as well.
Epperson never went into this prong of the test for Establishment Clause violations, probably because the justices could not
believe that the old anti-evolution laws had any effect in modern America. But a new requirement for equal time would have
an effect—and Overton concluded that the effect would be purely
religious.

This conclusion involved a two-step analysis. Overton first

found that the concept and tenets of creation science, as defined in the Arkansas law, were inescapably religious and identical to the Genesis account. This left "no doubt that a major effect of the Act is the advancement of particular religious beliefs." He then determined that the law had no saving nonreligious effects. Specifically, he concluded that the statutory section requiring balanced treatment "lacks legitimate educational value because 'creation science' as defined in that section is simply not science." Accepting expert testimony that science is "what scientists do," Overton noted that no recognized scientific journal had published a creationist article. Expert testimony from Canadian philosopher of science Michael E. Ruse further characterized science as tentative, empirically testable explanations of occurrences in terms of natural law. Viewing the creation as a non-repeatable, supernatural event uncritically accepted by faith, Overton flunked creation science on all counts. "Since creation science is not science," the court ruled, "the conclusion is inescapable that the *only* real effect of Act 590 is the advancement of religion."[22]

Strictly speaking, this conclusion was not inescapable. "Evidence showing that creationism was not science does not dispositively prove that it is religion," ACLU counsel Jack Novik later pointed out, "but it does tend toward that conclusion." Bryan had once given plenty of non-religious reasons for restricting evolutionary teaching, but Overton was satisfied that the Arkansas statute primarily benefited religion. As such, the statute was unconstitutional. Battered by criticism from both sides for his handling of the suit and personally convinced that the law was unconstitutional, Clark decided not to appeal.[23]

The *McLean* decision overturned the equal-time requirement solely for violating religious freedom. Overton did not find the statute unduly vague. Quite to the contrary, he found it "all too clear." Nor did he adopt the plaintiffs' view of academic freedom that the legislature could not prescribe the curriculum for public schools. The state simply could not use this authority to promote religion. Turning to the defendant's alternative points, Overton added that this constitutional restriction against advancing religion applied here even if most Americans favored teaching creationism. "The application and content of First

Amendment principles are not determined by public opinion polls or by a majority vote," he pointed out. Public opinion, acting through the legislature, still had its place in fixing the school curriculum, but its free rein to prescribe creationism or to proscribe evolution was checked by the Establishment Clause. Yet public opinion exerted some influence even within these limits. Overton appealed to it in refuting the defense contention that the religious nature of evolution justified restricting evolutionary teaching. Citing *Epperson, Willoughby,* and *Wright,* Overton observed that "it is clearly established in the case law, and perhaps also in common sense, that evolution is not a religion and that teaching evolution does not violate the Establishment Clause."[24] Thanks to the Constitution and common sense, in Arkansas, evolutionary teaching was legal and creationist instruction was illegal.

Evolutionists hailed the decision as a clear-cut triumph and moved to consolidate their victory. "I believe that the case will deal creation-science a fatal blow," an ACLU attorney hastily proclaimed.[25] The most prestigious scientific journal in America, *Science,* promptly reprinted the entire twenty-page decision, as did at least three books by advocates of evolutionary teaching.[26] Throughout the country, the number of creationist bills introduced into state legislatures dropped following Overton's ruling—and none were passed.[27] In Texas, a state senator took this opportunity to ask Attorney General Jim Maddox for a ruling whether *McLean* also called into question the ten-year-old state Board of Education anti-dogmatism regulations. After Maddox opined that those rules violated *McLean* by singling out evolution for special restrictions, the civil-liberties group People for the American Way vowed to challenge the rules in court, and the Board backed down. On April 19, 1984, the Board replaced its strict anti-dogmatism regulations with a simple requirement that all "[t]heories shall be clearly distinguished from fact and presented in an objective educational manner." Texas biology textbooks no longer needed to identify evolution as only one of several explanations of human origins.[28] The middle way had shifted against creationism.

Ever faithful, creationists struggled to minimize their losses by deflecting the blame away from their cause. With a disaster clearly looming in Little Rock, Bird denounced Attorney General Clark's efforts even before the trial began and dissuaded potential expert witnesses from appearing. During and after the trial, popular television evangelists Pat Robertson and Jerry Falwell accused Clark of cavorting with the ACLU—precipitating a defamation action against Robertson.[29] "If the law is unconstitutional it'll be because of something in the language that's wrong," the original Senate sponsor of the bill added. "So we'll just change the wording and try again."[30] Ellwanger did just this by preparing and distributing a new model equal-time act.[31] Following the decision, ICR scientist Duane T. Gish accused the judge of bias while Bird described the decision as "constitutionally erroneous and factually inaccurate."[32] Henry Morris reiterated the party line: "There is already no constitutional or legal impediment to teaching creation science along with evolution science in any state—regardless of publicity to the contrary—except in Arkansas after a biased judicial decision following a poor state defense."[33] All placed their hope on Louisiana, where the state attorney general had deputized Bird to give creationists their day in court to defend the last surviving equal-time statute.

Door to Accommodation

The Louisiana litigation was moving as slow as a backwater bayou in the summertime. With the law not scheduled to take effect until the fall of 1983 and plenty of work to do in Arkansas, the ACLU held off filing its complaint against the Louisiana statute. Then, shortly after he was excluded from the Arkansas suit, Bird stole a march on his adversaries by initiating his own legal action in the Baton Rouge federal court on December 2, 1981. On behalf of Senator Keith and fifty-four other plaintiffs, Bird sought to compel state educational agencies to comply with the act. A day later, the ACLU struck back with its own suit in the New Orleans federal court challenging the constitutionality of the law. The second action, *Aguillard v. Treen*, named twenty-six organizational and individual plaintiffs, beginning with local Louisiana educator Donald Aguillard and including such familiar participants as the National Association of Biology Teachers, the National Science Teachers Association, and the American Association for the Advancement of Science. Bird was named a special assistant attorney general for both cases and assumed overall responsibility for defending the statute. The ACLU coordinated the assault.

The *McLean* decision did not automatically resolve the Louisiana litigation. Many of the more damning features of the Arkansas act were absent from the Louisiana law, including the creationist findings of fact, the Genesis-like definition for creation science, and the hasty adoption of the proposal in the exact form supplied by religiously motivated private citizens. These differences obscured both the purpose behind enactment of the Louisiana legislation and the potential effects of its implementation.

"This case differs vastly from *McLean*," Bird's pre-trial brief asserted, "because the Balanced Treatment Act is (1) a substantially different statute with (2) an entirely different definition of creation-science and with (3) a markedly different legislative purpose." Elaborating on the new definition of creation science, Bird rejected all the traditional features of the biblical account that figured so prominently in the Arkansas statute, leaving only the broad concept that some organic and inorganic matter initially appeared in complex form, rather than merely evolving from ever simpler forms. Turning to legislative purpose, Bird pointed to the lengthy deliberations on the measure by both houses as substantiating the stated purpose for the law of "protecting academic freedom." To resolve these issues, Bird demanded a trial on the scientific merits of creation science and the educational merits of the Louisiana law.[34]

For its part, the ACLU relied on the arguments that carried the day in Arkansas. The law "does not have any secular legislative purpose in that creation-science is inherently religious, it is religious apologetics calculated to advance a particular religious belief, it is not science and it has no educational merit," an ACLU pretrial brief argued. As such, "teaching creation-science in the public schools advances religious beliefs even if attempts are made to eliminate overt references to the Bible, the Creator or other religious concepts." The brief cited *McLean* as determinative authority on both points and suggested that a second trial was unnecessary to void the Louisiana law.[35] After the stunning victory for evolution in Little Rock, the ACLU had nothing further to gain from another trial, while creationists had nothing more to lose.

Both Louisiana federal courts balked before even reaching these arguments. First the *Aguillard* court ducked by deferring any action until the resolution of the other suit. Then the *Keith* court avoided the First Amendment issues by ruling that, because Bird's legal action boiled down to a dispute between state officials over the implementation of a state law, the issue "must and should be resolved by Louisiana state courts."[36] Since this taint did not infect a straight-forward action to declare the law unconstitutional, the dismissal of *Keith* in June of 1982 simply revived activity in *Aguillard*. Acting without a trial the following November, Judge Adrian Duplantier again sidestepped the federal constitutional issues by overturning the statute for reasons wholly unrelated to creationism. According to Duplantier, the Louisiana constitution entrusted total authority over school curriculum matters to the state education board. The legislature wrongly usurped this authority in "dictating to the public schools not only that a subject *must* be taught, but also *how* it must be taught."[37]

No court dealing with the creationism controversy ever went this far in limiting legislative authority. Even *McLean* maintained that the legislature could control public education so long as it did not abridge constitutional rights in the process. The federal appellate court reviewing the decision referred this thorny question of state constitutional law to the elected Louisiana Supreme Court. Late in 1983, the state high bench rejected the federal trial court's limitation on the "plenary power of the people of a state exercised through its legislature." In doing so, the state court stressed that its decision did not "involve any scientific or religious questions related to creation-science or evolution-science."[38] These questions then returned to the federal court.

Early in 1985, Judge Duplantier disposed of these questions as quietly as possible by entering a second pre-trial summary judgment against the Louisiana equal-time act. The new judgment, granted in response to an ACLU motion, voided the statute as a patently unconstitutional establishment of religion. Creationism is inherently a religious doctrine, Duplantier opined. "Because it promotes the beliefs of some theistic sects to the detriment of others, the statute violates the fundamental First Amendment principle that a state must be neutral in its treatment of religions."[39]

Reaching this result in a summary judgment meant that Duplantier found the case against the statute so convincing on the key issue of religious effect that no conceivable trial testimony could save the law. "There is no doubt that the defendants could produce a great deal of evidence on collateral issues, as did the proponents of the similar Arkansas statute," the judge noted. "We are convinced that whatever that evidence would be, it could not affect the outcome." That anticipated evidence aimed at erecting a non-religious prop for the statute by demonstrating the scientific merits of the broad concept of origin by "complex initial appearance," and was outlined in a 630-page "brief" filed with the court in opposition to the summary judgment motion. Duplantier avoided a public trial of this controversial issue by his ruling. "We decline the invitation to judge that debate. Whatever 'science' may be, 'creation,' as the term is used in the statute, involves religion." Although this hands-off approach to the scientific merits of creationism sufficed for his holding that the statute had an unconstitutional religious effect, Duplantier let his own opinion on the issue slip by adding that "the sole reason why the Louisiana legislature would require the teaching of creationism is that it comports with [a particular] religious doctrine." This observation presupposed a view that no reasonable legislator could accept creationism except on religious grounds and underlaid Duplantier's alternative holding that the law had an unconstitutional religious purpose.[40] Here again, a judge's opinion about what reasonable people believe influenced his legal judgment.

In a triumphant remark reminiscent of earlier comments by Union lawyers following *Scopes, Epperson,* and *McLean,* Louisiana ACLU Executive Director Martha Kegel proclaimed, upon hearing Duplantier's decision, "This is the death knell for the entire creation science movement across the country." A tolling bell, however, can summon warriors for battle as well as celebrants to a wake, and at least some creationists opted to continue the fight. The sponsor of the Louisiana statute, Bill Keith, insisted that the judgment improperly ignored defense arguments about the scientific merits of creationism and accused the judge of bias. With Wendell Bird's strong encouragement, the state promptly filed legal notice to appeal the ruling.[41]

A three-judge panel of the Fifth Circuit U.S. Court of Appeals heard Bird's arguments in May of 1985. Those arguments alleged that Duplantier erred in denying a full trial on the scientific and educational merits of creation science. Federal court rules required that, when deciding motions for summary judgment, courts view disputed facts in a light most favorable to the party resisting the motion and accept uncontroverted affidavits as true. Further, the motion should not be granted where there is a "genuine issue as to any material fact."[42] Bird maintained that the state had presented five uncontroverted affidavits, plus a 630-page brief chock-full of scientific references, all to the effect that creation science was a scientific doctrine suitable for teaching in public schools. "Our allegations were not viewed in the most favorable light," Bird argued. At the very least, he charged, the state had raised genuine issues of material fact requiring a trial.[43]

New York ACLU attorney Allan Blumstein countered that Bird's so-called "facts" were immaterial. Duplantier voided the statute because it was enacted with a wrongful religious purpose, and that remained true even if later affidavits alleged that creation science had scientific elements. Further, Blumstein added, "secular and religious material are so intertwined [in creation science] that you can't sort them out."

This mix was even apparent in the five affidavits that served as the basis for Bird's claims. Only two of the five came from scientists. One of these was by W. Scot Morrow, an associate professor of chemistry at Wofford College, a small church-affiliated school in Spartanburg, South Carolina. Morrow's short affidavit failed to cite any scientific research supporting his conclusion "that creation-science is scientific, non-religious, and educationally worthwhile in comparison with evolution." The other was a detailed statement by San Francisco State University biology professor Dean H. Kenyon, a well-known scientist with a long-standing interest in the religious implications of evolution. His affidavit focused on scientific evidence against current evolutionary theories rather than for any particular doctrine of creation, and therefore could be read as supporting the Louisiana law only by accepting Bird's premise that the term "creation science," as used in the statute, meant all non-evolutionary theories of origins. Of the three remaining affidavits, two came from theologians teaching at small church colleges and one was by a local school administrator.[44] These affidavits clearly did not impress the appellate court.

Two panel judges expressed their doubts about the Louisiana law from the bench. "This is a religious effort, that's what it is," Chief Judge John R. Brown asserted. Bird disagreed, claiming that the law only provided for teaching purely scientific evidence for a creation, which need not involve discussing God or a creator. "For a system that's based upon creation, there has to be a creator," Brown shot back. Judge E. Grady Jolly added, "If that's not a law with respect to the establishment of religion, I just can't see it." Jolly expressed particular concern that the state could not find a single current textbook presenting creation science in a non-religious manner suitable for public-school use.[45]

Two months after this exchange, the appellate panel unanimously affirmed Duplantier's ruling. "In truth," Jolly wrote for the court, "this particular case is a simple one, subject to a simple disposal: the Act violates the establishment clause of the First Amendment because the purpose of the statute is to promote a religious belief." To reach this conclusion, Jolly dismissed the statute's express purpose of "protecting academic freedom" as a sham. "Academic freedom embodies the principle that individual instructors are at liberty to teach that which they deem to be appropriate in the exercise of their professional judgment," he observed. "The Balanced Treatment Act is contrary to the very concept it avows: it requires, presumably upon risk of *sanction* or *dismissal* for failure to comply, the teaching of creation-science whenever evolution is taught."[46] This in itself did not render the statute unconstitutional, because states may limit academic freedom. It did free the judges to look for the actual purpose underlying the Act, however, and they found it in religion.

This finding was rooted in common knowledge and history.

"We must recognize that the theory of creation is a religious belief," Jolly wrote. "Nor can we ignore the fact that through the years religious fundamentalists have publicly scorned the theory of evolution and worked to discredit it." Looking at the language of the law in light of its historical setting, Jolly concluded that the "scheme of the statute, focusing on the religious *bête noir* of evolution as it does, demonstrates the religious purpose of the statute. Indeed, the Act continues the battle William Jennings Bryan carried to his grave. The Act's intended effect is to discredit evolution by counterbalancing its teaching at every turn with the teaching of creationism, a religious belief." [47] As such, the law was unconstitutional.

Jolly did not leave the matter by simply defending evolutionary teaching as most decisions from *Epperson* to *McLean* had done, however, but introduced a measure of accommodation to those creationists who sincerely wanted to include scientific (rather than religious) concepts of creation in public-school instruction. "We do not, indeed cannot, say that the theory of creation is to all people solely and exclusively a religious tenet. We also do not deny that the underpinnings of creationism may be supported by scientific evidence," Jolly conceded. But this did not justify mandating the teaching of creation science under the guise of academic freedom, because schoolteachers already could present truly scientific elements of creationism. "No court of which we are aware has prohibited voluntary instruction concerning purely scientific evidence that happens, incidentally, to be consistent with a religious doctrine or tenet," Jolly affirmed. [48] In this backhanded way, the appellate panel cracked open a door to accommodation of creationist instruction by individual science teachers while slamming shut the door to establishing creation science in public schools by legislative mandate.

Rejecting these comments as a mere sop, Louisiana, led by its persistent Special Assistant Attorney General Wendell Bird, pressed on with the appeal. Bird did not follow the normal course of appealing directly to the U.S. Supreme Court, however, but sought a rehearing *en banc* by the entire fifteen-member Fifth Circuit appellate bench. This represented his best hope. The Supreme Court, in effect led by aging liberal Justice William Brennan, had just decided a series of Establishment Clause cases signaling a tough stand against mixing religion and public education. These rulings, issued by a deeply divided Court just days prior to the panel decision in *Aguillard*, struck down a twenty-year-old New York City program providing public remedial education for parochial-school students, a Grand Rapids scheme of offering public-education classes in church schools, and an Alabama statute imposing a moment of silence for student prayer in public schools.[49]

These decisions ran counter to other trends. Repeatedly proclaiming, "I don't believe we should ever have expelled God from the classroom," Ronald Reagan had been elected president five years earlier, promising to appoint federal judges willing to accommodate religion in public education. During the campaign, he embraced official school prayer, voiced support for teaching biblical creationism, and questioned the theory of evolution. His administration had actively intervened before the Supreme Court on the losing side of all three 1985 school-house religion cases, leading *Newsweek* magazine to report, "There is still no Reagan court." But while five years in office had provided Reagan the opportunity to appoint only one of the nine justices on the Supreme Court, he had named six of the fifteen Fifth Circuit appellate-court jurists. Bird appealed to these judges. Indeed, Louisiana creationism-law sponsor Bill Keith opined that God had delayed the lawsuit this long so that more Reagan appointees could join the bench.[50]

Losing litigants can only suggest a rehearing *en banc* by written petition to the full court, and a majority of the judges must agree before such an unusual procedure occurs.[51] Bird's petition betrayed a bitter frustration with being denied a trial on the merits of the law. He had faithfully assembled a massive brief and five affidavits affirming that creation science was scientific rather than religious and that the Louisiana statute promoted the secular objective of academic freedom. Yet, Bird charged, "The panel and district court *absolutely failed* to view the state's factual allegations (even its uncontroverted affidavits) in the most favorable light—and in actuality failed to consider them at all." To the contrary, he complained, the panel found that creationism was a religious belief and the law lacked a secular purpose even though these findings "directly conflict with the plethora of authority cited by the State and with the uncontroverted (and only) affidavits in the case."[52] After summarizing this plethora of authority in the few pages alloted for his petition, Bird demanded—or at least forcefully suggested— a rehearing before the full court.

Late in 1985, a bare majority of the court denied Bird's petition without comment, but seven judges dissented. Their dissent was explained by Judge Thomas Gee in a sharp opinion that represented the first published judicial support for creationist claims since *Scopes*. On the basis of the state's affidavits, Gee asserted that "there *are* two bona fide views" of origins. Once this is accepted, Gee reasoned, "It follows that the Louisiana statute requires no more than that . . . the subject of origins will be discussed in a balanced manner if it is discussed at all. I see nothing illiberal about such a requirement, nor can I imagine that Galileo or Einstein would have found fault with it." Establishment Clause concerns melted under this light, according to Gee, because "requiring the truth to be taught on any subject displayed its own secular warrant, one at the heart of the scientific method itself." This was too glib. Under settled precedent, a state could not mandate even the teaching of a recognized fact solely for a wrongful religious purpose; it simply was tougher to deny the existence of any secular motive in such a case. Yet in a taunting reference to *Scopes*, Gee suggested, "By requiring that the whole truth be taught, Louisiana aligned itself with Darrow; striking down that requirement, the panel holding aligns us with Bryan."[53] Jolly thereupon added a highly unusual published response: "I offer my apologies to the majority of this court for aligning it with the forces of darkness and anti-truth."[54] Clearly a profound split in world view divided the Fifth Circuit bench.

Gee's dissent reflected a view of evolution and creationism far different from the view reflected in judicial decisions from *Epperson* to *McLean*. The confident categorization of evolution as science and creationism as religion was gone, replaced by unabashed acceptance of alternative scientific views on origins. This dissent justified Bird's hope for support from judges named by Reagan to the bench. A majority of the judges opposed to rehearing the case were chosen by President Jimmy Carter, while the seven dissenters included four Reagan appointees, two named by President Richard Nixon, and only one Carter appointee. Underscoring the shifting nature of this balance, one of the three panel judges retired before the petition for rehearing, and the new judge joined the dissent.[55] One more such replacement, and the balance would have tipped. But creationism fell short again.

Without other alternatives for saving the statute, Louisiana turned to the U.S. Supreme Court. In the petition requesting Supreme Court review, Bird again raised procedural concerns in his bid for a trial on the merits of creation science. "[T]he decision under review failed to 'take as true' the State's factual assertions in its uncontroverted affidavits," Bird wrote, "and instead resolved disputed factual issues by improper judicial notice contrary to the only evidence in the case."[56] Not so, answered the ACLU in its written reply, "the real issue in this case is *not* whether defendant's after-the-fact, created-for-litigation affidavits establish that the doctrine of 'creation-science' has a scientific component to it," but rather if the creationism law had a fatal religious purpose.[57] As often happens in litigation, each side framed the issue in terms whereby it could win. If (as Bird maintained) the issue was whether creation science was a scientific concept with educational merit, then the state had raised sufficient factual questions to warrant a trial. If (as the ACLU countered) the issues were whether creation science embodied a religious belief and whether the law was enacted to promote that belief, then the state's facts were largely immaterial and summary disposition of the case was justified. The Supreme Court opted to frame the issue for itself, and scheduled its courtroom showdown on creation science for December 10, 1987.

Belling the Cat

The scene was far different from when the creation-evolution controversy first reached the courts in *Scopes*. The sweltering summer heat of Dayton gave way to a cool late-autumn day in

Washington. The carnival atmosphere of an open-air trial fea-
turing the most famous orators of the era was replaced by the
High Bench's august courtroom. The tenor of the arguments
reflected the cooler, more dignified physical environment.

Bird opened the oral arguments for the state. "Creation science means the scientific evidence for creation and inferences
from those scientific evidences," Bird began. "The teaching of
the Bible as part of the implications of the statute would be unconstitutional," he later added. Repeatedly invoking the state's
five expert affidavits affirming that creation science was a scientific (and not a religious) doctrine, Bird stressed that the statute sanctioned only the teaching of scientific material. According to Bird, "creation science" was "a technical term that should
be resolved as a factual matter." The lower courts simply determined "out of thin air" that creation science was a religious
concept and used this to void the statute for having the unconstitutional religious purpose of promoting that concept. Asking
for the Supreme Court to send the case back to the district court
for a trial where experts could show that creation science was
scientific, Bird asserted, "The courts did not rely on the record.
The courts said what 'creation science' means without looking
at the record."[58]

"But couldn't we look at the record, and see if the court was
right?" Justice Sandra Day O'Connor asked, as the justices began peppering Bird with questions. No, Bird replied, because
the unresolved factual issues about creation science and legislative purpose required a trial. Under close interrogation from
several justices about legislative purpose, Bird noted that lawmakers probably had a variety of reasons for enacting the law,
and he conceded that "undoubtedly some legislators had a desire to teach religious doctrine in the classroom." But he maintained that the predominant legislative purpose was to promote
"fairness and academic freedom" by including alternative scientific views in the curriculum. Bird faced the toughest questioning from centrist Justice John Paul Stevens, who repeatedly
asked if creation and evolution represented separate theories that
could be balanced in classroom instruction. While Bird maintained that they were distinct and mutually exclusive scientific

theories, Stevens argued that a person could view the two as working together in origins, and that therefore the equal-time concept failed to make sense to him.

Following Bird, New York ACLU attorney Jay Topkis argued against the statute. " 'Creation,' this is a term we are all familiar with," Topkis began. He then quoted from a dictionary definition that "creation" meant an "act of creating or fact of being created . . . by divine power or its equivalent." Creation required a creator, Topkis maintained, and creationist teaching therefore involved religious doctrine inappropriate for public schools.

Antonin Scalia, a new Reagan appointee to the Court, repeatedly interrupted Topkis to question whether creation always must involve a creator, citing both the state's evidence of scientists who described creation science as non-religious and the example of the ancient Aristotelian scientific theory of "a first cause, an unmoved mover." After Topkis conceded that Aristotelianism was not religious, Scalia proclaimed, "Then you could believe in a creation without a creator." When conservative Chief Justice William H. Rehnquist picked up this line of questioning, Topkis simply asserted that creation science meant "basically the Fundamentalist point of view." Topkis repeatedly lashed out at Bird for concocting non-religious meanings for the term, once comparing his adversary to Tweedledum in Alice's Wonderland. "He wants words to mean what he says they mean. It didn't fool Alice, and I doubt very much it will fool this Court." This prompted Rehnquist to quip, "Don't overestimate us."

Under questioning by Lewis F. Powell and other moderate justices, Topkis admitted that religion could constitutionally be taught in public schools if done in a neutral fashion for educational reasons. He also conceded to Scalia that a school principal could stop a teacher from teaching factual errors, even if the correction was religiously motivated. The statute failed, according to Topkis, because it mandated teaching a religious belief for a religious reason. Dismissing creation science as "Christian apologetics," he asserted, "There is nothing in the legislative history that speaks of a secular purpose." When Stevens asked if the legislators had not spoken of protecting academic freedom, Topkis replied, "Oh sure, we've got to give God equal time."

In addition to hearing these oral arguments, the Supreme Court received sixteen written briefs submitted by organizations or individuals interested in the case. The scientific community's scorn for creationism was communicated to the justices in briefs submitted either jointly or separately by the National Academy of Sciences, seventeen state academies of science, dozens of professional scientific associations, and an unprecedented array of prominent American scientists, including seventy-two Nobel laureates. Briefs opposing the statute were also filed by the states of New York and Illinois, the mainline National Council of Churches, and such long-time foes of creationism laws as the National Education Association, People for the American Way, the American Jewish Congress, and Americans United for Separation of Church and State. Combined, these organizations represented millions of Americans nationwide. Briefs supporting the law came primarily from a few conservative religious organizations, most notably the ever faithful National Association of Evangelicals and the Concerned Women for America—a new, half-million-member, grass-roots group headed by the wife of fundamentalist leader Tim LeHaye.

Viewed together, these briefs posed one clear question for the Supreme Court: Was creation science religion or science? No brief claimed that creation science was anything other than a religious or scientific concept. Every brief opposing the Louisiana law asserted or plainly assumed that creation science was solely religious and not scientific. The Nobel laureates' brief perhaps did so most starkly. "This case is crucial to the future of scientific education in this nation," the laureates warned. "Our capacity to cope with problems of food production, health care, and even national defense will be jeopardized if we deliberately strip our citizens of the power to distinguish between phenomena of nature and supernatural articles of faith. 'Creation-science' simply has no place in the public-school science classroom."[59] In contrast, every brief supporting the law maintained that creation science was scientific (or at least as scientific as evolution) and was not religious (or no more so than evolution). For example, the National Association of Evangelicals' brief maintained, "This case is about the arbitrary judicial exclusion of scientific evidence about origins from public school instruction as provided by a state statute."[60] These written arguments mirrored the oral ones presented to the court by Bird and Topkis. The battle lines were neatly drawn.

The Supreme Court announced its decision six months after hearing the case. In its written opinions, the nine-member Court split four ways. Four justices joined William Brennan in the lead opinion striking down the Louisiana Act as violating the Establishment Clause. Two other justices agreed with Brennan's conclusion, but not all his reasoning, and therefore wrote or joined concurring opinions. Two conservative justices, Scalia and Rehnquist, dissented—and would have sent the law back to the district court for a full trial. The different conclusions reflected markedly differing views of creation science.

Brennan saw an unconstitutional religious purpose spurring passage of the law, and a clear religious taint to creation science. After stating the Establishment Clause requirement that government must act with a secular purpose, Brennan's opinion examined the legislative history of the creationism law. "The preeminent purpose of the Louisiana legislature was clearly to advance the religious viewpoint that a supernatural being created humankind," Brennan wrote; "it is not happenstance that the legislature required the teaching of a theory that coincided with this religious view." Indeed, he noted that "the term 'creation science,' as contemplated by the legislature that adopted this Act, embodies [this] religious belief." Further, Brennan referred to the old anti-evolution laws voided by *Epperson* and observed that the "same historic and contemporaneous antagonisms between the teachings of certain religious denominations and the teaching of evolution are present in this case." Expanding on this point, Brennan noted: "The legislative history documents that the Act's primary purpose was to change the science curriculum of public schools in order to provide persuasive advantage to a particular religious doctrine that rejects the factual basis of evolution in its entirety." This a state cannot do without violating the Establishment Clause.[61] Brennan had belled the cat by identifying creation science with the fundamentalist religion while rejecting Bird's attempt to define it simply as scientific evidence of origin by complex initial appearance.

Following the example of the appellate panel, Brennan leavened this sweeping repudiation of creationism laws with a measure of accommodation to those sincerely interested in teaching creationist *scientific* concepts. In the course of rejecting the claim that the law advanced academic freedom, he quoted with apparent favor from testimony by a Louisiana educator that "[a]ny scientific concept that's based on established fact can be included in our curriculum already, and no new legislation allowing this is necessary." Brennan added that "teaching a variety of scientific theories about the origins of humankind to schoolchildren might be validly done with the clear secular intent of enhancing the effectiveness of science instruction."[62] Only time will tell how wide a door this opened.

Powell and fellow moderate Byron R. White wrote concurring opinions that also dismissed creation science as religious dogma. In a probing opinion joined by O'Connor, Powell bound the Louisiana statute to fundamentalism by examining the origins of creation science in the work of the Institute for Creation Research and the Creation Research Society. He pointed out that both organizations affirm the literal truth of the Bible as the basis for their work and seek to promote Christian evangelism. "Here, it is clear that religious belief is the Balanced Treatment Act's 'reason for existence.' The tenets of creation-science parallel the Genesis story of creation, and this is a religious belief," he wrote. "[T]he statements of purpose of the sources of creation-science in the United States make clear that their purpose is to promote religious belief. I find no persuasive evidence in the legislative history that the legislature's purpose was any different."[63] Taking simpler means to the same end, White noted in a one-page opinion that both lower courts reviewing the Act "construed the statutory words 'creation science' to refer to a religious belief" and "concluded that the State legislature's primary purpose was to advance religion." He knew of no reason to disagree.[64]

Scalia, in a tough dissenting opinion joined by Rehnquist, took quite a different view of both creation science and creationist lawmaking. Accepting creationist claims at face value, Scalia wrote, "We have no basis on the record to conclude that creation science need be anything other than a collection of scientific data supporting the theory that life abruptly appeared on the earth." This view provided Scalia with a rationale for validating the Louisiana statute. To him, the stated secular purpose of promoting academic freedom by including creationism in the science curriculum was credible, and constitutional, even if "creation science coincides with the beliefs of certain religions," so long as that theory was founded on scientific evidence. "Perhaps what the Louisiana Legislature has done is unconstitutional because there *is* no such evidence, and the scheme they have established will amount to no more than a presentation of the Book of Genesis," Scalia wrote. "But we cannot say that on the evidence before us."[65]

Scalia attributed the Court's "unprecedented readiness" to find a solely religious purpose for the law "to an intellectual predisposition created by the facts and the legend of *Scopes*." But even anti-evolutionism could have a scientific basis, he argued. If it did, "[t]he people of Louisiana, including those who are Christian fundamentalists, are quite entitled, as a secular matter, to have whatever scientific evidence there may be against evolution presented in their schools."[66] Popular opinion could control public science instruction, Scalia was insisting, so long as the sole purpose was not to promote religion. Bryan had never claimed anything more than this, and perhaps his view could still prevail if his non-religious objections to evolution became widely accepted. In *Aguillard*, however, the widely held "intellectual predisposition" that creationism laws spring from religious motivations held a clear majority of the Court, and the Balanced Treatment Act fell by the wayside.

The long legal battle over the Louisiana law had finally ended. "Somewhere in heaven John Scopes is smiling," rejoiced ACLU Executive Director Ira Glasser upon hearing of the decision. Down in Louisiana, Donald Aguillard smiled too: "I'm excited, I'm pleased, I'm relieved. I'm thrilled that after six years we finally have a decision." Describing Brennan's majority opinion as "exactly the kind of opinion we had hoped for," Jay Topkis pronounced that it "lays to rest the whole idea of allowing religion to be foisted on children in the schools by demanding equal time for creationism." Harvard paleontologist and popular writer Stephen Jay Gould, who had joined in submitting an anti-creationist brief to the Court, made perhaps the most expansive claim regarding the impact of *Aguillard* when he later declared that it "ended an important chapter in American social history, one that stretched back to the Scopes trial of 1925."[67]

Other evolutionists were less confident. "While, as biologists and educators, we have great cause for rejoicing over the recent U.S. Supreme Court decision in the Louisiana 'equal treatment for "creation science" ' case, we must, nevertheless, be careful," warned a prominent notice in the journal of the American Institute of Biological Sciences. "The actual decision in the Louisiana case was weaker than Judge William Overton's earlier ruling" because the decision suggested that " '[c]reation science' can still be brought into science classrooms if and when teachers and administrators feel that it is appropriate." People for the American Way Executive Director Arthur J. Kropp voiced similar fears. "The battle to stop this thinly veiled fraud isn't over," he cautioned darkly; the "ruling only forces the religious right to dig deeper into creationism disguises."[68]

In fact, creationists were already moving on to other legal battles and using other tactics. Supported by the Concerned Women for America and opposed by People for the American Way, seven fundamentalist families in Tennessee were waging a protracted lawsuit over whether their children had a constitutional right to opt out of public elementary-school classes using a popular series of basic readers. The families alleged that the texts undermined the children's religious beliefs in violation of the Free Exercise Clause by presenting certain themes. Although those themes included such peculiar topics of religious concern as mental telepathy, false supernaturalism, and feminism, much of the anxiety focused on evolution. A federal appellate court flatly rejected the families' claims two months after the Supreme Court decision in *Aguillard*. The court reasoned that the school simply was trying "to acquaint students with a multitude of ideas and concepts," and could do so without violating the Free Exercise Clause so long as it did not compel students to believe or say that they believed in an idea or concept contrary to their religion.[69]

Other creationists sought to exploit openings suggested by the *Aguillard* decision. "For some time, educators have recognized teachers' academic freedom to cite secular scientific uses of the term *creation*," reported the popular fundamentalist journal *Moody Monthly* in a 1988 article. "But the Supreme Court has now approved the teaching of 'any and all facets' of the origin of humankind. This includes facts, alternative theories, and critiques of prevailing theories." The article cautioned teachers against teaching anything called "creation science" as science, however, because the Court classified this as a religious doctrine.[70] Wendell Bird adopted a similar approach, maintaining that *Aguillard* "did not question the constitutionality of teaching scientific creationism" in public schools and suggesting that the next major case might involve defending a teacher punished for doing so. Fittingly, Paul Ellwanger went to work drafting a new model statute granting teachers this authority.[71]

Ever optimistic, Bird also dreamed of overturning *Aguillard* some day. Alluding to public-opinion surveys showing strong support for "balanced-treatment laws," he predicted that "86 percent of the public can't be stopped in the long run, especially given the age of the justices [with] four in the majority over 75 years old." This strategy would require a president willing to appoint new justices friendly to the creationist cause. With Reagan's second term drawing to a close, evangelist Pat Robertson already was preparing to offer himself as a Republican candidate to fill that role when *Aguillard* was decided. "Everyone in America who believes he or she was created by God will be outraged. The Supreme Court has written into the Constitution a questionable scientific theory of the origin of life," Robertson declared upon hearing of the ruling. "This is going to help my position wonderfully."[72]

These signs of life, and even of optimism, within the creationist legal movement following *Aguillard* testified to the resilience of the underlying cause. The sixty-five-year-old creation-evolution legal controversy would endure—and it will endure in some form, whatever happens in courts or legislatures—because its impetus comes from social forces lying far beyond the reach of the law. Judge Overton recognized this when he observed after *McLean*, "The controversy between biblical fundamentalism and evolution is one which will continue, I believe, forever."[73] A movement that survived *Scopes, Epperson, Daniel, McLean*, and all the skirmishes in between, will endure *Aguillard* as well. Creationists stand as living testimony to the word from Scripture that "faith is the substance of things hoped for, the evidence of things not seen."[74]

Conclusion

The controversy over evolutionary teaching is as lively today as ever. More than a century of scientific research on the theory of evolution has not settled the matter for the general public. Americans remain deeply divided in their beliefs about the origin and development of the human species, and a significant number care strongly enough about those beliefs to dispute how to teach the subject in school. If the issue solely involved science, it could be addressed in that forum without reaching the wider public consciousness. But, for many people, belief in evolution has implications beyond science. The cleric-geologist Edward Hitchcock threw down the gauntlet a year after the publication of *Origin of Species* when he warned readers of his high-school textbook that the theory of evolution was "intended and adopted to vindicate atheism."[1] Assurances to the contrary by Asa Gray, Joseph LeConte, and other late nineteenth-century textbook writers failed to dispel the concern. With a rapidly increasing number of teenagers attending secondary school during the twenties, concern over evolutionary teaching in those institutions burst into demands for legal relief that continued into the eighties.

Convictions on both sides of the controversy have been too strong to permit a compromise. From the beginning, partisans saw the well-being of American young people at stake. Launching his crusade against evolutionary teaching, William Jennings Bryan proclaimed, "There is that in each human life that corresponds to the mainspring of a watch—that which is absolutely necessary if the life is to be what it should be, a real life and not a mere existence. That necessary thing is *a belief in God*." After describing such belief as the sole source for morality, Bryan declared, "If there is at work in the world to-day anything that tends to break this mainspring, it is the duty of the moral, as well as the Christian, world to combat this influence in every possible way. I believe there is such a menace to fundamental morality." That menace was the Darwinian theory of human evolution.[2]

Clarence Darrow assumed an equally intransigent position on the opposite side. To him, the Genesis account of creation was a myth, Christianity a delusion, and heaven a mere dream. "Is the structure and capacity of man able to know aught of the origin of the universe, of its design or its purpose, or its beginning or its end? He must take it as he finds it," Darrow declared. "To make assertions not based on facts; to construct fantastic theories because he wants to dream; to entertain beliefs because he fears the truth shows only his craven fear of life and death."[3]

The basic issue has not really changed since the twenties. Reporting on his work as a creation-science leader, Henry M. Morris wrote in 1982 that "there have been multitudes of young people, and even hundreds of scientists, who have been won to creationism. Many of them were nominal Christians, but were lukewarm and doubting Christians because they were confused by their long indoctrination in evolution." In this way, Morris continued, creationism becomes "the *Cutting Edge* of the Gospel, the sharp weapon of foundational truth, in the great battle for the eternal souls of men and women for whom Christ died."[4] Evolutionary paleontologist George Gaylord Simpson reflected just the opposite view. " 'Why make so much fuss about evolution? It is only one of a thousand things that might be taught in high schools. Students can't learn them all. Naturally, you emphasize it because it is your specialty,' " Simpson rhetorically stated. "On the contrary, it is my specialty because I think it is supremely important." In the course of relating how he came to this conclusion, he noted that "a sharpening sense of values showed me that if life is the most important thing about our world, the most important thing about life is its evolution."[5]

These comments reflected two different views of life clashing over evolutionary teaching. Both sides were more than willing to seek legal protection for their cause. Ultimately, however, the law could not resolve the controversy because neither side would accept an adverse result as final. Creationists petitioned legislatures, courts, and school boards for relief from evolutionary teaching, while evolutionists sought similar relief from creationist instruction. When either side won a victory, the other one typically redoubled its efforts.

Because the creation-evolution controversy remained unresolved in popular opinion, it could not be settled in law. The legal issue first arose during the twenties when state legislatures outlawed evolutionary teaching in response to public demands, and continued to arise during the eighties as state lawmakers persisted in enacting statutes designed to bring public instruction in origins into line with popular opinion. In 1927, the Tennessee Supreme Court upheld the first anti-evolution law as a legitimate legislative response to the "popular prejudice" against evolution.[6] Forty years later, the U.S. Supreme Court that effectively reversed this ruling described such statutes as discomforting to "the modern mind."[7] Both courts assumed that prevailing popular opinion backed their decision. As the split in popular opinion over the issue subsequently became apparent in California, the state attorney general opined that the degree to which evolution could be taught as true in public schools turned "upon the degree of [its] scientific certainty as perceived by contemporary society" while the *Segraves* court enforced a state anti-dogmatism policy as a necessary accommodation for the beliefs of creationist students receiving public evolutionary instruction.[8] The 1982 *McLean* decision overturning the Arkansas equal-time statute appealed to "common sense" to refute allegations that evolutionary teaching was religious in nature, while the courts facing a similar Louisiana statute recognized "that the underpinnings of creationism may be supported by scientific evidence," and opened the door to "teaching a variety of scientific theories about the origins of humankind."[9]

Advocates litigating these cases recognized the importance of popular opinion all along. Attorneys on both sides in *Scopes* consciously aimed their arguments beyond the court to the public at large. "The people will determine this issue," Bryan told the court, and Darrow agreed.[10] Despite the best efforts of both sides, however, the people remained deeply divided on the issue of evolutionary teaching. Reflecting that split in the days immediately following the trial, Darrow's co-counsel Arthur Garfield Hays perceived that *Scopes* has so "aroused public opinion" that no further anti-evolution statutes would pass, while a key Bryan backer, financier George F. Washburn, believed that the trial had moved "the public conscience" to support more such laws.[11]

The deep split in opinion about evolutionary teaching persisted into the eighties, and a legal resolution appeared as elusive then as ever. For his part, Henry Morris attributed the creationists' judicial setbacks not so much to "constitutional and scientific" factors as to the evolutionary bias of national cultural leaders that must be overcome by education "if creationism is to prevail in the mind of the judge."[12] Speaking from the other side, ACLU lead counsel Jack D. Novik observed following *McLean*, "Notwithstanding the Arkansas victory, and regardless of the outcome in the Louisiana litigation, the problem of creationism will persist because it is a legal problem only in part. The law can provide only temporary relief." According to Novik, the real solution lay in "meaningful scientific education" that could enable the public "to move beyond the past with confidence and to face the future with intelligence."[13]

Both sides then agreed on the importance of science education to any ultimate resolution of the legal controversy over creation and evolution. That is precisely why they had fought so hard over the content of public biology teaching. But this point simply underscored the dilemma: a lasting legal victory on the issue of evolutionary teaching awaited a verdict of popular opinion on evolution while that verdict was itself at least partially dependent on the content of public instruction. At most, as Novik recognized, legislation and judicial decisions offered temporary relief, giving the winning side an opportunity to break this cycle through education. In the long run, however, the law reflects prevailing popular opinion. Otherwise, the law will be changed or ignored.

Appendix

The following bibliographic data are for the initial editions of multiple-edition high-school life-science textbooks published between 1859 and 1920 and contained in the Library of Congress (first post-1859 date in parenthesis for earlier texts).

Author	Title	Publisher	Date
A. Lincoln	*Familiar Lectures on Botany*	Collins	1831('60)
E. Hitchcock	*Elementary Geology*	Newman	1840('60)
A. Wood	*Class Book of Botany*	Barnes	1845('60)
L. Agassiz & A. Gould	*Principles of Zoology*	Gould	1848('73)
J. Loomis	*Elements of Geology*	Gould	1852('79)
A. Gray	*First Lessons in Botany*	Ivison	1857('68)
S. Tenney	*Geology*	Butler	1859('77)
J. Dana	*Text-Book of Geology*	Bliss	1863
S. Tenney	*Manual of Zoology*	Scribner's	1865
J. Steele	*Fourteen Weeks in Geology*	Barnes	1870
A. Wood	*Lessons in Plants*	Barnes	1870
S. Tenney	*Elements of Zoology*	Scribner's	1875
J. Steele	*Fourteen Weeks in Zoology*	Barnes	1877
A. Wood & J. Steele	*Fourteen Weeks in Botany*	Barnes	1879
C. Bessey	*Botany*	Holt	1880
A. Packard	*Zoology*	Holt	1883
C. Bessey	*Essentials of Botany*	Holt	1884
C. Holder & J. Holder	*Elements of Zoology*	Appleton	1884

Author	Title	Publisher	Date
W. Killerman	*Elements of Botany*	Potter	1884
J. LeConte	*Compend of Geology*	Appleton	1884
J. Bergen	*Elements of Botany*	Ginn	1896
A. Heilprin	*The Earth and Its Story*	Silver	1896
G. Atkinson	*Elementary Botany*	Holt	1898
J. Coulter	*Plant Relations & Plant Studies* (2 vols.)	Appleton	1899
L. Bailey	*Botany*	Macmillan	1900
A. Brigham	*Textbook of Geology*	Appleton	1900
C. Davenport & G. Davenport	*Introduction to Zoology*	Macmillan	1900
V. Kellogg	*Elementary Zoology*	Holt	1901
N. French	*Animal Activities*	Longmans	1902
E. Andrews	*Botany All the Year Round*	American	1903
D. Jordan, V. Kellogg, & H. Heath	*Animal Studies*	Appleton	1903
G. Atkinson	*Botany for High Schools*	Holt	1910
J. Bergen & O. Caldwell	*Botany for High Schools*	Ginn	1911
G. Hunter	*Essentials of Biology*	American	1911
J. Peabody & A. Hunt	*Elementary Biology* (2 vols.)	Macmillan	1912
G. Hunter	*Civic Biology*	American	1914
R. Hegner	*Practical Zoology*	Macmillan	1915
C. Hodge & J. Dawson	*Civic Biology*	Ginn	1918

Notes

Chapter One: Scene of the Crime

1. James Edward Peabody and Arthur Ellsworth Hunt, *Elementary Biology: Plants* (New York: Macmillan, 1912), 118.
2. Edward J. Pfeifer, "United States," in *The Comparative Reception of Darwinism*, ed. Thomas F. Glick (Austin: Univ. of Texas Press, 1974), 196 and 204.
3. V. M. Spalding, "Botany in High School," *The Academy*, 5 (1890), 317; A. Hunter Dupree, *Asa Gray, 1810–1888* (Cambridge: Harvard Univ. Press, 1959), 362–69; and Charles Carpenter, *History of American Schoolbooks* (Philadelphia: Univ. of Pennsylvania Press, 1963), 223.
4. Asa Gray, *First Lessons in Botany and Vegetable Physiology* (New York: Ivison, 1857), 173.
5. Asa Gray, *The Elements of Botany for Beginners and for Schools* (New York: Ivison, 1887), 175.
6. Gray, *First Lessons*, 174.
7. Gray, *Elements*, 177.
8. Gray, *First Lessons*, 174–75.
9. Gray, *Elements*, 175–77 (emphasis added).
10. Gray, *First Lessons*, 175.
11. Gray, *Elements*, 177.
12. Gray, *First Lessons*, 88.
13. Gray, *Elements*, 85.
14. *Ibid.*, 177.
15. Gray, *First Lessons*, 196.
16. For example, first edition: Louis Agassiz and A. A. Gould, *Principles of Zoology* (Boston: Gould, 1848), 182; and last edition: Louis Agassiz and A. A. Gould, *Principles of Zoology* (Boston: Gould, 1873), 214.
17. Agassiz and Gould, *Principles* (1848), 206; and Agassiz and Gould, *Principles* (1873), 238.
18. Agassiz and Gould, *Principles* (1848), 206; and Agassiz and Gould, *Principles* (1873), 283.

19. Edward Hitchcock and Charles H. Hitchcock, *Elementary Geology* (New York: Ivison, 1860), 377–93.

20. Hitchcock and Hitchcock, *Geology*, 373–74.

21. Compare the material referred to in the preceding cite with Edward Hitchcock, *Elementary Geology* (New York: Ivison, 1857).

22. Sanborn Tenney, *Geology for Teachers, Classes, and Private Students* (New York: Butler, 1877) and Justin R. Loomis, *Elements of Geology Adapted to the Use of Schools and Colleges* (New York: Sheldon, 1879).

23. Agassiz and Gould, *Principles* (1873); Almira Lincoln Phelps, *Familiar Lectures on Botany* (New York: Mason, 1860); and Alphonso Wood, *Class Book of Botany* (New York: Barnes, 1860).

24. Carpenter, *American Schoolbooks*, 226–27.

25. James D. Dana, *A Text-Book of Geology Designed for Schools and Academies* (Philadelphia: Bliss, 1863), 3, 63–72, 243–45, and 328–36.

26. *Ibid.*, 252–54.

27. *Ibid.*, 260.

28. *Ibid.*, 257–58.

29. *Ibid.*, 258–59.

30. *Ibid.*, 236 and 259–61.

31. *Ibid.*, 336 and 340.

32. James D. Dana, *Text-Book of Geology Designed for Schools and Academies* (New York: Ivison, 1874), 261–63.

33. *Ibid.*, 263.

34. *Ibid.*, 345.

35. James D. Dana and William North Rice, *Revised Text-Book of Geology* (New York: Ivison, 1897), 464.

36. *Ibid.*, 464.

37. Carpenter, *American Schoolbooks*, 218.

38. J. Dorman Steele, *Fourteen Weeks in Zoology* (New York: Barnes, 1877); and Alphonso Wood and J. Dorman Steele, *Fourteen Weeks in Botany* (New York: Barnes, 1879).

39. For example, C. F. Holder and J. B. Holder, *Elements of Zoology* (New York: Appleton, 1884); A. S. Packard, *Zoology* (New York: Holt, 1883); Sanborn Tenney, *A Manual of Zoology for Schools, Colleges, and the General Reader* (New York: Scribner's, 1867); and Sanborn Tenney, *Elements of Zoology: A Test-Book* (New York: Scribner's, 1875).

40. J. Dorman Steele and J. W. P. Jenks, *A Popular Zoology* (New York: Barnes, 1887), xii.

41. J. Dorman Steele, *Fourteen Weeks in Zoology* (New York: American Book, 1905), 8.

42. J. Dorman Steele, *A Fourteen Weeks' Course in Geology* (New York: Barnes, 1971), 254.

43. Charles E. Bussey, *The Essentials of Botany* (New York: Holt, 1884), 102.

44. Charles E. Bussey, *The Essentials of Botany* (New York: Holt, 1896), 320–22.

45. Bussey, *Botany* (1884), 100; and Bussey, *Botany* (1896), 102.

46. Byran D. Halsted to Charles E. Bussey, Dec. 2, 1908, in Ronald C. Torbey,

Saving the Prairies: The Life Cycle of the Founding School of American Plant Ecology, 1895–1955 (Berkeley: Univ. of California Press, 1981), 9.

47. Torbey, *Prairies*, 39.
48. Carpenter, *American Schoolbooks*, 227.
49. Joseph LeConte, *A Compend of Geology* (New York: Appleton, 1884), 242.
50. *Ibid.*, 282.
51. *Ibid.*, 363.
52. *Ibid.*, 390.
53. *Ibid.*, 390.
54. Joseph LeConte, *A Compend of Geology* (New York: American, 1898), 416.
55. Lester D. Stephens, *Joseph LeConte: Gentle Prophet of Evolution* (Baton Rouge: Louisiana State Univ. Press, 1982), 149–54.
56. LeConte, *Compend* (1884), 390.
57. Pfeifer, "United States," 198–202.
58. For example, LeConte, *Compend* (1884), 354, 363, and 376.
59. Joseph Y. Bergen, *Foundations of Botany* (Boston: Ginn, (1901), 394–95.
60. L. H. Bailey, *Botany: An Elementary Text for Schools* (New York: Macmillan, 1900), 209.
61. *Ibid.*, 232.
62. David Starr Jordan, Vernon Lyman Kellogg, and Harold Heath, *Animal Studies: A Text-book of Elementary Zoology for Use in High Schools and Colleges* (New York: Appleton, 1903), 351.
63. *Ibid.*, 265.
64. *Ibid.*, pp. 252, 282, 312, 430, and 440, for example.
65. George Francis Atkinson, *Botany for High Schools* (New York: Holt, 1912), 488; Albert Perry Brigham, *A Textbook of Geology* (New York: Appleton, 1900), 460; and Dana and Rice, *Revised Text-Book*, 464.
66. Vernon Lyman Kellogg and Rennie Wilbur Doane, *Elementary Textbook of Economic Zoology and Entomology* (New York: Holt, 1915), 336.
67. Brigham, *Geology*, 460.
68. Charles Benedict Davenport and Gertrude Crotty Davenport, *Elements of Zoology To Accompany the Field and Laboratory Study of Animals* (New York: Macmillan, 1911), 460–70.
69. Atkinson, *Botany*, 488.
70. E. F. Andrews, *Botany All the Year Round: A Practical Text-book for Schools* (New York: American Book, 1903), 250.
71. E. F. Andrews, *A Practical Course in Botany* (New York: American Book, 1911), 362.
72. Paul DeHart Hurd, *Biological Education in American Secondary Schools, 1890–1960* (Washington: Am. Institute of Biological Studies, 1961), 27–28; and George W. Hunter, *Science Teaching at Junior and Senior High School Levels* (New York: American Book, 1934), 32.
73. Hunter, *Science Teaching*, 32.
74. Gerald Skoog, "The Topic of Evolution in Secondary School Biology Textbooks: 1900–1977," *Science Education*, 63 (1979), 623–25. Biologist Robert A. Hellmann reached a similar conclusion based on a cursory qualitative re-

view of ten high-school or college life-science textbooks dating from 1883 to 1935. The persuasiveness of Hellmann's conclusion is weakened, however, by the small number of texts reviewed and the lack of any express justification for selecting these ten textbooks from among those published during the period. Robert A. Hellmann, "Evolution in American School Biology Books from the Late Nineteenth Century Until the 1930's," *The American Biology Teacher*, 27 (1965), 778–80.

75. Skoog, "Topic of Evolution," 625; quote from Peabody and Hunt, *Elementary Biology*, 118.
76. Oscar W. Richards, "The Present Status of Biology in Secondary Schools," *School Review*, 31 (1923), 144.
77. George William Hunter, *A Civic Biology: Presented in Problems* (New York: American Book, 1914), 194.
78. *Ibid.*, 183 and 194–96.
79. *Ibid.*, 405.
80. Clifton F. Hodge and Jean Dawson, *Civic Biology* (Boston: Ginn, 1918), 331–35.
81. *Ibid.*, 331.
82. *Ibid.*, 330.
83. John M. Coulter, "Biology in Secondary Schools," *School Review*, 1 (1893), 148.
84. Hurd, *Biological Education*, 10–11.
85. Herbert E. Walter, "The Nature and Amount of Biological Work That Can Profitably Be Attempted in Secondary School," *School Review* 8 (1900), 172.
86. Francis E. Lloyd and Marice A. Bigelow, *The Teaching of Biology in the Secondary School* (New York: Longmans, 1904), 138.
87. *Ibid.*, 287.
88. Hurd, *Biological Education*, 20.
89. Marion R. Brown, "The History of Zoology Teaching in the Secondary Schools of the United States," *School Science*, 2 (1902), 207.
90. *Ibid.*, 263.
91. Oran L. Raber, " 'Evolution' in the High School," *School Science and Mathematics*, 14 (1914), 324.
92. *Ibid.*, 325.
93. *Ibid.*, 325–26.
94. Biology Committee of the National Education Association Commission on the Reorganization of Secondary Education, "Revised Report," *School Science and Mathematics*, 16 (1916), 507.
95. Charles William Finley, *Biology in Secondary Schools* (New York: Columbia Univ. Bureau of Publications, 1926), 23.
96. *Ibid.*, 25.
97. *Ibid.*, 23.
98. Edward A. Krug, *The Shaping of the American High School* (Madison: Univ. of Wisconsin Press, 1969), 368–75.
99. Ronald L. Numbers, "Creationism in 20th-Century America," *Science*, 218 (1982), 539; and Kenneth K. Bailey, *Southern White Protestantism in the Twentieth Century* (New York: Harper, 1964), 72–73.

100. *Ibid.*, xi.
101. *Ibid.*, 5; and Hurd, *Biological Education*, 9.
102. Krug, *American High Schools*, 5, 189, and 439. These increases were not attributable to compulsory attendance laws because such laws did not effectively require high-school attendance prior to 1920. Krug, *American High Schools*, 170,n.2.
103. John F. Woodhull, *The Teaching of Science* (New York: Macmillan, 1918), 223.
104. Ruth Miller Elson, *Guardians of Tradition: American Schoolbooks in the Nineteenth Century* (Lincoln: Univ. of Nebraska Press, 1964), 17.
105. For example, Lloyd and Bigelow, *Teaching of Biology*, 138–39 and 286–87; and George Ransom Twiss, *A Textbook in the Principles of Science Teaching* (New York: Macmillan, 1917), 210.
106. William Jennings Bryan, *The Bible and Its Enemies* (Chicago: Bible Institute, 1921), 34.
107. James R. Moore, *The Post-Darwinian Controversies: A Study of the Protestant Struggle To Come to Terms with Darwin in Great Britain and America, 1870–1900* (Cambridge, U.K.: Cambridge Univ. Press, 1979), 73–74.
108. Bryan quote and further discussion of these causal concerns in Lawrence W. Levine, *Defender of the Faith: William Jennings Bryan: The Last Decade, 1915–1925* (New York: Oxford Univ. Press, 1965), 277. For additional discussion of these causal concerns see Chapter 2, notes 63–65.

Chapter Two: Outlawing Evolution, 1920–25

1. William Jennings Bryan ("WJB") to W. A. McRae, April 5, 1924, William Jennings Bryan Papers (Library of Congress, Washington) (papers hereafter cited as Bryan Papers).
2. Arthur S. Link and Richard L. McCormick, *Progessivism* (Arlington Heights, Ill.: Davidson, 1983), 2.
3. For a variety of interpretations of these reforms, see, for example, Benjamin Parke DeWitt, *The Progressive Movement; a Non-partisan, Comprehensive Discussion of Current Tendencies in American Politics* (New York: Macmillan, 1915) and John D. Hicks, *The Populist Revolt: A History of the Farmers' Alliance and the People's Party* (Minneapolis; Univ. of Minn. Press, 1931) (early views of progressivism as a drive by common folk to regain control from big business and its lackeys in government); Richard Hofstadter, *The Age of Reform: From Bryan to F.D.R.* (New York: Knopf, 1955) and George M. Mowry, *The Era of Theodore Roosevelt, 1900–1912* (New York: Harper, 1958) (later views of progressivism as a middle-class effort to regain status and individualism); Samuel P. Hays, *The Response to Industrialism, 1885–1914* (Chicago: Univ. of Chicago Press, 1957), Robert H. Wiebe, *The Search for Order, 1877–1920* (New York: Hill and Wang, 1967), and Samuel Haber, *Efficiency and Uplift: Scientific Management in the Progressive Era, 1890–1920* (Chicago: Univ. of Chicago Press, 1964) (saw progressivism as an attempt to resolve social problem with modern business, scientific, or sociological

techniques); John D. Buenker, *Urban Liberalism and Progressive Reform* (New York: Scribner, 1973) (identified contribution of urban immigrants to progressivism); and Gabriel Kolko, *The Triumph of Conservatism: A Reinterpretation of American History, 1900–1916* (New York: Free Press, 1963) (reinterpreted progressivism as conservative reforms by business elites).

4. Link and McCormick, *Progressivism*, 2; and David Kennedy, "Overview: The Progressive Era," *The Historian*, 37 (1975), 453–68.

5. Link and McCormick, *Progressivism*, 22.

6. Lawrence Goodwyn, *The Populist Moment: A Short History of the Agrarian Revolt in America* (New York: Oxford Univ. Press, 1978), xviii.

7. For example, Richard Hofstadter, *The Progressive Movement, 1900–1915* (Englewood Cliffs, N.J.: Prentice-Hall, 1963), 14.

8. Arthur S. Link, *American Epoch: A History of the United States Since the 1890's* (New York: Knopf, 1955), 255.

9. WJB to Inter. News Service, Dec. 4, 1922, Bryan Papers.

10. Marie Acomb Riley, *The Dynamics of a Dream* (Grand Rapids: Eerdmans, 1938), 119.

11. C. M. Aldridge to WJB, May 12, 1925, Bryan Papers; and WJB to C. M. Aldridge, undated, Bryan Papers.

12. WJB to John Roach Straton, July 1, 1925, Bryan Papers; and WJB to John Roach Straton, July 16, 1925, Bryan Papers.

13. Ferenc Morton Szasz, *The Divided Mind of Protestant America, 1880–1930* (University, Ala.: Univ. of Alabama Press, 1982), 125.

14. David Burner, *The Politics of Provincialism: The Democratic Party in Transition, 1918–32* (New York: Knopf, 1968), 8.

15. WJB to S. C. Singleton, Dec. 23, 1921, Bryan Papers.

16. Louis W. Koenig, *Bryan: A Political Biography of William Jennings Bryan* (New York: Putnam, 1971), 609.

17. WJB to W. A. McRae, April 5, 1924, Bryan Papers.

18. Burner, *Politics of Provincialism*, 12–14; William E. Ellis, "Evolution, Fundamentalism, and the Historians: An Historiographical Review," *The Historian*, 44 (1981), 27; Koenig, *Bryan*, 609–11; and Lawrence W. Levine, *Defender of the Faith: William Jennings Bryan: The Last Decade, 1915–1925* (New York: Oxford Univ. Press, 1965), 188–205.

19. WJB quoted in Levine, *Defender of the Faith*, 274.

20. WJB to R. L. Dean, March 11, 1925, Bryan Papers; and WJB to Robert L. Hutchinson, May 3, 1925, Bryan Papers.

21. Ferenc M. Szasz, "Three Fundamentalist Leaders," Diss. Univ. of Rochester 1969, 93.

22. C. Allyn Russell, "William Bell Riley: Architect of Fundamentalism," *Minnesota History*, 43 (1972), 21.

23. Ferenc M. Szasz, "The Progressive Clergymen," *Mid-America*, 55 (1973), 14; and Russell, "Riley," 21.

24. William Bell Riley quoted in Szasz, "Progressive Clergymen," 15. With respect to terminology, "Evangelicalism" and "Fundamentalism" will be used somewhat interchangeably to refer to the religious movement for biblical literalism of the past 120 years. The former term will be used exclusively

for the period before 1919, however, because the later term was not even coined until then. Some followers (including William Bell Riley) used the two terms interchangeably. If there is a distinction between the two terms, it is that fundamentalists represented a militant or ultraconservative subgroup of evangelicals. See, George M. Marsden, *Fundamentalism and American Culture: The Shaping of Twentieth-Century Evangelicalism: 1870–1925* (New York: Oxford Univ. Press, 1980), 4.

25. John Roach Straton quoted in Szasz, "Leaders," 70.
26. John Roach Straton, "The Secrets of Success in the Early Church," in *God Hath Spoken* (Philadelphia: Bible Conference Committee, 1919), 414 (transcript of proceedings of World's Conference on Christian Fundamentals).
27. John Roach Straton quoted in Szasz, "Fundamentalist Leaders," 72.
28. Hillyer H. Straton, "John Roach Straton, Prophet of Social Righteousness," *Foundations*, 5 (1962), 24 and 29.
29. John Roach Straton, "How Can We Get the Most from Our Legislature?," *Baltimore Evening Sun*, Jan. 8, 1914, p. 6.
30. H. Straton, "Straton," 18.
31. J. Straton, "Secrets," 413–14.
32. John Roach Straton and Charles Francis Potter, *Evolution Versus Creation* (New York: Doran, 1924), 32 and 106.
33. Szasz, "Fundamentalist Leaders," 99.
34. For example, Jack S. Blocker, Jr., *Retreat from Reform* (Westport, Conn.: Greenwood, 1976), 3–6; Levine, *Defender of the Faith*, 103–5; and Szasz, "Progressive Clergymen," 14. See also Paul A. Carter, *The Decline and Revival of the Social Gospel: Social and Political Liberalism in American Protestant Churches, 1920–40* (Ithaca: Cornell Univ. Press, 1962), ch. 3; and James H. Timberlake, *Prohibition and the Progressive Movement, 1900–1920* (Cambridge: Harvard Univ. Press, 1963), 2. Some historians viewed the prohibition movement as defensive and backward looking, but reform nonetheless. For example, Joseph R. Gusfield, *Symbolic Crusade: Status Politics and the American Temperance Movement* (Urbana: Univ. of Ill. Press, 1963), 7; Hofstadter, *Age of Reform*, 4; and Wiebe, *Search for Order*, 301. The historiography of the prohibition movement was reviewed in Jack S. Blocker, Jr., "The Modernity of Prohibitionists: An Analysis of Leadership Structure and Background," in *Alcohol, Reform and Society*, ed. Jack S. Blocker, Jr. (Westport Conn.: Greenwood, 1979), 148–50.
35. Blocker, *Retreat from Reform*, 10.
36. *Ibid.*, 15.
37. The coincidence of anti-evolution and dry sentiment among Arkansas voters was analyzed in Virginia Gray, "Anti-Evolution Sentiment and Behavior," *Journal of American History*, 57 (1970) 365.
38. Kenneth K. Bailey, *Southern White Protestantism in the Twentieth Century* (New York: Harper, 1964), 37.
39. *Ibid.*, 36–38 and 45–47.
40. John W. Porter, *Random Remarks* (Louisville: Baptist Book Concern, 1917), 74.

41. T. T. Martin, *Hell and the High Schools: Christ or Evolution, Which?* (Kansas City: Western Baptist, 1923), 9.

42. Joseph F. Kett, "Adolescence and Youth in Nineteenth Century America," *Journal of Interdisciplinary History*, 2 (1971), 263–86.

43. For example, WJB, *Equal Opportunity for All Children* (New York: Child Welfare Comm., 1925), 3–4.

44. Burner, *Politics of Provincialism*, 13.

45. Cora Wilson Steward to WJB, Feb. 14, 1924, Bryan Papers.

46. Bailey, *Protestantism*, 25–30.

47. *Ibid.*, 29–30; quote from Presbyterian Church in the United States, General Assembly, *Minutes 1904* (Richmond, 1904), 38.

48. Jeremy P. Felt, *Hostages of Fortune: Child Labor Reform in New York State* (Syracuse: Syracuse Univ. Press, 1965), 31–36; and Walter I. Trattner, *Crusade for Children: A History of the National Child Labor Committee and Child Labor Reform in America* (Chicago: Quadrangle, 1970), 25–45.

49. Bailey, *Protestantism*, 41; and Szasz, *Divided Mind*, 62–63.

50. Hugo, C. Bailey, "Edgar Gardner Murphy and the Child Labor Movement," *Alabama Review*, 18 (1965), 50–51; Herbert J. Doherty, Jr., "Alexander J. McKelway," *Journal of Southern History*, 24 (1958), 178; and Alton DuMar Jones, "The Child Labor Reform Movement in Georgia," *Georgia Historical Quarterly*, 49 (1965), 401.

51. WJB, *The Bible and Its Enemies* (Chicago: Bible Institute, [1921]), 37.

52. For a further discussion of this apolitical tradition, see Ernest R. Sandeen, *The Roots of Fundamentalism: British and American Millenarianism, 1800–1930* (Chicago: Univ. of Chicago Press, 1970), 267–69.

53. Charles R. Eerdman, "The Church and Socialism," in *The Fundamentals: A Testimony to the Truth* (Chicago: Testimony, [1905–15]), XII, 118. Printing and distribution of *The Fundamentals* was funded by the founders of the Union Oil Company, which may have accounted for the dearth of liberal political commentary but makes the absence of any conservative political comment even more noteworthy.

54. Mark A. Matthews, *Gospel Sword Thrusts* (New York: Revell, 1924), 11, 114, 128; and Szasz, *Divided Mind*, 125. For background on Matthews, see Szasz, "Progressive Clergymen," 11–12.

55. Levine, *Defender of the Faith*, 276–77.

56. For example, Kenneth Kyle Bailey, "The Anti-Evolution Crusade of the Nineteen-Twenties," Diss. Vanderbilt Univ. 1953, 24–28; Willard B. Gatewood, Jr., *Preachers, Pedagogues, and Politicians* (Chapel Hill: Univ. of N.C. Press, 1966), 12; Hofstadter, *Age of Reform*, 288–89; Richard Hofstadter, *Anti-Intellectualism in American Life* (New York: Knopf, 1963), 117–41; William E. Leuchtenburg, *The Perils of Prosperity, 1914–32* (Chicago: Univ. of Chicago Press, 1958), 223; and Moore, *Post-Darwinian Controversies*, 74.

57. Sandeen, *Roots of Fundamentalism*, 130–31, 207, 233–35, and 266–69.

58. George M. Marsden, *Fundamentalism and Culture*, 4–6; and Szasz, *Divided Mind*, 136–38. Another perspective on this is offered in Theodore Dwight Bozeman, *Protestants in an Age of Science* (Chapel Hill: Univ. of N.C. Press, 1977), 172.

59. Marsden, *Fundamentalism and Culture*, 62; and Sandeen, *Roots of Fundamentalism*, 132.
60. Goodwyn, *Populist Moment*, xviii.
61. Marsden, *Fundamentalism and Culture*, 132–35.
62. WJB, "The Prince of Peace," in *Speeches of William Jennings Bryan*, ed. WJB (New York: Funk and Wagnalls, 1909), 267 and 269.
63. J. Dorman Steele and J. W. P. Jenks, *A Popular Zoology* (New York: Barnes, 1887), 254 and 276–78 (quotes from pp. 276 and 277); and J. Dorman Steele, *Fourteen Weeks in Popular Geology* (New York: American Book, 1898), 19–20 and 255–56.
64. Sandeen, *Roots of Fundamentalism*, 132–39.
65. "The 1878 Niagara Creed," in *ibid.*, 273–77.
66. For background on the series and an index of articles, see *The Fundamentals*, XII, 3–5 and 124–28.
67. James Orr, "Science and Christian Faith," in *The Fundamentals*, VII, 103.
68. Dupree, *Asa Gray*, 362–69.
69. George Frederick Wright, "The Passing of Evolution," in *The Fundamentals*, VII, 20.
70. "Evolution in the Pulpit," and Henry H. Beach, "Decadence of Darwinism," in *The Fundamentals*, VI, 27–48 (quote, p. 48).
71. Marsden, *Fundamentalism and Culture*, 141. A similar view was expressed in Sandeen, *Roots of Fundamentalism*, 233–47; and Szasz, *Divided Mind*, 84–91.
72. "Report of Committee on the Correlation of Bible Conferences," in *God Hath Spoken*, 22.
73. William B. Riley, "The Great Divide, or Christ and the Present Crisis," in *ibid.*, 27 and 45.
74. George E. Guille, "Satan—His Person, Power and Purpose," in *ibid.*, 221.
75. W[illia]m B. Riley, "The Great Commission," in *ibid.*, 441.
76. "Report of Committee on the Correlation of Colleges, Seminaries, and Academies," in *ibid.*, 19–20.
77. R. A. Torrey, "God—His Relations to Man in Creation and in Regeneration," in *ibid.*, 143.
78. William Bell Riley quoted in Szasz, *Divided Mind*, 107.
79. Harry F. Huntington to WJB, April 1, 1921, Bryan Papers; and L. P. Putnam to WJB, May 11, 1921, Bryan Papers.
80. WJB, *Bible and Enemies*, 39.
81. WJB, *In His Image* (New York: Revell, 1922), 94. "The Menace of Darwinism" was reprinted several times, often in slightly different versions. The most easily accessible version is contained in this collection of lectures Bryan gave at Union Theological Seminary in 1922.
82. *Ibid.*, 91.
83. *Ibid.*, 93.
84. WJB to Editor, *Capital Times*, April 5, 1922, Bryan Papers; and WJB to Mayor Hylan, June 12, 1923, Bryan Papers.
85. WJB, *Bible and Enemies*, 34.
86. *Ibid.*, 37.
87. WJB, *Image*, 93.

88. *Ibid.*, 107.

89. WJB, *Bible and Enemies*, 29.

90. WJB, *Image*, 93.

91. *Ibid.*, 125.

92. David Starr Jordan to WJB, Nov. 24, 1919, Dec. 12, 1919, and Jan. 17, 1921, Bryan Papers; and Vernon Kellogg, *Headquarters Nights: A Record of Conversations and Experiences at the Headquarters of the German Army in France and Belgium* (Boston: Atlantic Monthly Press, 1917), 22–30.

93. WJB, *Image*, 125–26; and WJB, *Bible and Enemies*, 37–38.

94. For example, WJB, *Image*, 88.

95. *Ibid.*, 122. Similar views expressed in WJB, *Bible and Enemies*, 33; and WJB, "God and Evolution," *New York Times*, Feb. 26, 1922, sec. 7, p. 8.

96. WJB to John A. Taylor, April 17, 1925, Bryan Papers. A general discussion of Bryan's support for religious minorities is in Levine, *Defender of the Faith*, 257–58.

97. WJB, *Image*, 122.

98. Marsden, *Fundamentalism and Culture*, 169; Ronald L. Numbers, "Creationism in 20th Century America," *Science*, 218 (1982), 538; Sandeen, *Roots of Fundamentalism*, 266–69; and Szasz, *Divided Mind*, 107.

99. Harry F. Huntington to WJB, April 1, 1921, Bryan Papers.

100. An excellent compilation of this legislation is in Richard David Wilhelm, "A Chronology and Analysis of Regulatory Actions Relating to the Teaching of Evolution in Public Schools," Diss. Univ. of Texas 1978, 61–65.

101. G. W. Ellis to WJB, March 13, 1922, Bryan Papers.

102. Ernest L. Crandell to WJB, Feb. 25, 1922, Bryan Papers.

103. Bailey, "Anti-Evolution Crusade," 61–62. Quote in William Bell Riley to WJB, Feb. 7, 1923, Bryan Papers.

104. WJB to Editor, *Capital Times*, April 5, 1922, Bryan Papers.

105. R. Halliburton, Jr., "The Nation's First Anti-Darwin Law," *Southwestern Social Science Quarterly*, 41 (1960), 124.

106. J. L. Walton, quoted in "House Puts Knife to Darwinism," *Daily Oklahoman*, Feb. 22, 1923, p. 1.

107. G. W. Moothart to WJB, Dec. 5, 1922, Bryan Papers.

108. This summary of the House floor action is compiled from "House Outlaws Darwinism from Public Schools," *Morning Tulsa Daily World*, Feb. 22, 1923, p. 1; "House Puts Knife to Darwinism," *Daily Oklahoman*, Feb. 22, 1923, p. 1; " 'Who's a Monkey?' House in Evolution Row," *Muskogee Daily Phoenix*, Feb. 22, 1923, p. 1; Halliburton, "Anti-Darwin Law," 125–27; and *Journal of the House of Representatives, Regular Session: Ninth Legislature of the State of Oklahoma* (Oklahoma City: Great Western, [1923]), 4–6.

109. Amendment to House Bill No. 197 (Oklahoma, 1923).

110. This summary of the Senate floor action is compiled from *Journal of the Senate, Regular Session: Ninth Legislature of the State of Oklahoma* (Oklahoma City: Novak & Walker, [1923]), vi–vii, 1648–51, 1660–62, and 1671–74; "Bill Outlawing Monk Ancestry Goes to Walton," *Morning Tulsa Daily World*, March 23, 1923, p. 1; "Free School Book Bill Goes to Walton," *Muskogee*

Daily Phoenix, March 23, 1923, p. 1; "Free School Book Bill Is Sent Walton," *Daily Oklahoman*, March 23, 1923; and Halliburton, "Anti-Darwin Law," 128–29.

111. J. C. Walton to WJB, May 26, 1923, Bryan Papers.
112. WJB to Mayor Hylan, June 12, 1923, Bryan Papers. Similar comments in WJB to W. J. Singleton, April 11, 1923, Bryan Papers; and WJB to C. H. Thurber, Dec. 22, 1923, Bryan Papers.
113. WJB to W. J. Singleton, April 11, 1923, Bryan Papers.
114. John C. Trice, "Public Schools Must Be Free from Any Sectarian Views," *Florida Times Union*, April 19, 1923, p. 8.
115. House Concurrent Resolution No. 7 (Florida, 1923).
116. Bailey, "Antievolution Crusade," 66.
117. WJB to *Chicago Tribune*, June 14, 1923, Bryan Papers.
118. House Concurrent Resolution No. 7 (Florida, 1923).
119. Norman F. Furniss, *The Fundamentalist Controversy, 1918–31* (1954; rpt. Hamden, Conn.: Archon, 1963), 69.
120. WJB to Ginn and Company, Dec. 22, 1923, Bryan Papers. See also WJB to H. Revell Co., Jan. 5, 1924, Bryan Papers.
121. Kenneth K. Bailey, "The Enactment of Tennessee's Antievolution Law," *Journal of Southern History*, 16 (1950), 475; and W. B. Marr to WJB, March 13, 1925, Bryan Papers.
122. House Bill No. 185 (Tennessee, 1925).
123. Ralph Perry, "Bar Teaching of Evolution," *Nashville Banner*, Jan. 28, 1925, p. 3.
124. Historian Kenneth K. Bailey concluded that the bill was not passed in undo haste. Bailey, "Tennessee's Law," 488. For the official record of the Senate action, see *Senate Journal of the Sixty-fourth General Assembly of the State of Tennessee* (Nashville: Senate Chief Clerk, [1925]), 254, 466, 467, and 516–17.
125. *Ibid.*, 477–79; and Howard Eskridge, "Senate Passes Evolution Bill," *Nashville Banner*, March 13, 1925, p. 1.
126. "Lie Is Passed in Legislature," *Nashville Banner*, Feb. 5, 1925, p. 7; and Bailey, "Tennessee's Law," 477–78.
127. Jno. A. Shelton to WJB, Feb. 5, 1925, Bryan Papers.
128. WJB to Jno. A. Shelton, Feb. 9, 1925, Bryan Papers.
129. This summary of the Senate floor action is compiled from *Tennessee Senate Journal*, 516–17; Thomas Fauntleroy, "Darwinism Outlawed in Tennessee Senate," *Memphis Commercial Appeal*, March 14, 1925, p. 1; "Evolution Is Given Hard Jolt," *Knoxville Journal*, March 14, 1925, p. 1; and Howard Eskridge, "Senate Passes Evolution Bill," *Nashville Banner*, March 13, 1925, p. 1.
130. Senate Bill No. 133 (Tennessee, 1925).
131. Biographical data on legislators from Ernest N. Heston, ed., *Tennessee Hand-Book and Official Directory: 1925* (Nashville: Secretary of State, 1925), 48–51 and 54–60.
132. "Governor's O.K. on Evolution Ban in Schools," *Knoxville Journal*, March 24, 1925, p. 1.

133. Austin Peay, quoted in "Governor Signs Evolution Bill," *Nashville Banner*, March 24, 1925, p. 10.

Chapter Three: Enforcing the Law, 1925–60

1. "Plan Assault on State Law on Evolution," *Chattanooga Daily Times*, May 4, 1925, p. 5.
2. *The Fight for Free Speech* (New York: American Civil Liberties Union (ACLU), 1921), 17–18.
3. *Ibid.*, 6.
4. *Ibid.*, 4–5.
5. *Ibid.*, 8.
6. "Report of Committee on the Correlation of Bible Conferences," in *God Hath Spoken* (Philadelphia: Bible Conference Committee, 1919), 22 (transcript of proceedings of World's Conference on Christian Fundamentals).
7. Thomas Stewart and Arthur Garfield Hays in *The World's Most Famous Court Trial: State of Tennessee v. John Thomas Scopes* (1925; rpt. New York: Da Capo, 1971), 218–19 (unedited trial transcript hereinafter cited as *Court Trial*).
8. *Free Speech 1925–1926: The Work of the American Civil Liberties Union* (New York: ACLU, 1926), 4 and 21–23.
9. "Evolution Case Started at Rhea," *Chattanooga Daily Times*, May 6, 1925, p. 1.
10. John T. Scopes and James Presley, *Center of the Storm: Memoirs of John T. Scopes* (New York: Holt, 1967), 56–62.
11. *Goetz v. Smith*, 152 Tenn. 451, 278 S.W. 417 (1925).
12. "Discuss Teaching of Evolution," *Nashville Banner*, May 6, 1925, p. 10.
13. "Material Criticism Denies Supernatural," *Memphis Commercial Appeal*, May 5, 1925, p. 1.
14. "Commoner Believes Evolution Tommyrot," *Memphis Commercial Appeal*, May 11, 1925, p. 1.
15. See W. B. Riley to L. L. Minor, May 18, 1925, William Jennings Bryan Papers (Library of Congress, Washington) (papers hereafter cited as Bryan Papers).
16. WJB to L. M. Aldridge, undated [May 13, 1925], Bryan Papers; and WJB to James W. Freeman, June 10, 1925, Bryan Papers.
17. WJB to Howard A. Kelly, June 17, 1925, Bryan Papers.
18. J. Frank Norris to WJB, undated [June or July, 1925], Bryan Papers.
19. Arthur Garfield Hays, "The Strategy of the Scopes Defense," *The Nation*, Aug. 5, 1925, pp. 157–58. See also, Hays in *Court Trial*, 219. An account of the changing ACLU defense strategy is recalled by John Scopes in Scopes and Presley, *Center of Storm*, 71–73, and by Roger Baldwin in Peggy Lamson, *Roger Baldwin: Founder of the American Civil Liberties Union* (Boston: Houghton Mifflin, 1976), 167–68. The narrow initial ACLU strategy is suggested in "Plan Assault," 5.
20. Expressing his views on the topic of evolution and religion, Darrow declared in one public speech, "Can the human mind conceive of any wilder

delusion or more absurd conceit than the thought that the transitory, weak, and pulling pieces of protoplasm on this insignificant microscopic Earth are the special objects of the Universe." Clarence Darrow, "Purpose of the Universe," Clarence Darrow Papers (Library of Congress, Washington) (papers hereafter cited as Darrow Papers). Darrow and Malone's offer of services reprinted in, Clarence Darrow and Dudley Field Malone to John R. Neal, in Scopes and Presley, *Center of Storm*, 66–67.

21. Luther Burbank, quoted in Kenneth Kyle Bailey, "The Anti-Evolution Crusade of the Nineteen-Twenties," Diss. Vanderbilt Univ. 1953, p. 127. For further discussion of the role of Colby and Hughes, see Scopes and Presley, *Center of Storm*, 69–73.

22. WJB in *Court Trial*, 316–17.

23. S. K. Hicks to WJB, May 25, 1925, Bryan Papers; and WJB to F. P. Dunnington, July 16, 1925, Bryan Papers. The first name of S. K. Hicks, local counsel supporting the law, was Sue. His name inspired the country ballad made famous by Johnny Cash, "A Boy Named Sue."

24. Stewart in *Court Trial*, 196.

25. *Ibid.*, 57.

26. S. K. Hicks to WJB, June 12, 1925, Bryan Papers.

27. George F. Washburn to WJB, July 23, 1925, Bryan Papers.

28. WJB to William Bell Riley, June 7, 1925, Bryan Papers; J. Frank Norris to WJB, undated [June or July, 1925], Bryan Papers; and John Roach Straton to WJB, July 12, 1925, Bryan Papers.

29. WJB to S. K. Hicks, June 16, 1925, Bryan Papers.

30. J. Frank Norris to WJB, undated [June or July, 1925], Bryan Papers. For additional discussion of Bryan's efforts to assemble scientific expert witnesses for the *Scopes* trial, see Ronald L. Numbers, "Creationism in 20th-Century America," *Science*, 218 (1982), 540.

31. WJB and Clarence Darrow in *Court Trial*, 297.

32. George McCready Price to WJB, July 1, 1925, Bryan Papers.

33. For example, Louis T. More to WJB, June 15, 1925, Bryan Papers; and Alfred W. McCann to WJB, June 20, 1925, Bryan Papers.

34. Howard A. Kelly to WJB, June 15, 1925, Bryan Papers.

35. Samuel Untermayer to WJB, June 25, 1925, Bryan Papers.

36. WJB to W. B. Marr, June 15, 1925, Darrow Papers.

37. "Defense Motion To Quash the Indictment" in *Court Trial*, 47–50.

38. Hays in *Court Trial*, 56–57.

39. Stewart in *Court Trial*, 67 and 71.

40. "Opinion on Overruling Motion To Quash," in *Court Trial*, 107–8.

41. Darrow in *Court Trial*, 146.

42. Stewart in *Court Trial*, 148; and WJB in *Court Trial*, 181. Judge Raulston ruled in favor of this point in "Ruling in Excluding Experts," in *Court Trial*, 202.

43. Hays in *Court Trial*, 137 and 203; and Dudley Field Malone in *Court Trial*, 185.

44. Stewart and Hays in *Court Trial*, 219. This exchange between Stewart and Hays most clearly revealed the public education aspect of the trial strategy employed by the defense.

45. Stewart in *Court Trial*, 137; William Jennings Bryan, Jr., in *Court Trial*, 150–53; David W. Louisell and Christopher B. Mueller, *Federal Evidence* (Rochester: Lawyers Co-operative, 1979), 629–30, 633, 649–56, and 687–88; and Jack B. Weinstein and Margaret A. Berger, *Weinstein's Evidence* (New York: Bender, 1982), 702[01] and 703[01].

46. John T. Raulston in *Court Trial*, 137.

47. "Ruling," in *Court Trial*, 203.

48. WJB in *Court Trial*, 172.

49. Raulston and WJB in *Court Trial*, 284.

50. WJB in *Court Trial*, 177.

51. *Ibid.*, 299. Looking back at the trial from the vantage point of 1984, creationist leader Henry Morris viewed acknowledging the day/age theory as Bryan's "most serious mistake" at Dayton. "Darrow," Morris noted, "of course, made the most of it, ridiculing the idea of people claiming to believe the Bible was inspired when its meaning was so flexible that one could make it say whatever he wished!" Henry M. Morris, *History of Modern Creationism* (San Diego: Master Book, 1984), 66. This comment, however, reflected the gap separating current creationists, who generally believe in a literal six-day creation, from their anti-evolutionist ancestors, who commonly equated the days of creation with geologic ages. The day/age interpretation was advanced during the nineteenth century by such leading anti-evolutionary geologists as Edward Hitchcock and J. W. Dawson; popularized around the turn of the century by the highly influential *Scofield Reference Bible*; and accepted by Bryan, Riley, Straton, and most other anti-evolution leaders of the twenties. For a concise description of various evangelical interpretations of the Genesis account, see Bernard Ramm, *The Christian View of Science and Scripture* (Grand Rapids: Eerdmans, 1954), 120–56.

52. "Editorial Paragraphs," *The Nation*, July 22, 1925, p. 1.

53. Technically, Darrow put Bryan on the stand to discuss if teaching evolution conflicted with the Bible in violation of the statute. That issue involved interpreting the proscription contained in the statute—a task for the judge rather than for the jury. See above, Chapter 3, note 41 and accompanying text.

54. Darrow in *Court Trial*, 311.

55. WJB and Darrow in *Court Trial*, 317.

56. WJB in *Court Trial*, 307.

57. For example, coverage of the events in Dayton dominated the front page of the *New York Times* after each day of the eight-day trial. In contrast, coverage of the *Scopes* appellate argument was relegated to one column on page 8 of the *New York Times* after the first day of oral argument.

58. Issues for overturning Scopes's conviction relating to the conduct of the trial (including the exclusion of expert witnesses) were precluded from appeal by the failure of the defense to timely file the requisite bill of exceptions. *Scopes v. State*, 152 Tenn. 424, 278 S.W. 57 (1925).

59. "Both Sides Heard in Scopes Appeal," *New York Times*, June 1, 1926, p. 8.

60. "Argument of Clarence Darrow," *Scopes v. State*, 154 Tenn. 105, 289 S.W. 363 (1927), 28, Darrow Papers.

61. "Reply Brief and Argument for the State of Tennessee," *Scopes*, 154 Tenn. 105, p. 16.

62. "Brief and Argument of the Tennessee Academy of Science as Amicus Curiae," *Scopes*, 154 Tenn. 105, p. 16.

63. "Reply Brief," 61.

64. William Jennings Bryan, Jr., in "Both Sides Heard," 8.

65. Quote from Arthur Garfield Hays, in "Both Sides Heard," 8.

66. *Scopes*, 154 Tenn. at 111, 289 S.W. at 364.

67. *Ibid.*, at 105, 289 S.W. at 366.

68. *Ibid.*, at 117–18, 289 S.W. at 366.

69. Dudley Field Malone in "Malone Criticizes Decision," *New York Times*, Jan. 16, 1927, p. 28.

70. Stewart, Raulston, and Darrow in *Court Trial*, 311–12.

71. "Will Ask Court To Rehear Case," *Nashville Banner*, Jan. 17, 1927, p. 1.

72. *Scopes*, 154 Tenn. at 121, 289 S.W. at 367.

73. "Will Ask Court," 1.

74. Malone, quoted in "Malone Criticizes Decision," 28.

75. Joseph Wood Krutch, "Darrow vs. Bryan," *The Nation*, July 29, 1925, p. 136; "Foreign Amazement at Tennessee," *The Literary Digest*, July 25, 1925, 18; "The Conduct of the Scopes Trial," *The New Republic*, Aug. 19, 1925, 332; H. L. Mencken's editorials are reprinted in Jerry D. Tompkins, ed., *D-Days at Dayton: Reflections on the Scopes Trial* (Baton Rouge: Louisiana State Univ. Press, 1965), 35–51; and Russell D. Owen, "Issues and Personalities," in "The Significance of the Scopes Trial," *Current History Illustrated*, 22 (1925), 883 (published by the *New York Times*).

76. Paxton Hibben, *The Peerless Leader: William Jennings Bryan* (New York: Farrar, 1929), 402.

77. For example, Richard Hofstadter, *Anti-Intellectualism in American Life* (New York: Knopf, 1963), 131; Richard Hofstadter, William Miller, and Daniel Aaron, *The United States: The History of a Republic* (Englewood Cliffs, N.J.: Prentice-Hall, 1952), 636; and Richard Hofstadter, William Miller, and Daniel Aaron, *The American Republic: From Reconstruction* (Englewood Cliffs, N.J.: Prentice-Hall, 1970), 389.

78. Ray Ginger, *Six Days or Forever? Tennessee v. John Thomas Scopes* (Boston: Beacon, 1958), 214.

79. William E. Leuchtenburg, *The Perils of Prosperity, 1914–1932* (Chicago: Univ. of Chicago Press, 1958), 223.

80. *Ibid.*, 223.

81. George M. Marsden, *Fundamentalism and American Culture: The Shaping of Twentieth-Century Evangelicalism: 1870–1925* (New York: Oxford Univ. Press, 1980), 185–95. For further discussion of the northern urban origins of key fundamentalist leaders, see Paul A. Carter, *The Twenties in America* (New York: Crowell, 1968), 85; Paul A. Carter, "The Fundamentalist Defense of the Faith," in *Change and Continuity in Twentieth Century America: The 1920's*,

ed. John Braeman, Robert H. Bremner, and David Brody (Columbus: Ohio State Univ. Press, 1968), 204–5; and Ernest R. Sandeen, *The Roots of Fundamentalism: British and American Millenarianism, 1800–1930* (Chicago: Univ. of Chicago Press, 1970), 266–67.

82. Lawrence W. Levine, *Defender of Faith: William Jennings Bryan: The Last Decade, 1915–1925,* (New York: Oxford Univ. Press, 1965), 354.

83. Lewis W. Koenig, *Bryan: A Political Biography of William Jennings Bryan* (New York: Putnam, 1971), 654.

84. Marsden, *Fundamentalism and Culture,* 185–86.

85. Dudley Field Malone, in Ginger, *Six Days,* 191.

86. Evidence for this includes the mixed view presented in the southern media of the public opinion impact of the *Scopes* trial. Ginger, *Six Days,* 191; and Bailey, *Southern White Protestantism in the Twentieth Century* (New York: Harper, 1964), 90–91. Further evidence comes from the electoral success of persons connected with the *Scopes* affair. Tennessee Governor Peay was re-elected in 1926, lead prosecutor Thomas Stewart was elected to the U.S. Senate, and local prosecutor S. K. Hicks was elected to the state House of Representatives.

87. Ginger, *Six Days,* 211–14; Marsden, *Fundamentalism and Culture,* 189; Paolo E. Coletta, *William Jennings Bryan: III. Political Puritan: 1915–1925* (Lincoln: Univ. of Nebraska Press, 1969), 279; Numbers, "Creationism," 540–41; and Ferenc Morton Szasz, *The Divided Mind of Protestant America, 1880–1930* (University, Ala.: Univ. of Alabama Press, 1982), 123. A later article has carried this revisionist historiography still further by suggesting that the *Scopes* trial was not immediately perceived as a fundamentalist defeat by either camp. Paul M. Waggoner, "The Historiography of the Scopes Trial: A Critical Re-evaluation," *Trinity Journal,* 5 (1984), 156–61.

88. Bailey, "Anti-Evolution Crusade," 212–16; Coletta, *Bryan,* 279; Marsden, *Fundamentalism and Culture,* 189; and Szasz, *Divided Mind,* 125.

89. Anti-evolution bill introductions listed in Richard David Wilhelm, "A Chronology and Analysis of Regulatory Actions Relating to the Teaching of Evolution in Public Schools," Diss. Univ. of Texas 1978, pp. 62–64.

90. Cameron Morrison to WJB, Feb. 5, 1924, Bryan Papers; Bailey, "Anti-evolution Crusade," 67–69; and Wilhelm, "Chronology," 90.

91. Compare Maynard Shipley, *The War on Modern Science: A Short History of the Fundamentalist Attacks on Evolution and Modernism* (New York: Knopf, 1927), 111, with Maynard Shipley, "Growth of the Anti-Evolution Movement," *Current History,* 32 (1930), 330. For further discussion of local restrictions on evolutionary teaching imposed during the late 1920s, see Bailey, "Anti-evolution Crusade," 71–72 and 223–24; Bailey, *Protestantism,* 88; Ginger, *Six Days,* 223; Szasz, *Divided Mind,* 123; and Wilhelm, "Chronology," 88–91.

92. Population data are taken from Robert Hunt Lyman, ed., *The World Almanac and Book of Facts for 1926* (New York: World, [1926]), 307 and 320. For purposes of categorizing Mississippi as the most rural state, the Census Bureau defined rural areas to include all areas not within incorporated territory having 2500 or more people. For purposes of this study, in contrast,

rural legislators are those representing counties with fewer than 100,000 people.

93. House Bill No. 77 (Mississippi, 1926).

94. T. T. Martin, *Hell and the High School; Christ or Evolution, Which?* (Kansas City: Western Baptist, 1923), 9.

95. T. T. Martin, quoted in Shipley, *War on Science*, 65; and T. T. Martin in "Ben M'Kenzie Will Speak Here Sunday," *Jackson Daily Clarion-Ledger*, Feb. 3, 1926, p. 2.

96. "Legislature Under Headway Is Making Rapid Progress, Important Matters Pending," *Jackson Daily Clarion-Ledger*, Feb. 7, 1926, p. 2.

97. This summary of House floor debate is compiled from "Evolution Measure Passes Lower House," *Jackson Daily Clarion-Ledger*, Feb. 9, 1926, p. 1; "Evolution Bill Comes Up Today," *Jackson Daily Clarion-Ledger*, Feb. 24, 1926, p. 2; and R. Halliburton, Jr., "Mississippi's Contribution to the Anti-Evolution Movement," *Journal of Mississippi History*, 35 (1973), 177–79.

98. This summary of Senate floor debate is compiled from "Evolution Measure Is Passed in Senate by Decisive Margin," *Jackson Daily Clarion-Ledger*, Feb. 25, 1926, p. 1; and Halliburton, "Mississippi's Contribution," 179.

99. Bible Crusaders Win Notable Victory," *Jackson Daily Clarion-Ledger*, Feb. 25, 1926, p. 4.

100. "Governor Signs Anti-Evolution Bill," *Jackson Daily Clarion-Ledger*, March 12, 1926, p. 4.

101. Darrow in *Court Trial*, 137.

102. This conclusion is based on a review of the *Arkansas Gazette* and the *Arkansas Democrat* (the two leading Little Rock newspapers) for the two-month period preceding the election. For example, the initiative was not even mentioned on the editorial page of the *Democrat* on the day before the election. Virginia Gray suggested greater interest in the initiative campaign from her review of Arkansas newspapers. Virginia Gray, "Anti-Evolution Sentiment and Behavior: The Case of Arkansas," *Journal of American History*, 57 (1970), 357.

103. "Political Debate Will Be Broadcast from KGHI," *Arkansas Gazette*, Nov. 4, 1928, p. 4.

104. "If You Would Serve Arkansas with Your Ballot," *Arkansas Gazette*, Oct. 30, 1928, p. 6.

105. "Dean Jones Scores Evolution Measure," *Arkansas Gazette*, Nov. 2. 1928, p. 2.

106. "Against Act No. 1," *Arkansas Gazette*, Nov. 4, 1928, p. 9.

107. "Urges Passage of Evolution Measure," *Arkansas Gazette*, Oct. 31, 1928, p. 19.

108. "Bigotry . . . and Worse," *Arkansas Gazette*, Nov. 5, 1928, p. 3.

109. "The Bible or Atheism, Which?," *Arkansas Gazette*, Nov. 4, 1928, p. 12.

110. "Against Act No. 1," 9.

111. Gray, "Anti-Evolution Sentiment," 365.

112. Mississippi Attorney General Opinion in Bailey, *Protestantism*, 87.

113. Arkansas Attorney General Opinion in Wilhelm, "Chronology," 253.

114. Repeal measures listed in Wilhelm, "Chronology," 72.

115. Harbor Allen, "The Anti-Evolution Campaign in America," *Current History*, 24 (1926), 894. See also, *Free Speech, 1926: The Work of the American Civil Liberties Union* (New York: ACLU, 1927), 20.

116. *The Fight for Civil Liberty, 1927–28* (New York: ACLU, [1928]), 43; *The Fight for Civil Liberty: The Story of the Activities of the American Civil Liberties Union, 1928–29* (New York: ACLU, 1929), 23 and 30; *The Fight for Civil Liberty; 1930–31* (New York: ACLU, 1931), 27 (quote); and *"Sweet Land of Liberty," 1931–1932* (New York: ACLU, 1932), 34. A new action could not be brought on behalf of John Scopes because he had voluntarily left his teaching job for graduate school shortly after the trial ended. Funds for his studies were raised through the ACLU in New York. Scopes had been offered continued employment at the high school in Dayton after the trial.

117. Wilhelm, "Chronology," 210–14.

118. See Chapter 3, notes 77, 78, and 82 above.

119. Willard B. Gatewood, Jr., *Preachers, Pedagogues, and Politicians* (Chapel Hill: Univ. of N. C. Press, 1966), 233. A similar view is expressed in Elber L. Watson, "Oklahoma and the Anti-Evolution Movement of the 1920's," *Chronicles of Oklahoma*, 42 (1965), 406.

120. Arthur S. Link and John B. Catton, *American Epoch: A History of the United States Since the 1890's* (New York: Knopf, 1973), II, 39; Bailey, "Antievolution Crusade," 243.

121. Marsden, *Fundamentalism and Culture*, 189–91.

122. Allen, "Anti-Evolution Campaign," 893.

123. C. H. Thurber to WJB, Nov. 21, 1923, Bryan Papers.

124. WJB to C. H. Thurber, Dec. 22, 1923, Bryan Papers.

125. C. H. Thurber to WJB, Nov. 21, 1923, Bryan Papers.

126. The popularity of Hunter's text was noted in George W. Hunter, *Science Teaching at Junior and Senior high School Levels* (New York: American Book, 1934), 32; and Gerald Skoog, "The Topic of Evolution in Secondary School Biology Textbooks: 1900–1977," *Science Education*, 63 (1979), 625.

127. WJB to W. B. Marr, June 11, 1925, Darrow Papers.

128. W. B. Riley to L. L. Minor, May 18, 1925, Bryan Papers.

129. Bailey, "Antievolution Crusade," 224.

130. George William Hunter, *A Civic Biology: Presented in Problems* (New York: American Book, 1914), 193–96; and George W. Hunter, *A New Civic Biology* (New York: American Book, 1926), 250–57.

131. Hunter, *Civic Biology*, 253, 404–6, and 423; and Hunter, *New Civic Biology*, 383, 411–12, and 436.

132. Shipley, "Anti-Evolution Movement," 330–32.

133. Otis W. Caldwell and Florence Weller, "High School Biology Content as Judged by Thirty College Biologists," *School Science and Mathematics*, 32 (1932), 411–12 and 419–20. This article included a parallel survey of thirty leading college biology professors. Ninety percent of these biologists indicated that the relationship between heredity and environment should appear in high-school texts but few thought that theories of the origin of life should be presented. The one text presenting such theories was not identified by name.

134. Oscar Riddle, "Preliminary Impressions and Facts from a Questionnaire on Secondary School Biology," *American Biology Teacher*, 3 (1941), 157.

135. H. J. Muller, "One Hundred Years Without Darwinism Are Enough," *School Science and Mathematics*, 49 (1959), 314–18 (reprint of 1958 speech).

136. George Gaylord Simpson, *This View of Life: The World of an Evolutionist* (New York: Harcourt, 1964), 33. This quote is from a chapter of this book reprinting Simpson's earlier speech on evolutionary teaching. On page 56, he acknowledged borrowing his title from Muller, though he got it a little wrong.

137. Events surrounding this bill are compiled from House Bill No. 161 (Missouri, 1959); "Legislator Raps Evolution Theory," *Jefferson City Daily Capital News*, Jan. 21, 1959, p. 2; and Walter H. Toberman, *Official Roster, 1959–1960; State, District, and County Officers of the State of Missouri* (Jefferson City: Von Huffmann, [1959]), 24–28.

138. Skoog, "Topic of Evolution," 623–24 and 627.

139. Judith V. Grabiner and Peter D. Miller, "Effects of the Scopes Trial," *Science*, 185 (1974), 832 and 837.

140. *Ibid.*, 833–35; Skoog, "Topic of Evolution," 626–27; and Wilhelm, "Chronology," 173 (Texas restriction).

141. Grabiner and Miller, "Effect of Scopes," 185.

142. Hunter, *Science Teaching*, 32.

143. WJB, "Text of Bryan's Proposed Address in Scopes Case," in *Court Trial*, 336. Bryan never gave this address at trial but did give it twice during the week between the trial and his death.

144. Stewart in *Court Trial*, 197.

145. Senator Dent in "Senators Devote Whole Day to Debate on One Measure; Great Crowds Hears Arguments," *Jackson Daily Clarion-Ledger*, Feb. 25, 1926, p. 3.

146. "Brief for State," 78.

147. Gordon McKenzie in *Court Trial*, 168.

148. "Commoner Believes Evolution Tommyrot," 2.

149. Shipley, *War on Science*, 373.

150. *Historical Statistics of the United States; Colonial Times to 1970* (Washington: Bureau of the Census, 1975), 967.

151. Vannevar Bush, *Science: The Endless Frontier* (1945; rpt. Washington: National Science Foundation, 1960), 86.

152. A. Hunter Dupree, *Science in the Federal Government: A History of Politics and Activities to 1940* (Cambridge: Harvard Univ. Press, 1957), 340–42.

153. *Historical Statistics*, 224 and 966.

154. Dupree, *Science in Government*, 41; and Daniel S. Greenberg, *The Politics of Pure Science* (New York: Times Mirror, 1967), 8–9.

155. Congressional Research Service, *U. S. Science and Engineering Education and Manpower: Background; Supply and Demand; and Comparison with Japan, the Soviet Union, and West Germany* (Washington: GPO, 1983), 166–73 (quotes from 167 and 169).

156. *Ibid.*, 179 (quote from President Eisenhower's 1958 State of the Union address as set forth in this source).

157. George H. Gallup, ed., *The Gallup Poll: Public Opinion 1935–1971* (New York: Random House, 1972), II, 1547.
158. Arnold B. Grobman, *The Changing Classroom; The Role of the Biological Sciences Curriculum Study*, (Garden City, N.Y.: Doubleday, 1969), 94–95 and 204.
159. *Yearbook of American and Canadian Churches, 1983* (Nashville: Abingdon, 1983), 270; *Historical Statistics*, 391–91; and Marsden, *Fundamentalism and Culture*, 194–95. This period of institution building by evangelicals was described in Joel A. Carpenter, "Fundamentalist Institutions and the Rise of Evangelical Protestantism, 1929–1942," *Church History*, 49 (1980), 62–75.
160. Gallup, ed., *Gallup Poll*, II, 1482.
161. Bruce R. Reichenbach, "C. S. Lewis on the Desolation of De-Valued Science," *Christian Scholar's Review*, 11 (1982), 99–111 (quote from Lewis on page 99 of this source).
162. Numbers, "Creationism," 541.

Chapter Four: Legalizing Evolution, 1961–70

1. "Opinion," in *The World's Most Famous Court Trial: State of Tennessee v. John Thomas Scopes* (1925; rpt. New York: Da Capo, 1971), 105–6.
2. Joseph Story, *Commentaries on the Constitution of the United States* (1833; rpt. New York: Da Capo, 1970), III, 728.
3. *Everson v. Board of Education*, 330 U.S. 1, 15 (1947).
4. Laurence H. Tribe, *American Constitutional Law* (Mineola, N.Y.: Foundation Press, 1978), 813.
5. *McCollum v. Board of Education*, 333 U.S. 203, 212 (1948).
6. *Engel v. Vitale*, 370 U.S. 421, 424 (1962).
7. *Abington School Dist. v. Schempp*, 374 U.S. 203, 222 (1963).
8. *Freedom Through Dissent; 42nd Annual Report, July 1, 1961 To June 30, 1962* (New York: ACLU, [1962]), 22.
9. *Schempp*, 374 U.S. at 225.
10. See Chapter 2, notes 102–4 and 125–27, above.
11. Judith V. Grabiner and Peter D. Miller, "Effects of the Scopes Trial," *Science*, 185 (1974), 185; and Gerald Skoog, "The Topic of Evolution in Secondary School Biology Textbooks: 1900–1977," *Science Education*, 63 (1979), 624.
12. Skoog, "Topic of Evolution," 633. According to project director Arnold B. Grobman, three different BSCS texts were produced "to avoid any implication concerning a national curriculum" and to "provide maximum flexibility." Each version stressed a different approach to biology (biochemical, ecological, and cellular), with all three incorporating evolution. Arnold B. Grobman, *The Changing Classroom: The Role of the Biological Sciences Curriculum Study* (Garden City, N.Y.: Doubleday, 1969), 62, 88, and 95.
13. John A. Moore, "Creationism in California," in *Science and Its Public: The Changing Relationship*, ed. Gerald Holton and William A. Blanpied (Dordrecht, Holland: D. Reidel, 1976), 192–93. A similar explanation for the ac-

ceptance of the BSCS textbooks appeared in Grabiner and Miller, "Effects of Scopes," 836.

14. "Creation-Science Report" (San Diego: Creation-Science Research Center, [1975]), 1 (retrospectively written in 1975 by the association cofounded and run by Nell Segraves); Ronald L. Numbers, "Creationism in 20th-Century America," *Science*, 218 (1982), 543; and Author's interview with Nell and Kelly Segraves, Dec. 19, 1983.

15. Dorothy Nelkin, *Science Textbook Controversies and the Politics of Equal Time* (Cambridge: MIT Press, 1977), 81–82.

16. House Bill No. 301 (Arizona, 1964); and Senate Bill No. 178 (Arizona, 1965). For a discussion of the Phoenix resistance to the BSCS textbooks by the director of the BSCS project, see Grobman, *Changing Classroom*, 205–7.

17. Federal Communications Commission, "Applicability of the Fairness Doctrine in the Handling of Controversial Issues of Public Importance," *Federal Register*, 29 (1964), 10416. See also, Thomas M. Durbin, "The Fairness Doctrine and the Equal Opportunities Doctrine in Political Broadcasting," Library of Congress, Congressional Research Service Issues Brief No. IB82087 (1982), 2–4; and Don R. Pember, *Mass Media Law* (Dubuque: Brown, 1977), 418–19.

18. Susan Epperson and Bruce Bennett in "Proceedings," in *Appendix, Epperson v. Arkansas*, 393 U.S. 97 (1968), 40. This collection of the lower-court trial documents is cited hereafter as *Appendix*.

19. Skoog, "Topic of Evolution," 627.

20. "Response to Motion of the State of Arkansas," in *Appendix*, 30–35.

21. Skoog, "Topic of Evolution," 633.

22. "Teacher at Central High Challenges Constitutionality of Evolution Law," *Arkansas Gazette*, Dec. 7, 1965, 1; and Susanna McBee and John Neary, "Evolution Revolution in Arkansas," *Life*, Nov. 22, 1968, p. 89.

23. "Complaint," in *Appendix*, 6–7.

24. "Intervention of Hubert H. Blanchard, Jr.," in *Appendix*, 10–11.

25. McBee and Neary, "Evolution Revolution," 89.

26. "Complaint," in *Appendix*, 4.

27. "Intervention," in *Appendix*, 10.

28. "Motion," in *Appendix*, 27.

29. "Suit Attacking Evolution Act Slated Today," *Arkansas Gazette*, April 1, 1966, p. 4A.

30. "Defendants' First Amendment to the State of Arkansas' Answer," in *Appendix*, 20.

31. "Separate Answer to the Intervention of Hubert H. Blanchard, Jr.," in *Appendix*, 26.

32. "Defendants' First Amendment," in *Appendix*, 18; and "Separate Answer," in *Appendix*, 25.

33. Epperson in "Proceedings," in *Appendix*, 27–29.

34. Hubert H. Blanchard, Jr. in "Proceedings," in *Appendix*, 62.

35. Bennett in "Proceedings," in *Appendix*, 42.

36. *Ibid.*, 59.

37. *Ibid.*, 66, 47, and 69.

38. "Proceedings," in *Appendix*, 76–93.

39. Murray O. Reed in "Proceedings," in *Appendix*, 49.

40. "Bennett Gets No Room To Roam, Trial of Evolution Law Cut Short," *Arkansas Gazette*, April 2, 1966, p. 1.

41. M. L. Moser, Jr. in *ibid.*, 1.

42. Murray O. Reed, "Memorandum Opinion," in *Appendix*, 99–100.

43. Bud Lemke, "Science Teacher Takes Stand in Evolution Hearing," *Arkansas Democrat*, April 1, 1966, p. 1; and "Judge Reed To Study Briefs in Evolution Suit," *Arkansas Democrat*, April 2, 1966, p. 2.

44. Richard David Wilhelm, "A Chronology and Analysis of Regulatory Actions Relating to the Teaching of Evolution in Public Schools," Diss. Univ. of Texas 1978, p. 219.

45. *Baker v. Carr*, 369 U.S. 186, 237 (1962).

46. This summary of House floor debate is compiled from " 'Monkey Law' Repeal Bill Before House Committee," *Nashville Banner*, April 5, 1967, p. 7; "House Votes Down 'Monkey Law'," *Nashville Banner*, April 12, 1967, p. 1; "House Act Fails To Stir Scopes," *Nashville Tennessean*, April 13, 1967, p. 1; and "House Moves To Halt Wiggle of Monkey Law," *Memphis Commercial Appeal*, April 13, 1967, p. 1. Data on legislators from Joe C. Carr, *Tennessee Blue Book; 1967–68* (Nashville: Secretary of State, [1967]), 22–46. For purposes of this analysis, counties with a population over 100,000 people in the 1970 federal census are characterized as urban and all other counties are characterized as rural.

47. George M. Marsden, *Fundamentalism and American Culture: The Shaping of Twentieth-Century Evangelicalism, 1870–1925* (New York: Oxford Univ. Press, 1980), 185–91.

48. "Teacher Fired on Evolution," *Knoxville Journal*, April 15, 1967, p. 1; and " 'Evolutionist' Holds Last Science Class," *Nashville Tennessean*, April 15, 1967, p. 1.

49. This summary of Senate floor debate is compiled from Bill Kovach, " 'Monkey Law' Left Out on a Limb," *Nashville Tennessean*, April 21, 1967, p. 1; and "Senate Passes Bill To Soften "Monkey Law'," *Memphis Commercial Appeal*, April 21, 1967, p. 1.

50. *Rules of Order of the Senate of the Eighty-fifth General Assembly; State of Tennessee; SESSION 1967* ([Nashville]: Senate Chief Clerk, [1967]), 5.

51. This summary of legal activity on behalf of Gary Scott is compiled from "Rehired Teacher To Test 'Monkey Law,' Anyway," *Nashville Tennessean*, May 13, 1967, p. 1; "Overthrow of Monkey Law Asked," *Knoxville Journal*, May 16, 1967, p. 3; and Nellie Kenyon and W. A. Reed, Jr., "Teacher Urges Court To Tree Monkey Law," *Nashville Tennessean*, May 16, 1967, p. 1.

52. This summary of Senate floor action is compiled from Bill Kovach, "Darwin Theory Wins Over 'Monkey Law'," *Nashville Tennessean*, May 17, 1967, p. 1; "Scott To End Suit; Scopes Welcomes Action in Assembly," *Nashville Banner*, May 17, 1967, p. 2; William Bennett, "State's 'Monkey Law' Repealed by Senators," *Memphis Commercial Appeal*, May 17, 1967, p. 1; and " 'Monkey Law' Repeal Sent to Governor," *Knoxville Journal*, May 17, 1967, p. 1.

53. Walter Smith, "Monkey Law Dead, But Dayton Residents Recall Famed

Trial," *Nashville Banner*, May 19, 1967, p. 14; Duren Cheek, "Peay Signed 'Damn Fool' Monkey Law," *Nashville Tennessean*, May 19, 1967, p. 16; and "Scott To End Suit," 2.

54. Grabiner and Miller, "Effects of Scopes," 836.

55. In his U. S. Supreme Court oral argument in *Epperson*, the state's attorney defending the law stated that "the Supreme Court of Arkansas which ordinarily and in almost all of its cases renders an opinion with reason to back it up, has failed—I shouldn't say failed to, but has not filed an opinion which is usually written by one of its justice with reasoning for its decision. They merely issued a per curiam opinion in this case which they very rarely do." Don Langston in "Proceedings," *Epperson*, 393 U.S. 97, pp. 10–11, Abe Fortas Papers (Yale University Library, New Haven, Conn.) (papers hereafter cited as Fortas Papers).

56. *State v. Epperson*, 242 Ark. 922, 416 S.W.2d 322 (1967).

57. [John M.] Harlan, "No. 7—Epperson v. Arkansas," John Marshall Harlan Papers (Princeton University Library, Princeton, N. J.) (papers hereafter cited as Harlan Papers).

58. "Jurisdictional Statement," *Epperson*, 393 U.S. 97, p. 23.

59. Warren invoked these rights in "Complaint," in *Appendix*, 6–7; and "Intervention," in *Appendix*, 10–11. All these rights were also cited by the trial court in "Memorandum Opinion," in *Appendix*, 97–99.

60. Eugene R. Warren, "Proceedings," 3. Warren set forth his written argument in "Brief for Appellants," *Epperson*, 393 U.S. 97, p. 9.

61. Warren, "Proceedings," 4–9.

62. "Brief of the National Education Association of the United States and the National Science Teachers Association as *Amici Curiae*," *Epperson*, 393 U.S. 97, p. 6.

63. *Ibid.*, 13a.

64. *Ibid.*, 21.

65. *Ibid.*, 24.

66. "Brief of American Civil Liberties Union and American Jewish Congress, as *Amici Curiae*," *Epperson*, 393 U.S. 97, pp. 15–21.

67. *Ibid.*, 2.

68. Langston and unidentified Supreme Court justices in "Proceedings," 9–11. Justice Black noted "the defense's languid interest in the case." *Epperson v. Arkansas*, 393 U.S. at 110 (1968) (Black, J., concurring).

69. Langston in "Proceedings," 15.

70. "Motion To Dismiss," *Epperson*, 397 U.S. 97, pp. 3–4.

71. Langston in "Proceedings," 15. Further arguments on this point were in "Brief for Appellee," *Epperson*, 393 U.S. 97, pp. 30–31.

72. Langston in "Proceedings," 19.

73. *Epperson*, 393 U.S. at 109 (Black, J., concurring).

74. "Bennett Takes Sizable Lead for Fifth Term," *Arkansas Gazette*, July 27, 1966, p. 1; "Bennett Likely To Face Runoff with Purcell," *Arkansas Gazette*, July 28, 1966, p. 1; and "Purcell Defeats Bennett, Says 'Faith' Restored," *Arkansas Gazette*, Aug. 10, 1966, p. 1.

75. "In Court's Failure, the Barrier Remains," *Arkansas Gazette*, June 8, 1967, p. 6a.

76. *Epperson*, 393 U.S. at 102 and 102, nn. 9 and 10; *Epperson*, 393 U.S. at 115 (Harlan, J., concurring); and *Epperson*, 393 U.S. at 116 (Stewart, J., concurring).

77. This account of the Court conference on *Epperson* is based on Fortas's handwritten notes taken at the conference in "No. 7 Epperson v. Arkansas, 10-18-68," Fortas Papers. According to Fortas's notes, the justices citing vagueness were Warren, William Douglas, Brennan, and Byron White, while those citing the Establishment Clause were Harlan, Fortas, and Thurgood Marshall. Harlan's Court file indicates that even he had earlier viewed the case as a question of free speech with the establishment arguments "pretty thin." "Epperson v. Arkansas; No. 7," Dec. 14, 1967, Harlan Papers.

78. Peter [L. Zimroth], "Epperson and Blanchard v. Ark. No 749 OT 1967 7 OT 68, 12/20/67," Fortas Papers. In a later note appended to this memo, the clerk reiterated his original recommendation but assured Fortas, "With you, I would like very much to strike the law down."

79. Evidence for this point (beyond the implications of the facts themselves) comes from Fortas's case file for *Epperson*, which indicates that Fortas sent a copy of his opinion to a personal friend named Arthur Goldschmidt. (Abe Fortas to Arthur Goldschmidt, Nov. 19, 1968, Fortas Papers.) No other such mailing is indicated. Goldschmidt, like Fortas, was a Jew who had attended a southern high school during the height of the anti-evolution crusade, gone to an Ivy League university, and served in government. In his reply to Fortas, Goldschmidt recalled the religious "arguments made in Breckinridge High School in 1925." (Arthur Goldschmidt to Abe Fortas, Nov. 22, 1968, Fortas Papers.) At least Goldschmidt, and presumably Fortas, had a personal interest in anti-evolution laws.

80. *Epperson*, 393 U.S. at 103–6.

81. For Bryan's non-religious purposes, see Chapter 2, notes 99–101, above. For Gray's analysis, see Chapter 3, note 111, above.

82. Addressing other issues, Justice Black criticized the defense for not keeping "this Court informed concerning facts that might easily justify dismissal of this alleged lawsuit." *Epperson*, 393 U.S. at 110 (Black, J., concurring).

83. Untitled file memo in *Epperson* Court file, Fortas Papers (the clerk who wrote this memo is not identified, but it was clearly written after Peter L. Zimroth left Fortas's service). Only one other advertisement supporting the anti-evolution initiative appeared in the Little Rock daily newspapers during the two-week period preceding the election. That ad, which also appeared twice, was a three-inch long, one-column wide statement alerting readers that the local public schools were teaching the "so-called science of Evolution" as true. The ad never expressly appealed to any religious opposition to such instruction. P. J. Park "To the Voters of Arkansas," *Arkansas Gazette*, Oct. 28, 1928, p. 32. Several ads against the initiative also appeared in the Little Rock newspapers during the campaign. Fortas's use of historical evidence is in *Epperson*, 393 U.S. at 102, nn. 9 and 10, and 107, nn. 15 and 16.

84. Compare *Epperson v. Arkansas*, No. 7—October Term, 1968, Circulated: 10–31–68 (draft opinion) with *Epperson v. Arkansas*, No. 7—October Term, 1968, Recirculated: 11-5 (draft opinion). Both drafts from William J. Brennan Pa-

pers (Library of Congress, Washington, D. C.) (papers hereafter cited as Brennan Papers).

85. "The Bible or Atheism, Which?" *Arkansas Gazette*, Nov. 4, 1928, p. 12. Fortas quoted from this ad in *Epperson*, 393 U.S. at 108, n. 16.

86. *Epperson*, 393 U.S. at 109.

87. E.W. to Abe, Nov. 5, 1968, Brennan Papers.

88. W.J.B., Jr., to Abe, Nov. 4, 1968, Brennan Papers.

89. *Epperson*, 393 U.S. at 113 (Black, J., concurring).

90. *McGowan v. Maryland*, 336 U.S. 420 (1961).

91. *Scopes*, 154 Tenn. at 105, 289 S.W. at 366.

92. *Epperson*, 393 U.S. at 102 and 107.

93. *Epperson*, 393 U.S. at 113 (Black, J., concurring). This comment was not in the first draft of Black's concurring opinion, and was added after he received Fortas's majority opinion. Black, J. to Mr. Justice Harlan, "No. 7; Epperson," Oct. 31, 1968, Harlan Papers.

94. *Epperson*, 393 U.S. at 112 (Stewart, J., concurring).

95. *Epperson*, 393 U.S. at 111–14 (Black, J., concurring).

96. Virginia Van Der Veer Hamilton, *Hugo Black: The Alabama Years* (Baton Rouge: Louisiana State Univ. Press, 1972), 15, 67, and 116–18.

97. Daniel J. Meador, *Mr. Justice Black and His Books* (Charlottesville: University Press, 1974), 77–78 and 158.

98. *Epperson*, 393 U.S. at 113 (Black, J., concurring). As discussed above, Fortas also had personal familiarity with the intense popular opposition to evolutionary teaching in the South during the twenties, but from the very different viewpoint of a Jewish public high-school student. In all probability, Black and Fortas took opposite sides on the issue in the twenties as well as in the sixties.

99. "The Supreme Court; Making Darwin Legal," *Time*, Nov. 22, 1968, p. 41.

100. "Supreme Court: Monkey Trial, 1968," *Newsweek*, Nov. 25, 1968, pp. 36–37.

101. McBee and Neary, "Evolution Revolution," 89.

102. *Smith v. State*, 242 So.2d 692, 693–94 (Miss. 1970).

103. Charles M. Hills, Jr., "Ban Against Teaching of Evolution Upheld," *The Jackson Clarion-Ledger*, Jan. 22, 1970, p. 1; and "Evolution Law Ruled OK Now," *Jackson Clarion-Ledger*, Feb. 4, 1970, p. 9.

104. This summary of House floor debate compiled from Charles M. Hills, Jr., "House Votes To Repeal State's Fair Trade Act," *Jackson Clarion-Ledger*, Jan. 21, 1970, p. 1; Hills, "Ban Upheld," 1; Charles M. Hills, Jr. and Lincoln Warren, Jr., "Committees Have Big Issues; Solons Debate Lesser Items," *Jackson Clarion-Ledger*, Jan. 26, 1970, p. 6a; and *Journal of the House of Representatives of the State of Mississippi* (Jackson: House of Representatives, 1970), 23 and 99.

105. Data on legislators from Heber Landner, *Directory of Mississippi Elective Officials: State, State Districts, County and County Districts, 1968–1972* (Jackson: Secretary of State, 1968), 4–7. For purposes of this analysis, counties with a population over 100,000 people in the 1970 federal census are characterized as urban and all other counties are characterized as rural.

106. "Evolution Law Ruled OK," 9.

107. *Smith*, 242 So.2d at 696–98.

108. *Science Framework for California Public Schools Kindergarten—Grades One Through Twelve*, quoted in Moore, "Creationism," 196.

109. Numbers, "Creationism," 543; Nelkin, *Textbook Controversies*, 67–68; Henry M. Morris, *History of Modern Creationism* (San Diego: Master Book, 1984), 231–32, and Tim LaHaye, "The Religion of Secular Humanism," in *Public Schools and the First Amendment*, ed. Stanley M. Elam (Bloomington: Phi Delta Kappa, 1983), 2–3.

110. Henry M. Morris, "Preface," in *Biology: A Search for Order in Complexity*, eds. John N. Moore and Harold Schultz Slusher (Grand Rapids: Zondervan, 1970), xx.

111. Grobman, *Changing Classroom*, 207–18; Nelkin, *Textbook Controversies*, 47; Mel [Gabler], "Comments Regarding Specific Points in Senator Mauzy's Letter to the TX Attorney General," (undated draft letter from late 1983 or early 1984); and Author's interview with Mel Gabler, April 12, 1984.

112. *Wright v. Houston Independent School Dist.*, 366 F.Supp. 1208, 1209 (S.D.Tex. 1972).

Chapter Five: Legislating Equal Time, 1970–81

1. George Marsden, in *Transcript, McLean v. Arkansas Bd. of Educ.*, 529 F.Supp. 1255 (E.D. Ark. 1982), 61 and 69–71 (document hereafter cited as *McLean Transcript*).

2. Ronald L. Numbers, "Creationism in 20th-Century America," *Science*, 218 (1982), 539–43. For this supportive evidence, see Chapter 3, notes 159–61, above.

3. R. Halliburton, Jr., "The Adoption of Arkansas' Anti-Evolution Law," *Arkansas Historical Quarterly*, 23 (1964), 283; and Frederic S. Le Clercq, "The Monkey Laws and the Public Schools: A Second Consumption?," *Vanderbilt Law Review*, 27 (1974), 209.

4. Le Clercq, "Monkey Laws," 210–13.

5. Henry M. Morris and Donald H. Rohrer, eds., *The Decade of Creation: Articles on Creationism from ICR Acts & Facts 1978–1979* (San Diego: Creation-Life, 1981), 7–9.

6. Ronald Reagan, quoted in Kenneth M. Pierce, "Puting Darwin Back in the Dock," *Time*, March 16, 1981, p. 80.

7. *Epperson v. Arkansas*, 393 U.S. 97, 107 (1968).

8. Dorothy Nelkin, in *McLean Transcript*, 109 and 116–17. See also, Dorothy Nelkin, *The Creation Controversy: Science or Scripture in the Schools* (New York: Norton, 1982), 21, 63, and 84–85.

9. For example, Henry M. Morris and Donald H. Rohrer, eds, *Creation: The Cutting Edge* (San Diego, Creation-Life, 1982), 8–9.

10. George Gaylord Simpson, *This View of Life: The World of an Evolutionist* (New York: Harcourt, 1964), 37–38.

11. "A Statement Affirming Evolution as a Principle of Science," *The Humanist,* Jan.–Feb. 1977, pp. 4–6. Morris's comment in Henry Morris, *History of Modern Creationism* (San Diego: Master Book, 1984), 311.

12. Langdon Gilkey, in *McLean Transcript,* 227.

13. Langdon Gilkey, "The Creationist Controversy: The Interrelation of Inquiry and Belief," in *Creationism, Science, and the Law: The Arkansas Case,* ed. Marcel C. La Follette (Cambridge: MIT Press, 1983), 135.

14. "Creation-Science Research Center," (San Diego: Creation-Science Research Center, n.d.), n.pag. (flyer).

15. "No. 86—The ICR Scientists," *Impact,* Aug. 1980, i–viii; and Henry M. Morris and Gary E. Parker, *What Is Creation Science?* (San Diego: Creation-Life, 1982), 272. See also Morris and Rohrer, eds., *Creation,* 210–12. Morris discussed the split in C-SRC and the aims of both resulting organizations in Morris, *History of Creationism,* 232–44.

16. Author's interview with Mel Gabler, Apr. 12, 1984; and Nelkin, *Creation Controversy,* 63–65.

17. Nelkin, *Creation Controversy,* 100 and 139.

18. "Resolutions of Learned Societies in the Textbook Controversy," *American Biology Teacher,* 35 (1973), 35.

19. Nelkin, *Creation Constroversy,* 156–59.

20. "The Statement Affirming Evolution," 4.

21. "The Christianity Today—Gallup Poll: An Overview," *Christianity Today,* Dec. 21, 1979, p. 14. Other polling data in Morris and Rohrer, *Creation,* 222; Morris, *History of Creationism,* 309–11; and Katherine Ching, "The Cupertino Story," *Origins,* 2 (1975), 42. In a 1975 pamphlet, Henry Morris urged local creationist groups to conduct such polls to support their requests for creationist instruction in local schools. Henry M. Morris, "Introducing Scientific Creationism into the Public Schools," (San Diego: Institute for Creation Research, 1975), 7.

22. For example, Morris and Rohrer, *Creation,* 220–22; Morris and Rohrer, *Decade,* 55–56; Duane T. Gish and Donald H. Rohrer, eds., *Up with Creation! ICR Acts/Facts/Impacts 1976–1977* (San Diego: Creation-Life, 1978), 122–24; Katherine Ching, "The Del Norte County Survey," *Origins,* 1 (1974), 94–95; Ching, "Cupertino," 42; and Nelkin, *Creation Controversy,* 117, Although the 1982 Gallup poll on personal beliefs regarding origins found that "[m]ost in the survey would like to see only their own view taught in the public schools," about a quarter of those believing in special creation or theistic evolution thought other views should be taught and nearly half of those believing in naturalistic evolution thought other views should be taught. George Gallup, "Public Evenly Divided Between Evolutionists, Creationists," (Los Angeles: Los Angeles Times Syndicate, 1982), 2 (press release).

23. Morris and Parker, *Creation Science,* 266. This survey found that 76 percent of the respondents favored teaching both creation and evolution, 10 percent favored only teaching creation, 8 percent favored only teaching evolution, and 6 percent were undecided. "76% for Parallel Teaching of Creation Theories," *San Diego Union,* Nov. 18, 1981, p. A–15.

24. *Wright v. Houston Independent School Dist.*, 366 F.Supp. 1208, 1208–09 (S.D.Tex. 1972).

25. *Ibid.*, 1209.

26. *Conley v. Gibson*, 355 U.S. 41, 45–46 (1957); and Charles Alan Wright and Arthur R. Miller, *Federal Practice and Procedure* (St. Paul: West, 1969), 598–604.

27. *Shull v. Pilot Life Ins. Co.*, 313 F.2d 445, 447 (5th Cir. 1963).

28. *Wright*, 366 F.Supp. at 1211, *aff'd*, 486 F.2d 137 (5th Cir. 1973), *cert. denied sub. nom.*, *Brown v. Houston Independent School Dist.*, 417 U.S. 969 (1974).

29. *Willoughby v. Stever*, Civil Action No. 1574–72 (D.D.C. Aug. 25, 1972); and *Crowley v. Smithsonian Inst.*, 462 F.Supp. 725, 725 (D.D.C. 1978).

30. *Willoughby*, Civil Action No. 1574–72, *aff'd mem.*, 504 F.2d 271 (D.C. Cir. 1974), *cert. denied*, 420 U.S. 927 (1975); and *Crowley*, 462 F.Supp. at 725, *aff'd*, 636 F.2d 738, 744 (D.C. Cir. 1980).

31. *Crowley*, 636 F.2d at 744.

32. Morris, "Introducing Scientific Creationism," 1.

33. Twenty-four creationism bills in twelve different states during the period from 1971 to early 1977 were identified in Richard David Wilhelm, "Chronology and Analysis of Regulatory Actions Relating to the Teaching of Evolution in Public Schools," Diss. Univ. of Texas 1978, pp. 64–65.

34. *Senate Journal of the Eighty-eighth General Assembly of The State of Tennessee* (Nashville: Senate Chief Clerk, [1973]), 345. Background data on each state senator is contained on unnumbered pages at the front of this book. For purposes of this analysis, counties with a population over 100,000 in the 1970 federal census are characterized as urban and all other counties are characterized as rural. Legislative districts containing any part of an urban county are treated as urban districts, with the rest designated as rural. For sources of data on the 1967 Senate vote, see Chapter 4, note 52, above.

35. Senate Bill No. 394 (Tenn. 1973).

36. Tom Gillem, "Prof's Textbook Campaign Led to Genesis Bill," *Nashville Tennessean*, April 30, 1973, p. 1.

37. Compare *Senate Journal*, 743, with voting results listed in Bill Kovach, "Darwin Theory Wins Over 'Monkey Law'," *Nashville Tennessean*, May 17, 1967, p. 1.

38. This summary of Senate floor action is compiled from *Senate Journal*, 742–44; Larry Daughtrey, "Senators Clam Up on CBS," *The Nashville Tennessean*, April 19, 1973, p. 1; "State Senate Races TV on Evolution Legislation," *Nashville Banner*, April 19, 1973, p. 20; and "Old 'Monkey Law' Evolves in Senate," *Memphis Commercial-Appeal*, April 19, 1973, p. 3.

39. This summary of House floor action is compiled from *House Journal of the Eighty-eighth General Assembly of the State Of Tennessee* (Nashville: House Chief Clerk, [1973]), 1152–58; Frank H. Thinland, "Creation Theories Could Crowd Books," *Nashville Tennessean*, April 19, 1973, p. 1; John Haile, "Genesis Bill Wins House Passage," *Nashville Tennessean*, April 27, 1973, p. 1; John Pope, "House Amends Proposal on Creation of Man," *Nashville Banner*, April 27,

1973, p. 16; and "House Alters Some Senate Theories on Creation," *The Memphis Commercial-Appeal*, April 27, 1973, p. 3. Background data on each House member are contained on unnumbered pages at the front of the *House Journal*.

40. Compare *House Journal*, 1056, with voting results listed in "House Act Fails To Stir Scopes," *Nashville Tennessean*, April 13, 1967, p. 1.

41. *Senate Journal*, 1046–50.

42. Larry Daughtrey, "Dunn Signature Withheld, But Genesis Bill Now Law," *Nashville Tennessean*, May 9, 1973, p. 1; and William Bennett, " 'Genesis Bill' Becomes Unsigned Law," *Memphis Commercial-Appeal*, May 9, 1973, p. 3.

43. "Complaint," *Daniel v. Waters*, 515 F.2d 485 (6th Cir. 1975), in Wilhelm, "Chronology," 234. For a further discussion of Le Clercq's legal theories, see Le Clercq, "Monkey Laws," 213–41.

44. "Complaint," *Steele v. Waters*, 527 S.W.2d 72 (Tenn. 1975), in Wilhelm, "Chronology," 239–40.

45. "Arguments Swirl in Appeal of Ban of 'Genesis Law'," *Memphis Commercial-Appeal*, March 7, 1975, p. 3.

46. *Daniel*, 515 F.2d at 492.

47. *Daniel*, 515 F.2d at 494 (Celebrezze, J., dissenting). Quotes taken from excerpts of earlier decisions set forth in this dissenting opinion.

48. *Daniel*, 515 F.2d at 489–91.

49. *Steele*, 527 S.W.2d at 74.

50. Harold Bigham, quoted in Irene Walker, "Bible-Science Unit Says Genesis Bill 'Sabotaged'," *Nashville Tennessean*, May 25, 1975, p. 25-C.

51. Katherine Ching, "The Textbook Controversy in Tennessee," *Origins*, 2 (1975), 97.

52. Oscar H. Mauzy to Jim Mattox, Oct. 24 1983 (letter from the chairman of the state Senate Committee on Jurisprudence to the state Attorney General); and Author's interview with Mel Gabler, April 12, 1984.

53. *Tex. Educ. Code Ann.*, tit. 19, sec. 81.63.

54. Gabler interview. In a press release issued in early 1984, the Gablers wrote that the Texas anti-dogmatism policy was "as 'middle-of-the-road' as is possible to prepare. It is midway between the 'two-model approach' demanded by scientific creationists and the evolutionists who seek to exclude any theory but their own and then want it taught as fact." The Mel Gablers, "For Immediate Release," March 13, 1984.

55. John A. Moore, "Creationism in California," in *Science and Its Public: The Changing Relationship*, ed. Gerald Holton and William A. Blanpied (Dordricht, Holland: D. Reidel, 1976), 199.

56. California State Board of Education, June 19, 1981 letter, in Kelly Segraves and Robert Grant, "EVOLUTION and the Christian Child in California Public Schools," (Pacific Grove, Cal.: Creation Creed Committee, 1982), 23. This pamphlet contained a duplicate of the Board letter redistributing the anti-dogmatism policy under court order.

57. Nelkin, *Creation Controversy*, 116.

58. *Ops. Att'y Gen.* 262, 263 (Cal. 1975). For background data on the two leg-

islators, John Stull and Robert H. Burke, see Darryl R. White and James D. Driscoll, *California Legislature: 1975* ([Sacramento]: Senate Secretary and House Chief Clerk, 1975), 39 and 190.

59. *Ibid.*, 271–73.

60. Kelly Segraves, "Resolved: That Scientific Creationism Must Be Taught in the Public Schools," in Stanley M. Elam, ed., *Public Schools and the First Amendment* (Bloomington: Phi Delta Kappa, 1983), 134–35; and Katherine Ching, "Creation in the Court," *Origins*, 6 (1979), 45.

61. Philip J. Hilts, "Fundamentalists Drop Wide Attack on Schools' Teaching of Evolution," *Washington Post*, March 5, 1981, p. A–2; Peter Gwynne, "'Scopes II' in California," *Newsweek*, March 16, 1981, p. 67; and Author's interview with Nell and Kelly Segraves, Dec. 19, 1983.

62. "Partial Transcript," *Segraves v. California*, No. 278978 (Sacramento Co. Cal. Super. Ct. June 12, 1981), 6 (case cited hereafter as *Segraves*).

63. This summary of the *Segraves* trial compiled from Philip J. Hilts, "Evolution on Trial Again California," *Washington Post*, March 2, 1981, p. A–2; Hilts, "Fundamentalists," p. A–2; Wallace Turner, "California Schools Upheld on Teaching Evolution," *New York Times*, March 7, 1981, p. 23; and Robert Crabbe, "Evolution or Creation in Class: California's 'Scopes' Trial," *Los Angeles Daily Journal*, March 3, 1981, p. 3.

64. Irving Perluss, quoted by Kelly Segraves in Segraves interview.

65. "Findings of Fact and Conclusions of Law," *Segraves*, 2.

66. "Judgment After Trial by Court," *Segraves*, 1–2.

67. California Board letter, in Segraves and Grant, "EVOLUTION," 23.

68. Kelly L. Segraves to "friend," Nov. 1981; and "Californians Will Monitor Evolution Teaching in Schools," *Christianity Today*, Feb. 5, 1982, p. 69.

69. Segraves interview.

70. Senate Bill No. 50 (Ky. 1976).

71. This summary of Kentucky legislative action is compiled from *Journal of the Senate of the General Assembly of the Commonwealth of Kentucky: Regular Session of 1976* (Frankfort: Legislative Research Comm., 1976), 133 and 347–49; *Journal of the House of Representatives of the General Assembly of the Commonwealth of Kentucky: Regular Session of 1976*, (Frankfort: Legislative Research Comm., 1976), 1878–1900; "Bible Instruction Bill Approved by the Senate," *Louisville Courier-Journal*, Feb. 2, 1976, p. B–2; "Crime Victim Aid Passed by House," *Louisville Courier-Journal*, March 16, 1976, p. D–4; and Maria Braden, "Carroll Signs Measure To Aid Crime Victims," *Frankfort State Journal*, March 31, 1976, p. 11.

72. "Brief of Indiana Textbook Commission," *Hendren v. Campbell*, No. S577-0139 (Marion Co. Ind. Super. Ct. No. 5, April 14, 1977), 4 (the court file hereafter cited as *Hendren*).

73. "Affidavit of Harold H. Negley," Feb. 21, 1977, *Hendren*, 2–3; and "Motion To Dismiss," *Hendren*, 6–7.

74. "Complaint," *Hendren*, 3–4.

75. Bill Mundy in "Transcript of Tapes and Notes Taken at a Hearing Before the Textbook Adoption Commission," *Hendren*, 9. For Commission ruling,

see "Determination of Commission on Textbook Adoption," in "Memorandum Opinion," *Hendren*, Appendix A.

76. "Memorandum Opinion," *Hendren*, 19–20.
77. *Ibid.*, 14–15.
78. Kelly Segraves reported that Judge Dugan later said that he would have banned dogmatic evolutionary texts on the same basis, but that this issue was never raised at trial. Segraves interview.
79. "Defendant Indiana Textbook Commission's Reply Brief," *Hendren*, 5.
80. Although the full extent of these creationist teaching activities is unknown, some indication of it is provided by the following partial listing of such activities during the seventies. State educational agencies approved the use of creationist texts or teaching in Georgia, Idaho, Indiana, Oklahoma, Oregon, and Tennessee. State legislative bodies in Alabama and Georgia passed resolutions in favor of creationist teaching. Local school boards adopted a policy of teaching creationism in Charleston, West Virginia; Clover Park, Washington; Cobb County, Georgia; Columbus, Ohio; Dallas, Texas; and Racine, Wisconsin. Controversies arose over creationist instruction by individual teachers in Lemmon, South Dakota, and Livermore, California, and over anti-creationist instruction by a student teacher in North Carolina. [Wendell R. Bird], "Freedom of Religion and Science Instruction in Public Schools," *Yale Law Journal*, 83 (1978), 516–17, nn. 8–9; Wendell R. Bird, "No. 71, Resolution for Balanced Presentation of Evolution and Scientific Creationism," *ICR Impact Series*, May 1979, p. iv, n. 14; Gish and Rohrer, eds., "Up with Creation," 81–82; Morris and Rohrer, *Creation*, 212; Robert M. O'Neil, "Creationism, Curriculum, and the Constitution," *Academe*, March–April 1982, p. 23; Hilts, "Evolution on Trial," p. A–2; and Joy Horowitz, "Battle Lines Drawn over Scientific Creationism in the Classroom," *Los Angeles Times*, March 6, 1981, p. V–1.
81. Kenneth M. Dolbeare and Phillip E. Hammond, *The School Prayer Decisions: From Court Policy to Local Practice* (Chicago: Univ. of Chicago Press, 1971), 33 and 44. A similar conclusion based on more and later evidence appears in Steven L. Wasby, *The Supreme Court in the Federal Judicial System*, 2nd ed. (New York: Holt, Rinehart & Winston, 1978), 301–3.
82. *Ibid.*, x and 7.
83. Wendell R. Bird, "Evolution in Public Schools and Creation in Students' Homes: What Creationists Can Do.," in *Decade of Creation*, eds. Morris and Rohrer, 119.
84. Bruce Catton, *Terrible Swift Sword*, (New York: Washington Square, 1967), 424.
85. [Bird], "Freedom of Religion," 518–19.
86. *Ibid.*, 523–26, 554, and 570.
87. *Ibid.*, 556 and 561.
88. *Ibid.*, 527–28 and 561.
89. John Ball, notes in law clerk's file, *McLean*, 529 F.Supp. 1255.
90. Henry M. Morris, "No. 26, Resolution for Equitable Treatment of Both Creation and Evolution," *ICR Impact Series*, [1975], i.

91. Bird, "Resolution," ii–iii.

92. *Ibid.*, i. Morris's earlier model resolution gave similar advice. Morris, "Resolution," ii.

93. For background on Paul Ellwanger and his small anti-evolution organization, Citizens for Fairness in Education, see Nelkin, *Creation Controversy*, 100 and 139; "No. 67, Creation Science and the Local School District," *ICR Impact Series*, Jan. 1979, pp. i–iv; and Paul Ellwanger to Mary Ann Miller, April 17, 1981, in "Appendix to Plaintiffs' Pre-Trial Brief," *McLean*, 529 F.Supp. 1255, sec. 15. *McLean* court file is cited hereafter as *McLean*.

94. Pierce, "Putting Darwin Back," 80; Alex Heard, "Creationist Movement Appears to Be Slowed by Loss in Arkansas," *Education Week*, Feb. 17, 1982, p. 4; Wendell R. Bird, "The First Amendment and Evolution/Creation Science in Public Schools: Freedom of Religious Exercize, Freedom of Belief, and Separation of Church and State," April 23–26, 1981, p. 1 (unpublished seminar paper for Christian Legal Society conference).

95. W. A. Blunt to Paul Ellwanger, July 2, 1981, in "Appendix," *McLean*, sec. 15.

96. Senate Bill No. 482 (Ark. 1981)

97. James L. Holsted, quoted in John Brummett, " 'Creation-science' Bill Prompted by Religious Beliefs, Sponsor Says," *Arkansas Gazette*, March 22, 1981, p. 1A

98. James L. Holsted, in *McLean Transcript*, 385–87; and Brenda Tirey, "Senate Approves Bill To Distribute Tax on Premiums to Fire Fighter Pension Fund," *Arkansas Gazette*, March 13, 1981, p. 10–A.

99. This summary of House action is compiled from "Legislators Pass 'Creation' Bill," *Arkansas Gazette*, March 18, 1981, p. 1; Ed Phillips and Marion Fulk, "House Stifles Debate, Passes Creationism Bill," *Arkansas Democrat*, March 18, 1981, p. 1; and House voting records at the Office of the Secretary of State, Little Rock, Arkansas. Background data on legislators from "Arkansas State Directory" (Little Rock: Heritage, 1981), 35–36.

100. Frank White, quoted in Andrew Polin, "Law Requires Schools Offer Theory Choice," *Arkansas Democrat*, March 20, 1981, p. 1. See also, John Brummett, "He Hasn't Read It, But White Signs Bill on 'Creation'," *Arkansas Gazette*, March 20, 1981, p. 1.

101. Polin, "Theory Choice," 1; and Brummett, "White Signs Bill," 1.

102. This summary of Senate action is compiled from *1981 Official Journal of the Proceedings of the Senate of the State of Louisiana* ([Baton Rouge]: Secretary of the Senate, 1981), 784–85 and 848–49; Allan Pursnell, "Senate Passes Bill Limiting Abortions," *State-Times* (Baton Rouge), June 3, 1981, p. 1; and "Defendants' Pre-Trial Brief," *Keith v. Louisiana Department of Education*, 553 F.Supp. 295 (M.D. La. 1982), 33–40. *Keith* court file is cited hereafter as *Keith*.

103. This summary of House action is compiled from *1981 Official Journal of the Proceedings of the House of Representatives of the State of Louisiana* ([Baton Rouge]: House Chief Clerk, 1981), 2932–34; Jack Wardlaw, "Equal Time for Creation Passes House," *Times-Picayune/States-Item* (New Orleans), July 7, 1981, p. 1; John LaPlante, "House OKs Creationism; Bill Goes Back to

Senate," *State-Times* (Baton Rouge), July 7, 1981, p. 12–A; and "Defendants' Pre-Trial Brief," *Keith*, 40–41.

104. This summary of Senate floor debate is compiled from *1981 Journal of Senate*, 2687–90; Jack Wardlaw, "Creation Bill Goes to Treen," *Times-Picayune/States-Item* (New Orleans), July 9, 1981, p. 1; and Candace Lee, "Creationism Bill Is Sent to Treen," *State-Times* (Baton Rouge), July 8, 1981, p. 1–B.

105. Background data on legislators and legislative districts from James H. Brown, *State of Louisiana Roster of Officials* (Baton Rouge: Secretary of State, 1981), 41–49. For purposes of this analysis, counties with a population over 100,000 people in the 1980 federal census are characterized as urban and all other counties are characterized as rural.

106. Wardlaw, "Creation Bill," 1; and Lee, "Creationism Bill," 1–B.

107. David C. Treen, quoted in Jack Wardlaw, "Creationism Teaching Bill Becomes Law," *Times-Picayune/States-Item* (New Orleans), July 22, 1981, p. 1. See also, Jack Wardlaw, "Treen Signs Bill To Repeal License Tax," *Times-Picayune/States-Item* (New Orleans), July 21, 1981, p. I–13; and John LaPlante, "Gov. Treen Signs Measure Requiring Creationism Lessons," *State-Times* (Baton Rouge), July 22, 1981, p. 1.

108. Roger Baldwin, quoted in "Remember Scopes Trial? ACLU Does," *Times-Picayune/States-Item* (New Orleans), July 22, 1981, p. 1.

Chapter 6: Outlawing Creation

1. *Williamsburg Charter Survey on Religion and Public Life* (Washington: Williamsburg Charter Foundation, 1988), 36–37 (James Davison Hunter wrote the survey analysis).

2. *The Williamsburg Charter Survey on Religion and Public Life: List of Tables* (Washington: Williamsburg Charter Foundation, 1988), tables 23, 29, 33, and 34.

3. William R. Overton, "Speech to Pennsylvania Appellate Judges," June 29, 1982, p. 22, in law clerk's file, *McLean v. Arkansas Board of Education*, 529 F.Supp. 1255 (E.D. Ark. 1982). *McLean* court file is cited hereafter as *McLean*.

4. *List of Tables*, table 35.

5. George Gallup, "Public Evenly Divided Between Evolutionists, Creationists," (Los Angeles: Los Angeles Times Syndicate, 1982), 1–2 (press release). According to this poll, belief in biblical creationism was weaker in other regions, but nowhere fell below 40 percent, while belief in atheistic evolution never topped 17 percent.

6. For example, see *Aguillard v. Edwards*, 765 F.2d 1251, 1257 (5th Cir. 1985).

7. See pages 72–74 of text. Reflecting this general view, Overton commented that before hearing the case against the Arkansas creationism law, he "had the notion that any serious controversy involving the teaching of evolution

in public schools had died in Dayton, Tennessee, back in the 1920's." Overton, "Speech," 1.

8. *List of Tables*, tables 16 and 24.

9. Jack D. Novik, "Litigating the Religion of Creation Science," *Federation of American Societies for Experimental Biology Proceedings*, 42 (1983), 3039; and Mark E. Herlihy, "Trying Creation: Scientific Disputes and Legal Strategies," in *Creationism*, ed. La Follette, 97.

10. *McLean v. Arkansas Board of Education*, 663 F.2d 47, 48 (8th Cir. 1981), *aff'g*, No. LRC 81–322 (W.D. Ark. Aug. 20, 1981); and Overton, "Speech," 21.

11. Marcel C. La Follette, "Creationism in the News: Mass Media Coverage of the Arkansas Trial," in *Creationism*, ed. La Follette, 194. In one notable exception, a vitriolic analysis of events in Arkansas that matched anything from the *Scopes* era for biting satire and wit appeared in Gene Lyons, "Repealing the Enlightenment," *Harper's*, April 1982, pp. 38–40 and 73–78.

12. *McLean*, 529 F.Supp. at 1257; and Overton, "Speech," 1.

13. Herlihy, "Trying Creation," 98–99.

14. Nelkin, *Creation Controversy*, 140–41; and Novik, "Litigating Creation Science," 3040. See also similar analysis of plaintiffs' scientific arguments by plaintiffs' counsel in Eric Holtzman and David Klasfeld, "The Arkansas Creationism Trial: An Overview of the Legal and Scientific Issues," in *Creationism*, ed. La Follette, 92.

15. Herlihy, "Trying Creation," 100.

16. "Plaintiffs' Outline of Legal Issues and Proof," in *Creationism*, ed. La Follette, 28. Similar statement in "Plaintiffs' Pre-Trial Brief," *McLean*, 50.

17. "Plaintiffs' Pre-Trial Brief," *McLean*, 59.

18. "Defendants' Trial Brief," *McLean*, 17.

19. *McLean*, 529 F.Supp. at 1269–70; and Overton, "Speech," 15. For a spectrum of perspectives on these defense expert witnesses by viewers of the trial, see Philip J. Hilts, "Creation Trial: Less Circus, More Law," *Washington Post*, Dec. 21, 1981, p. A-3; Walter Sullivan, "Creation Debate Is Not Limited to Arkansas Trial," *New York Times*, Dec. 27, 1981, p. 48; Novik, "Litigating Creation Science," 3041; Nelkin, *Creation Controversy*, 141–43; and Duane T. Gish, "What Actually Occurred at the Trial," *Impact* (ICR), March 1982, pp. ii–iii.

20. "Defendants' Trial Brief," *McLean*, 23–27; and *McLean*, 529 F.Supp. at 1274.

21. *McLean*, 529 F.Supp. at 1264.

22. *Ibid.*, 1266–72. For this portion of Ruse's testimony, see *McLean Transcript*, 246–47. The trial and judicial decision focused on the two older prongs of the test for Establishment Clause violation—religious purpose and effect. A third prong, creating excessive entanglement of government with religion, was added to the test by *Lemon v. Kurtzman*, 403 U.S. 602 (1971). The three prongs are independent, in that failing any one prong voids a statute. Almost in passing, the Arkansas statute was held to also violate this third prong of the test for forcing school officials to decide how to teach creationist religious doctrine. *McLean*, 529 F.Supp. at 1272.

23. Novik, "Litigating Creation Science," 3041; and Heard, "Creationist Movement Slowed," 4.

24. *McLean,* 529 F.Supp. at 1273–74; and Overton, "Speech," 20–21.

25. Robert Cearley, Jr., quoted in "Federal Judge Denies Arkansas Creation Law," *Moral Majority Report,* Jan. 25, 1982, p. 3.

26. "Creationism in Schools: The Decision in McLean Versus the Arkansas Board of Education," *Science,* 215 (1982), 934–43; Nelkin, *Creation Controversy,* 201–28; David B. Wilson, ed., *Did the Devil Make Darwin Do It? Modern Perspectives on the Creation-Evolution Controversy* (Ames: Iowa State Univ. Press, 1983), 206–22; and La Follette, ed., *Creationism,* 45–73.

27. Heard, "Creationism Movement Slowed," 4; and Frederick Edwords, "The Aftermath of Arkansas," *The Humanist,* March–April 1982, p. 55.

28. This summary of the activities in Texas is compiled from Oscar H. Muzey to Jim Mattox, Oct. 24, 1983 (requesting Attorney General opinion); Att'y Gen. Op. JM-134 (Tex. March 13, 1984); Michael Hudson to Members of the State Board of Education, March 21, 1984 (People for the American Way demand letter); and 9 *Tex. Reg.* 2351–54 (1984) (new regulations).

29. "Federal Judge Denies Law," 3; and Nelkin, *Creation Controversy,* 143–45.

30. James Holsted, quoted in Nelkin, *Creation Controversy,* 145.

31. Roger Lewin, "New Creationism Bill Already Drafted," *Science,* 214 (1981), 1224.

32. Gish, "What Actually Occurred," iii; and Wendell R. Bird and John W. Whitehead, "A Brief Statement on the Arkansas Decision," *Impact* (ICR), March 1982, p. iii.

33. Morris and Parker, *Creation Science,* 273.

34. "Plaintiffs' Pre-trial Brief," *Keith,* 2, 5, and 48.

35. "Defendants' Pre-Trial Brief," *Keith,* 62–63.

36. *Keith v. Louisiana Department of Education,* 553 F.Supp. 295, 297 (M.D.La. 1982).

37. *Aguillard v. Treen,* No. 81-4787 (E.D.La. Nov. 22, 1982), 6.

38. *Aguillard v. Treen,* 440 So.2d 704, 707, n. 6 (La. 1983).

39. *Aguillard v. Treen,* No. 81-4787 (E.D.La. Jan. 10, 1985), 9–10.

40. *Ibid.,* 3–7; and "Brief of the State in Opposition to ACLU Motion for Summary Judgment," *Aguillard,* No. 81-4787 (1985), 37–392.

41. The immediate response to the *Aguillard* decision is from Bridget O'Brian, "Creation Law Invalid, Judge Rules," *Times-Picayune/States-Item* (New Orleans), Jan. 11, 1985, p. 1.

42. Fed. R. Civ. P. 56.

43. This summary of the appellate-court argument is compiled from John Pope, "Creation Law Trial Is Urged," *Times-Picayune/States-Item* (New Orleans), May 9, 1985, p. A-37; and "Creationism Defense Asks Full Court Trial," *The Times* (Shreveport), p. 24-A.

44. These affidavits were reprinted in the appendix to "Brief of Appellants," *Edwards v. Aguillard,* 107 S.Ct. 2571 (1987). The *Edwards* court file is cited hereafter as *Edwards.* The theologians were Terry L. Miethe of Jerry Falwell's Liberty Baptist University and William G. Most of Loras College, a Roman Catholic institution. The school administrator was Assistant Superintendent Robert L. Clinkert from DuPage County, Illinois.

45. Pope, "Creation Law," p. A-37; and "Creationism Defense," p. 24-A.

46. *Aguillard,* 765 F.2d at 1253 and 1257.

47. *Ibid.*, 1256–57.

48. *Ibid.*

49. *Aguilar v. Felton*, 473 U.S. 402 (1985); *School Dist. of City of Grand Rapids v. Ball*, 573 U.S. 373 (1985); and *Wallace v. Jaffree*, 472 U.S. 38 (1985).

50. Ronald Reagan, quoted in George J. Church, "Politics from the Pulpit," *Time*, Oct. 13, 1980, p. 28; Kenneth M. Pierce, "Putting Darwin Back in the Dock," *Time*, March 16, 1981, p. 80; Aric Press, "A Reagan Court?" *Newsweek*, July 15, 1985, p. 69; Michael S. Serrill, "Rebuilding Jefferson's Wall," *Time*, July 15, 1985, p. 73; and author's interview with Bill Keith, Sept. 1985. In a later press release, Keith noted the importance to his cause of new Reagan appointees on the appellate bench. Creation Science Legal Defense Fund, "U.S. Supreme Court Accepts Appeal in Louisiana Creation-Science Case," May 5, 1986, p. 2.

51. Fed. R. App. P. 35 and 40.

52. "Suggestion for Rehearing *En Banc*," *Aguillard*, 765 F.2d 1251, 6 and 9.

53. *Aguillard v. Edwards*, 778 F.2d 225, 226–28 (5th Cir. 1985) (Gee, J., dissenting).

54. *Aguillard*, 778 F.2d at 228 (Jolly, J., responding).

55. "Judges of the Federal Courts," 778 F.2d. xv (1986). Contrary to this trend, Jolly was appointed by Reagan.

56. "Jurisdictional Statement," *Edwards*, iv–v.

57. "Motion to Affirm," *Edwards*, 21 and 26.

58. This summary of the Supreme Court argument is compiled from Al Kamen, "Creation Science Law Had Secular Intent, High Court Told," *Washington Post*, Dec. 11, 1986, p. A-13; Joe Atkins, "State's Creationism Case Gets Justices' Ears," *The Times* (Shreveport), Dec. 11, 1986, p. 2-A; "Justices Hear 2 Views on 'Creation' Law," *New York Times*, Dec. 11, 1986; Susan Feeney, "Creationist Law Aired Before Supreme Court," *Times-Picayune* (New Orleans), Dec. 11, 1986, p. 1; "Arguments Before the Court," *United States Law Week*, Dec. 16, 1986, pp. 3419–20; Tom Mirga, "High Court Hears Case Challenging Creationism Law," *Education Week*, Dec. 17, 1986, p. 1; Lyle Denniston, " 'Creation Science' Gets a Critical Reception," *American Lawyer*, March 1987, p. 95; and author's notes from oral argument, Dec. 10, 1986. The comments by Justice Stevens during oral arguments denying that evolution and creation were mutually exclusive views made their way into the Court's opinion. A curious footnote stated, "While the belief in the instantaneous creation of humankind by a supernatural creator may require the rejection of every aspect of the theory of evolution, an individual instead may choose to accept some or all of this scientific theory as compatible with his or her spiritual outlook." The authority cited for this statement was "Tr[anscript] of Oral Arg[ument] 23–29." *Edwards*, 107 S.Ct. at 2573, n. 11.

59. "*Amicus Curiae* Brief of 72 Nobel Laureates, 17 State Academies of Science, and 7 Other Scientific Organizations, in Support of Appellees," *Edwards*, 4. See also, "Brief of People for the American Way," *Edwards*, 13–14; "Brief

of Americans United for Separation of Church and State," Edwards, 11; "Brief *Amici Curiae* of the American Association of University Professors and the American Council on Education in Support of Appellees," *Edwards*, 11–12; "Brief of the Anti-Defamation League of the B'nai B'rith and Americans for Religious Liberty, *Amici Curiae*, in Support of Appellees," *Edwards*, 4 and 7–8; "Brief of the American Jewish Congress and the Synagogue Council of America as *Amici Curiae* in Support of Appellees," *Edwards*, 45; "*Amicus Curiae* Brief of the State of New York, Joined by the State of Illinois," *Edwards*, 4; "Brief of *Amicus Curiae*, American Federation of Teachers, AFL-CIO, in Support of Appellees," *Edwards*, 7–9; "Motion for Leave to File Brief of *Amici Curiae* and Brief of *Amici Curiae* Reverend Bill McLean, Bishop Ken Hicks, Right Reverend Herbert Donovan, and Most Reverend Andrew J. McDonald," *Edwards*, 9–11; "Brief for *Amicus Curiae* the National Academy of Sciences Urging Affirmance," *Edwards*, 12 and 27; "Brief *Amicus Curiae* of the New York Committee for Public Education and Religious Liberty," *Edwards*, 53 and 58; and "Brief for the Spartacist League and Partisan Defense Committee as *Amicus Curiae* on Behalf of Appellees," *Edwards*, 11.

60. "Brief of the Christian Legal Society and National Association of Evangelicals as *Amici Curiae* Supporting Appellants," *Edwards*, 4–5. See also "Brief *Amicus Curiae* of Concerned Women for America in Support of Appellants," *Edwards*, 9; "Brief of the Rabbinical Alliance of America," *Edwards*, 18–20; and "Brief for the Catholic League for Religious and Civil Rights, *Amicus Curiae*, in Support of Appellants," *Edwards*, 5.

61. *Edwards*, 107 S.Ct. at 2581–82.

62. *Ibid.*, at 2579 and 2583.

63. *Edwards*, 107 S.Ct. at 2588 (Powell, J., concurring).

64. *Edwards*, 107 S.Ct. at 2590–91 (White, J., concurring).

65. *Edwards*, 107 S.Ct. at 2595, 2602 and 2604 (Scalia, J., dissenting).

66. *Ibid.*, at 2604.

67. Ira Glasser, quoted in Stuart Taylor, Jr., "Evolution Debate Started by Darwin," *New York Times*, June 20, 1987, p. 6; Donald Aguillard, quoted in Frances Frank Marcus, "Elation, Relief and Sadness in Louisiana as Fight Ends," *New York Times*, June 20, 1987, p. 7; Jay Topkis, quoted in Susan Feeney, "La.'s Creationism Law Struck Down," *Times-Picayune* (New Orleans), June 20, 1987, p. A-4; and Stephen Jay Gould, "Genesis and Geology," *Natural History*, 97 (1988), 12.

68. Michael Zimmerman, "Keep Guard Up After Evolution Victory," *BioScience*, 37 (1987), 636; and Arthur J. Kropp, quoted in Tony Mauro, "La. Creation Law Fails Court Test," *The Times* (Shreveport), June 20, 1987, p. 10. Similar concern was expressed by Eugenie Scott, leader of the National Center for Science Education, which is the umbrella organization for the state-based Committees of Correspondence on Evolution. She wrote, "The Supreme Court decision says only that the Louisiana law violates the constitutional separation of church and state; it does not say that no one can teach scientific creationism—and unfortunately many individual teachers do.

Some school districts even require 'equal time' for creation and evolution." Eugenie C. Scott, "Creationism Lives," *Nature*, 329 (1897), 282 (letter).

69. *Mozart v. Hawkins County Bd. of Educ.*, 827 F.2d 1058, 1062, 1064, and 1069 (6th Cir. 1987).

70. Jon A. Buell and Michael J. Woodruff, "Balance Without the Bar," *Moody Monthly*, Sept. 1988, pp. 24 and 27 (Woodruff wrote the *Edwards* brief for the National Association of Evangelicals). Similar advice was given by the creationist Students of Origins Research. After summarizing the *Aguillard* ruling in a letter to members, that organization concluded: "So what does all this mean for science education? Mainly, that it is unwise to continue to use the term "creation-science" in the classroom. . . . The Court has left the door wide open for teachers to openly present scientific evidence that challenges evolutionary theory." "Understanding the Supreme Court Decision," *SOR Annual Report*, Oct. 15, 1987, p. 1.

71. Wendell R. Bird, quoted in Marcus, "Elation," 7; Wendell R. Bird, quoted in "After *Edwards v. Aguillard*: A Brief Analysis, and Prospect," *SOR Bulletin*, Aug. 1987, p. 4; and Paul Ellwanger, "Current Status of 'Uniform Origins Policy' Initiative," Dec. 18, 1987 (unpublished memorandum).

72. Pat Robertson, quoted in Mauro, "La. Creation Law," p. 10; and Pat Robertson, quoted in "Robertson: Court Ruling Disgraceful," *The Times* (Shreveport), June 20, 1987, p. 11.

73. Overton, "Speech," 21.

74. Hebrews 11:1 (King James Version).

Conclusion

1. Edward Hitchcock and Charles H. Hitchcock, *Elementary Geology* (New York: Ivison, 1860), 373–74.

2. William Jennings Bryan, *In His Image* (New York: Revell, 1922), 86–88.

3. Clarence Darrow, "Purpose of the Universe," n.d., n.pag., Clarence Darrow Papers (Library of Congress, Washington, D. C.) (handwritten speech).

4. "Introduction," in *Creation: The Cutting Edge*, eds. Henry M. Morris and Donald H. Rohrer (San Diego: Creation-Life, 1982), 8–9.

5. George Gaylord Simpson, *This View of Life: The World of an Evolutionist* (New York: Harcourt, 1964), 36–37.

6. *Scopes v. State*, 154 Tenn. 105, 117, 289 S.W. 363, 366 (1927).

7. *Epperson v. Arkansas*, 393 U.S. 97, 102 (1968).

8. Op. Att'y Gen. 262, 272 (Cal. 1975); and "Findings of Fact and Conclusions of Law," *Segraves v. California*, No. 278978 (Sacramento Co. Cal. Super. Ct. June 12, 1981), p. 2.

9. *McLean v. Arkansas Bd. of Educ.*, 529 F.Supp. 1255, 1274 (E.D. Ark. 1982); *Aguillard v. Edwards*, 765 F.2d 1251, 1256 (5th Cir. 1985); and *Edwards v. Aguillard*, 107 S.Ct. 2571, 2583 (1987).

10. William Jennings Bryan in *The World's Most Famous Court Trial: State of Tennessee v. John Thomas Scopes* (1925; rpt. New York: Da Capo, 1971), 317.

11. Arthur Garfield Hays, "The Strategy of the Scopes Defense," *The Nation*, Aug. 5, 1925, p. 158; and George F. Washburn to William Jennings Bryan, July 23, 1925, William Jennings Bryan Papers (Library of Congress, Washington, D. C.).

12. Henry M. Morris, *History of Modern Creationism* (San Diego: Master Book, 1984), 233 and 292.

13. Jack D. Novik, "Litigating the Religion of Creation Science," *Federation of American Societies for Experimental Biology Proceedings*, 42 (1983), 3042.

Bibliographic Note

Although many historical studies dealing with the controversy over creation and evolution exist, few focus on the legal aspects of the controversy. In these works, legal actions usually appear, if at all, as part of the social, biographical, or religious history divorced from their place in the ongoing legal tradition. The few books and articles that directly examine these legal actions typically deal with only one trial or the enactment of a particular statute. No existing work attempts to present a comprehensive survey of the creation-evolution legal controversy placed in its historical setting. In filling this void, the present study analyzes the ongoing legal controversy as one particularly rich point of continuing interaction between science and society, with that analysis set in the context of parallel legal developments.

Despite the novel approach of this study, I am deeply indebted to many of the existing historical books and articles examining the creation-evolution controversy. Those secondary works and the multitude of primary sources used for this study appear in the Notes section following the text and they will not be repeated here at length. Readers are directed to those references for materials on specific topics. This Bibliographic Note is intended only as a guide for general study and as a brief overview of the major resources used in the preparation of this book.

A handful of secondary works provide an introduction to the subject for a general reader. Two recent books discussing the religious roots of anti-evolutionism are George M. Marsden, *Fundamentalism and American Culture: The Shaping of Twentieth-Century Evangelicalism, 1870–1925* (New York: Oxford Univ. Press, 1980), and Ferenc Morton Szasz, *The Divided Mind of Protestant America, 1880–1930* (University, Ala: Univ. of Alabama Press, 1982). An older glimpse of the social setting for anti-evolutionism in the South during the twenties is provided by Kenneth K. Bailey, *Southern White Protestantism in the Twentieth Century* (New York: Harper, 1964), with a more recent sociological study of the current creationism appearing in Dorothy Nelkin, *The Creation Controversy: Science or Scripture in the Schools* (New York: Norton, 1982). An introduction to Bryan's anti-evolution activities is provided by Lawrence W. Levine, *Defender of the Faith:*

William Jennings Bryan: The Last Decade, 1915–1925 (New York: Oxford Univ. Press, 1965).

No comprehensive work examines the scientific history of the controversy. Theodore Dwight Bozeman, *Protestants in an Age of Science* (Chapel Hill: Univ. of North Carolina Press, 1977) looks back at the relationship of science and religion in the early nineteenth century. The responses of some later nineteenth-century scientists and religious leaders to Darwinism are examined in James R. Moore, *The Post-Darwinism Controversies: A Study of the Protestant Struggle to Come to Terms with Darwin in Great Britain and America, 1870–1900* (Cambridge, U.K.: Cambridge Univ. Press, 1979), while an expanded account of one such scientist's response appears in A. Hunter Dupree, *Asa Gray, 1810–1888* (Cambridge, Harvard Univ. Press, 1959). Ronald L. Numbers, "Creationism in 20th-Century America," in *Science*, 218 (1982), 538–44, provides a short overview of twentieth-century creationist scientific activities while a quasi-autobiographical account of such activities is in Henry M. Morris, *History of Modern Creationism* (San Diego: Master Book, 1984). A further analysis of relevant secondary works is provided by William E. Ellis, "Evolution, Fundamentalism, and the Historians: A Historiographical Review," in *The Historian*, 44 (1981), 15–35.

Using the material in school textbooks as an indicator of curricular content, this book traces the roots and impact of the creation-evolution legal controversy in part by examining the presentation of the topic of biological origins in high-school life-science texts. The most comprehensive collection of such textbooks that I could find is in the Library of Congress, and I made extensive use of that collection. Unfortunately, even that collection is incomplete, especially for recent years as limitations in shelf space and resources have forced that library to retain only a selection from among the ever increasing number of textbooks that it receives for copyright purposes. The most helpful works about high-school textbooks were Charles Carpenter, *History of American Schoolbooks* (Philadelphia: Univ. of Pennsylvania Press, 1963); Judith V. Grabiner and Peter D. Miller, "Effects of the Scopes Trial," in *Science*, 185 (1974), 832–37; Arnold B. Grobman, *The Changing Classroom: The Role of the Biological Sciences Curriculum Study* (Garden City, N.Y.: Doubleday, 1959); and Gerald Skoog, "The Topic of Evolution in Secondary School Biology Textbooks: 1900–1977" in *Science Education*, 63 (1979), 621–40. To provide a different view into the high-school life-science curriculum during the critical period leading up to the anti-evolution crusade, I read the three leading teaching journals of that era, *Academy, School Review*, and *School Science and Mathematics*, as well as other available journal articles and teaching manuals dating from that and later periods. An introductory discussion of the development of secondary education appears in Edward A. Krug, *The Shaping of the American High School* (Madison: Univ. of Wisconsin Press, 1969).

Two primary sources were used to investigate the enactment of every anti-evolution or creationism statute. First, I reviewed available official legislative records pertaining to each statute. This included the legislation itself, journals of the senate and house of representatives for each state passing such a law, official rosters and biographical material on legislators, and pertinent legislative voting records. Copies of many such records are preserved in the Library of

Congress, but some are only available from the states. The extensiveness and quality of these official records vary greatly from state to state. Second, I read all the newspapers from the state retained in the collections of the Library of Congress for the period when the legislation was under consideration. Typically, this provided me with first-hand accounts of legislative action written by capitol reporters for three to six newspapers, a wealth of editorial comment, insight into the surrounding political and social atmosphere, and a variety of letters to the editor.

These two sources were supplemented whenever possible by other primary and secondary materials. The William Jennings Bryan Papers in the Manuscripts Division of the Library of Congress provided a wealth of material on the enactment of the earliest anti-evolution statutes. I gleaned some material on the passage of later creationism statutes from trial transcripts, legal briefs, or other court documents generated by lawsuits challenging the constitutionality of those laws. As an added resource, several secondary accounts describe passage of the four original anti-evolution statutes of the twenties. These accounts include Kenneth K. Bailey, "The Enactment of Tennessee's Antievolution Law," in *The Journal of Southern History*, 16 (1950), 472–90, Virginia Gray, "Anti-Evolution Sentiment and Behavior," in *The Journal of American History*, 57 (1970), 352–66 (a quantitative analysis of the vote for the Arkansas anti-evolution initiative), and three articles by R. Halliburton, Jr., "The Adoption of Arkansas' Anti-Evolution Law," in *Arkansas Historical Quarterly*, 23 (1964), 271–83, "Mississippi's Contribution to the Anti-Evolution Movement," in *The Journal of Mississippi History*, 35 (1973), 175–82, and "The Nation's First Anti-Darwin Law," in *The Southwestern Social Science Quarterly*, 41 (1960), 123–34 (dealing with the Oklahoma textbook restriction).

Partisans and participants on both sides of the issue have produced a tremendous volume of material dealing with individual laws and regulations, especially those arising during the past two decades. Among the many such resources cited in the references to this book, two stand out as especially early evolutionist warnings of the resurgence in creationist legal activity, Frederic S. Le Clercq, "The Monkey Laws and the Public Schools: A Second Consumption?" in *Vanderbilt Law Review*, 27 (1974), 209–42, and John A. Moore, "Creationism in California," in *Science and Its Public: The Changing Relationship*, eds. Gerald Holton and William A. Blanpied (Dordricht, Holland: D. Reidel, 1976), 191–207. Further, ongoing reports to supporters about recent creationist activities appear in the monthly newsletter of the Institute for Creation Research, *Acts & Facts*, in the staunchly evolutionary bimonthly magazine *The Humanist*, and in *Origins*, an Adventist journal.

The heart of my research focused on the trials and other judicial actions spawned by the controversy over creation and evolution. These legal actions generated a rich body of primary source material, including trial transcripts, written briefs for both sides, and judicial opinions. I examined all three of these sources for *Epperson v. Arkansas*, 393 U.S. 97 (1968), *Hendren v. Campbell*, No. S577–0139 (Marion Co. Ind. Super. Ct. No. 5, April 14, 1977), *McLean v. Arkansas Bd. of Educ.*, 529 F. Supp. 1255 (E.D. Ark. 1982), and *Scopes v. State*, 154

Tenn. 105, 289 S.W. 363 (1927). Extensive available court documents were also reviewed for the other judicial actions discussed in this book.

I supplemented this basic research with a variety of other primary source material. The personal papers of several key participants in *Scopes* and *Epperson* provided a wealth of material, with the most valuable documents in the William Jennings Bryan Papers and the Clarence Darrow Papers, both housed at the Library of Congress, and the Abe Fortas Papers at Yale University Library. Many of the attorneys, parties, and witnesses involved in the major creation-evolution legal actions recorded their observations, most notably John T. Scopes and James Presley, *Center of the Storm: Memoirs of John T. Scopes* (New York: Holt, 1967) and a collection of essays by opponents of the creationism law in *McLean*, edited by Marcel C. La Follette, entitled *Creationism, Science, and the Law: The Arkansas Case* (Cambridge: MIT Press, 1983). Some insight into the pattern of ACLU activity emerged from reviewing that organization's annual reports. Conversations with researchers at the Institute for Creation Research, Nell and Kelly Seagraves, Mel Gabler, Wendell Bird, and *McLean* law clerk John Ball provided additional perspective, as did contemporaneous newspaper and journal articles about the lawsuits.

With one prominent exception, little in the way of secondary literature exists for the creation-evolution court actions. That one exception is *Scopes*, which has generated tremendous amounts of historical writing, including at least three books: L. Sprague De Camp, *The Great Monkey Trial* (Garden City, N.Y.: Doubleday, 1968); Ray Ginger, *Six Days or Forever? Tennessee v. John Thomas Scopes* (Boston: Beacon, 1958); and Mary Lee Settle, *The Scopes Trial: The State of Tennessee v. John Thomas Scopes* (New York: Watts, 1972). Further primary and secondary sources pertaining to these trials and judicial actions are cited in the appropriate references.

Index